QUICKSAND *and* CACTUS

Books by Juanita Brooks

Dudley Leavitt, Pioneer to Southern Utah (1942)

The Mountain Meadows Massacre (1950)

John Doyle Lee: Zealot, Pioneer Builder, Scapegoat (1961)

George Brooks, Artist in Stone (1965)

Uncle Will Tells His Story (1970)

The Christmas Tree (1972)

Frontier Tales: True Stories of Real People (1972)

History of the Jews in Utah and Idaho (1973)

On the Ragged Edge: The Life and Times of Dudley Leavitt (1973)

Emma Lee (1975)

Jacob Hamblin: Mormon Apostle to the Indians (1980)

Edited by Juanita Brooks

A Mormon Chronicle: The Diaries of John D. Lee, 1848–1876
(with Robert Glass Cleland, 1955)

On the Mormon Frontier: The Diary of Hosea Stout (1964)

*Journal of the Southern Indian Mission:
Diary of Thomas D. Brown* (1972)

*Not by Bread Alone:
The Journal of Martha Spence Heywood, 1850–1856* (1978)

When first that band of pioneers did look upon the scene
They thought they never saw a land so barren and so mean
Their hearts were filled with nameless fear
And O! Their spirits sank!
There was quick-sand in the river-bed, and CACTUS ON THE BANK!

Sing rol di riddle, di riddle, di ray
Sing rol de riddle di ray!

Juanita Brooks

QUICKSAND
and
CACTUS

A Memoir
of the Southern Mormon Frontier

Juanita Brooks

UTAH STATE UNIVERSITY PRESS
LOGAN, UTAH

1992

Published by

Utah State University Press
Logan, Utah 84322-7800

Manufactured in the United States of America

LIBRARY OF CONGRESS CATALOGING IN PUBLICATION DATA

Brooks, Juanita, 1898-1989
    Quicksand and cactus: a memoir of the southern Mormon frontier /
Juanita Brooks.
        p.   cm.
    Originally published: Salt Lake City: Howe Brothers, 1982.
    ISBN 0-87421-163-8
    1. Brooks, Juanita, 1898-1989.   2. Frontier and pioneer life—Utah.
3. Historians—Utah—Biography.   4. Utah—Biography.   5. Mormons—
Utah—History—20th century.   6. Mormons—Nevada—Biography.
7. Nevada—Biography.   8. Frontier and pioneer life—Nevada.
I. Title.
F826.B874   1992
979.2'03'092—dc20
[B]   92-36970
                                                                    CIP

Preface to the First Edition

By Richard Howe

THE STORY OF THE WRITING OF THIS BOOK, and of the career of its author over a span of thirty-five years, is in itself a dramatic one, told in detail by Charles S. Peterson in the following introduction. The manuscript of *Quicksand and Cactus* followed Juanita Brooks through fifteen books and more than forty articles, and in a haunting way remains much the same as it was originally conceived and begun in the early 1940s; as a memoir of the southern Mormon frontier it assumes an ironical meaning in light of her subsequent career as a writer. "If I had a book or two or a half-dozen before my name, or if I had been outstanding in any field," she wrote to historian Dale L. Morgan in August 1944, "then perhaps an autobiographical work would do."

The first part of the book was essentially written by 1946; that portion dealing with her life after the death of her first husband was completed by 1978. There remain several chapters, or portions of chapters, not published here, which deal with her life after her marriage to Will Brooks in 1933; some of these have been published separately, others remain unpublished. The first twenty-one chapters were completed earliest, and many were reworked several times; in some cases four or five versions of the same chapters and episodes exist.

We received the manuscript in the fall of 1980 from Karl Brooks, who has acted as agent and literary executor for his mother since her retirement to her home in St. George, Utah. While she clarified many episodes, dates, and names in the manuscript, she was not able to actively participate in the final stages of editing.

We were fortunate in having access to the personal papers and manuscripts of Mrs. Brooks, and especially her voluminous correspondence with Dale L. Morgan, whose friendship, help, and criticisms were of vital importance to this and later manuscripts. In her letters she outlined in detail and in sample chapter-by-chapter procession the chronology of the book and the subjects it would cover; he provided lengthy criticism and interpretation of the major themes and stylistic considerations he saw in her thinking and writing. And always he urged her toward the larger, more universal perspective he felt she was uniquely qualified to provide. In the final stages of editing we followed the instruction, direction, and growing sense of "completed book" that this correspondence produced. The major editorial problem was perhaps collating the various versions and drafts of many of the chapters, some written years apart. Morgan had urged the developing "pull of the outside" upon Juanita as a major theme; and too with the passage of years her work reflected a similar maturing. We strived to retain the character of her earlier writing and the broadening perspective and reflection evident in that of the later years.

The epilogue is a compilation of Mrs. Brooks' "Just a Copyin' — Word f'r Word" (*Utah Historical Quarterly*, Vol. 37, Fall 1969, pp. 375–95, used with permission); of elements of a chapter so-named, in progress for inclusion in this book; and of several paragraphs written in honor of Dale L. Morgan for the Utah Academy of Science, Arts, and Letters in 1971.

Several chapters have been published previously: "Old Tubucks," "The Outsider," and "Selah" were excerpted together under the title "Memories of a Mormon Girlhood" in Volume 77 (July–September 1964) of the *Journal of American Folklore*; "The Outsider" was later included in *Great Western Short Stories*, edited by J. Golden Taylor (Palo Alto: The American West Publishing Co., 1967); "The Christmas Tree" was later published under hard cover by the same name (Salt Lake City: Peregrine Smith, 1972, reprinted here with permission).

In addition, several episodes have appeared in other published works of Mrs. Brooks. "The Lord's Vineyard" contains several anecdotes in the life of Dudley Leavitt which were included in *On the Ragged Edge: The Life and Times of Dudley Leavitt*, *The Mountain Meadows Massacre*, *John Doyle Lee: Zealot, Pioneer Builder, Scapegoat*, and *Jacob Hamblin: Mormon Apostle to the Indians*. Later versions of scenes from "Simon and the Magic Sack" and "Over the Shovel Handles" appeared in *Jacob Hamblin* and in *Lore of Faith and Folly*, which was edited by Thomas E. Cheney, Austin E. Fife, and Juanita Brooks (Salt Lake City: University of Utah Press, 1971). A longer story of the dog Griz, from "Pa Goes Freighting," was published in *Frontier Tales: True Stories of Real People* (Logan, Utah: Western Text Society, 1972).

Several of the autobiographical reflections and episodes in *Quicksand and Cactus* were told by Mrs. Brooks in "Riding Herd: A Conversation with Juanita Brooks," with Davis Bitton and Maureen Ursenbach (*Dialogue: A Journal of Mormon Thought*, Vol. 9, 1974, pp. 11–33). A bibliography of her writing through 1974 is published there.

The Utah Historical Society (Salt Lake City) has microfilmed copies of most of Mrs. Brooks' unpublished papers, manuscripts, and correspondence, which are in possession of her family in St. George. The University of Utah (Salt Lake City) Marriott Library's Special Collections has a substantial collection of Dale Morgan's correspondence, including a copy of the 4 August 1944 letter to Bernard DeVoto (see Appendix B). J. S. Holliday of San Francisco, Morgan's literary executor, granted permission to reprint the portions of the Morgan letters used in the introduction and text of the book.

In addition to Morgan and the various publishers who read and commented on the manuscript in the 1940s (and who are discussed in the introduction), editors at American Heritage and Harper and Row stimulated Mrs. Brooks' renewed interest in *Quicksand and Cactus* in the early 1960s. In the late 1960s and early 1970s Richard Thurman and Norma Mikkelsen of the University of Utah Press encouraged work on and the eventual publication of the manuscript.

And special thanks are due Trudy McMurrin, whose handiwork is evident in the editorial development of the latter third of the book; her skillful insistence that Mrs. Brooks write in more detail of her single years will be especially appreciated. Charles S. Peterson, in addition to his considerable work on the introduction, offered suggestions and criticism as the book was in early proof.

Estelle Rebec of the Manuscripts Division, Bancroft Library, University of California, Berkeley, provided helpful access to Mrs. Brooks' letters to Dale Morgan in the collection of his papers there. Lynne Clark of Washington, Utah, contributed much time and effort in locating and preparing photographs from her vast collection of southern Utah images.

Contents

Contents

ILLUSTRATIONS

following page 156

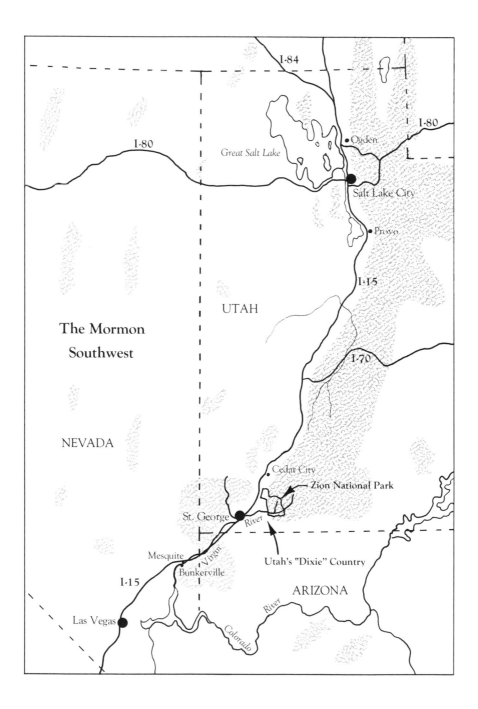

I·84

I·80

Great Salt Lake

Ogden

I·80

Salt Lake City

Provo

I·15

UTAH

The Mormon
Southwest

I·70

NEVADA

Cedar City

Zion National Park

St. George

River

Utah's "Dixie" Country

Mesquite

Virgin

Bunkerville

I·15

ARIZONA

River

Las Vegas

Colorado

Introduction

By Charles S. Peterson

QUICKSAND AND CACTUS, AN AUTOBIOGRAPHY BY JUANITA
BROOKS, could hardly be more appropriately named. Her life began
in the "Mormon Country" of southern Nevada and Utah's Dixie,
and after ripe, full years continues there at her home in St. George,
Utah. Born in 1898 of pioneering Mormon stock at Bunkerville,
Nevada, she has become one of the distinguished historians of the
American West, perhaps the most notable person to emerge from
the settlements of southwestern Utah and southern Nevada. She is
a product of what have been called the "Middle Years" of Mormon
Dixie, a remarkable pocket of local culture. Beginning in 1877,
when Brigham Young's overriding influence was quieted by death,
and ending about 1920, when modern forces began to penetrate
the region, Dixie's Middle Years were a time of great isolation
in which local influences flowered. Indeed, Mormon culture as a
distinctive folkway may well have reached its richest texture in these
years and in this setting.

The Mormons who pioneered this country were a chosen lot,
winnowed by the mission call, doubly sifted by a reenactment of

Charles S. Peterson is Professor of History in Utah State University, and
Editor of the *Western Historical Quarterly.* For several years in the late 1960s
and early 1970s he was Director of the Utah Historical Society, where he came
to know Juanita Brooks.

man's primordial struggle with desert wilderness, and burdened with a terrible and suppressed memory of how the wilderness in man sometimes runs rampant. In one of the great American tragedies, southern Utah Mormons killed upwards of one hundred California-bound emigrants in 1857 during an armed confrontation between settlers in the Territory of Utah and the United States government. The infamous mass killing northwest of St. George was in itself tragic beyond description. To the Mormon participants, the spectre of the Massacre remained an unspeakable threat from within, creating a fear that the entire Mormon mission, and indeed the promise of life implicit in Christ's atonement itself, were without meaning. Thus, the Mountain Meadows Massacre cast a brooding shadow of tragedy that molded and formed Dixie's character in the middle years, giving tragic counterpoint, profound anxiety, and uncommon dimension to the society into which Juanita Brooks was born.[1]

In *Quicksand and Cactus*, Brooks describes this society and her own attachment to it. Written over a period of decades, the book displays something of her changing perspective. Its early chapters consciously deal with her country and people. Deserts, mail contracts, rural routines, isolation, family, and community speak loudly. Sense of place is strong. Then, as her life advances and her world extends to include school and deep personal sorrow, her own experience becomes progressively more central. More and more she responds to the beckoning of what she calls "that great untravell'd world whose margin fades for ever and for ever when I move."[2] The final chapters, some of which were written in the 1960s and 1970s, become very much her personal story. With the exception of an epilogue about her role in the Utah Historical Records Survey, the book ends with her 1933 marriage to Will Brooks, a country sheriff at St. George.[3] As historian Dale Morgan wrote of the manu-

---

[1]The passages on the Middle Years of southwestern Utah's "Dixie" country have been abstracted with permission from my own "Life in a Village Society, 1877–1920," *Utah Historical Quarterly*, Vol. 49 (Winter 1981), pp. 78–96.

[2]See p. 161, below.

[3]Juanita Brooks, "Just a Copyin' — Word f'r Word," *Utah Historical Quarterly*, Vol. 37 (Fall 1969), pp. 375–395.

script nearly forty years ago, "It is a book that no one can read without a renewed sense of the worth of human living. It is, at the same time, a book to be read with delight."[4]

The reader will of course want to enjoy it to the fullest, but may well find that a brief treatment of her later life and accomplishment will enhance the story so ably told in the pages of her book.

Mrs. Brooks' life as a historian was initiated about the time she married Will Brooks. The two careers — marriage and history — demanded almost unimaginable commitment and self-control. Family life was paramount. As she put it, "In those days I always had one child on my knee and another under my apron."[5] Her home and its facilities were carefully managed. The telephone could be commanded from both the kitchen sink and an ironing board positioned at one end of her living room. When she talked by phone she could do dishes, and from the ironing board she could talk either by phone or to visitors in her living room.[6] She worked long nights at her typewriter, knowing full well that there is "no good writing, only good rewriting."[7] Similarly, as time advanced and she became a board member of the Utah Historical Society, she traveled to and from Salt Lake City, taking a night bus each way, thus minimizing time lost in sleep and travel.

She can be said to have been a major success as a wife and a mother. A loving and congenial relationship existed between herself and her children and, in time, grandchildren and great-grandchildren. There was also a touching and reassuring tenderness in her relationship with Will Brooks, who died while she was on one of her periodic bus trips "upstate" in 1970. After his death she memorialized him

[4]Morgan to Bernard DeVoto, 4 August 1944, Dale Morgan Collection, University of Utah Marriott Library Special Collections, Salt Lake City. See also Appendix B, below.

[5]I have often heard her make this comment myself.

[6]Austin and Alta Fife and A. Russell Mortensen are among those who have described this arrangement to me.

[7]She entitled a lecture delivered to a graduate seminar at Utah State University "There Is No Good Writing, Only Good Rewriting," in which she described her own experience.

and his family in *Uncle Will Tells His Story* (1970), a truly fine book on family and community history published well before the recent upsurge of regional and national interest made such books an "in" thing to do. To the society in which she lived, her homelife was and is a mark of fellowship and reliability. With the loyalty to the community that grew naturally from it, this commitment to home kept the folkways she reflected so intimately open to her and was an essential element in her writing career.

In 1934 her "A Close-Up of Polygamy" appeared in *Harper's Monthly Magazine.* Her role with the Utah Historical Records Survey was launched the same year. These developments influenced her life profoundly, impelling her in two fundamentally different directions. On the one hand she proceeded more deeply into her own locality. Collecting the country's lore had begun much earlier, as she absorbed the oral tradition from her grandfather's lips and first journeyed into the pages of the past through her grandmother's diary. As the Records Survey proceeded she became even more closely tied to home, even more a part of the Dixie tradition, more aware of its real character, and more determined to throw light upon it. Haunted especially by the Mountain Meadows Massacre and its hushed half-record, she developed an extraordinary passion for the full story of any historical document. As she later put it, her purpose in collecting and using records was to "see each [document] steadily and [to] see it whole."[8]

On the other hand, centrifugal forces brought Mrs. Brooks into an exciting intellectual ferment then working among a group of native and adopted Utahns who were approaching regional and Mormon themes from the perspective of new moods and with new methods of study. From diverse backgrounds and with little more than regional attachments to hold them, they were brought together by Depression-sponsored projects and by a common interest in letting the record of the past speak candidly and fully. They never associated closely and have indeed not been recognized as representing a movement. Yet in the richness of their production, in their ties to a place, in their shared access to records, and in their efforts to help each other find

[8]Brooks, "Just a Copyin'," p. 394.

publishers, may be seen a meaningful interaction that enhanced the individual value of their writing and gave it added impact.[9]

Certainly Mrs. Brooks' associates were a varied lot. Some were interested in history, some in fiction, and some in folklore. A surprising number had southern Utah connections. Some were associated — or came to be — with universities, some with historical societies. Still others were journalists or freelance writers, while some were would-be novelists and historians who worked full-time in other professions. Among the closest were Dale Morgan, Nels Anderson, Fawn Brodie, LeRoy Hafen, Wallace Stegner, Bernard DeVoto, Maurine Whipple, Austin and Alta Fife, Wayland Hand, and Russell Mortensen.

Perhaps the first to have a direct influence on Juanita Brooks was Nels Anderson. After dropping off a freight train as a teenage hobo, Anderson had lived in southern Utah, where he acquired deep roots. In 1934, after completing a master's degree in sociology at the University of Chicago, Anderson returned to St. George for a few months on a grant from Columbia University. In addition to doing the research for *Desert Saints* (1942), a superb book that approaches the Mormon experience from the perspective of desert settlers, he encouraged Juanita Brooks to try her hand at historical writing and to collect southern Utah's numerous diaries and memoirs.[10]

During that same period, Brooks was involved in various ways with several other southern Utah and Nevada writers. Perhaps most noted in the long run was her uncle LeRoy Hafen, who had taken a Ph.D. at the University of California under Herbert Eugene Bolton, then at the height of a brilliant career. By the mid-thirties Hafen was at the Colorado Historical Society and had initiated a long, productive career as a student of the fur trade. He became one of

---

[9]Suggestive as to the cooperation in this last respect was Morgan's assurance in 1942 that he and DeVoto would "give you a lift with a publisher . . . and if I have no influence in the book world, he has, at least!" Morgan to Brooks, 21 May 1944, Juanita Brooks Collection.

[10]Brooks, "Just a Copyin'," pp. 379–381; and Davis Bitton and Maureen Ursenbach, "Riding Herd: A Conversation with Juanita Brooks," *Dialogue*, Vol. 9 (1974), p. 22.

the most illustrious of the authors publishing with Arthur H. Clark Company of Glendale, California, ultimately issuing at least thirty volumes under its imprint.

Other collectors and writers from southern Utah whose paths Brooks crossed during the early years were William A. Palmer, Angus M. Woodbury, Maurine Whipple, and her Dixie College colleague Andrew Karl Larson. Whipple, whose *Giant Joshua* (1941) is still considered by some to be the most powerful and moving Mormon novel, drew heavily upon Brooks' intimate knowledge of Mormon Country and upon her fortitude and strength. Although Larson's writing career really did not begin until 1957 with the publication of *Red Hills of November*, he shared Brooks' affinity for Utah's Dixie, and in recent years has authored and edited an outpouring of books that clearly establishes him as second only to her as a regional voice of Mormon history.

Only less intimate in the circle of Brooks' contacts were Bernard DeVoto and Fawn Brodie. By the late 1930s and early 1940s DeVoto had in many ways shed himself of Utah. A brilliant, if "uneasy" son of Ogden, he was an expatriate in most respects. There was little in his hometown, Mormon society, or Utah generally that he had not ridiculed. Yet his great trilogy on the westering process (*The Year of Decision, 1846* [1943]; *Across the Wide Missouri* [1947]; *The Course of Empire* [1952]) showed a rarely paralleled sense for the forces that had claimed the North American continent, and an equally rare gift to produce readable history. He knew the publishing world and was known by it, and in his passion for conservation, was a prophet well ahead of his time. With his success and contacts he became, perhaps in spite of himself, a catalyst who opened doors to other Utahns, including Juanita Brooks.

Gifted and angry, Fawn Brodie, too, had already ventured far from Utah. In contrast to Brooks, both inclination and opportunity would continue to draw her away. Her tremendous talent was spent on national figures, including Thomas Jefferson and Richard M. Nixon, as she became one of America's best-known biographers. Yet in the 1940s she shared a profound interest in Mormon history with Brooks, and when she wrote *No Man Knows My History: The Life of Joseph Smith, the Mormon Prophet* (1945), she approached

Introduction

Mormon studies at a more sensitive point even than did Brooks. Called on to critique Brooks' early manuscripts, she found them to be filled with stylistic problems, but saw in them parallels to her own village background in northern Utah and the stuff of great history.

A central figure in all this, as well as Brooks' closest friend, was Dale L. Morgan. His instinct for perfection, indefatigable energy, and vast correspondence made him the central figure in Utah and Mormon history from the late 1930s to the mid–1950s. Trained but unable to find work as a commercial artist, he joined the WPA-sponsored Utah Writers' Project, which he headed from 1937 to 1941. Portending his prolific future, the Writers' Project had a bumper year in 1940 when it produced ten publications, including Morgan's *The State of Deseret*, an underrated milepost in Utah and Mormon historiography, which appeared as three issues of the *Utah Historical Quarterly*. Less impressive in the sheer bulk of its production, the next year was made equally important for the Writers' Project by the appearance of Morgan's *Utah: A Guide to the State*, which was acclaimed to be among the best of a highly regarded series. As Ray A. Billington, long dean of western historians, pointed out, the *Utah Guide* also confirmed that Morgan "could write magnificently, blending . . . poetic imagery and word sense with the exactness of expression required by the canons of history." Evident also was the fact that he could write Mormon history "with complete objectivity."[11]

During the war years Morgan took employment in Washington, D.C. On his own time he continued to do research on Utah history and published works in two prestigious series, *The Humboldt: Highroad to the West* (1943) in Farrar and Rinehart's Rivers of America Series and *The Great Salt Lake* (1947) in Bobbs–Merrill Company's American Lakes Series. A difficult period ensued in the late 1940s and early 1950s during which Morgan became increasingly convinced that Utah had neither the research materials nor the economic incentives to hold him. In 1954 he joined the Bancroft Library at the University of California, where he produced what are perhaps

[11]Ray A. Billington, "Introduction," in Dale L. Morgan, *The Great Salt Lake*, new edition (Albuquerque: University of New Mexico Press, 1973), pp. vii–ix.

the best books ever written on the fur trade and mountain men. By the time of his death in 1971 he had written or edited over forty books and countless articles. The cost to Utah and Mormon studies of his shift in emphasis was immense. Unfinished when he died was a union catalogue on Mormon history, multi-volume works on Utah and the Mormon experience, and *A Mormon Bibliography*.

The intellectual vitality of these years was also apparent at the Utah Historical Society, which Morgan did much to foster as an independent voice for history. Mormon history had its institutional voices at the Church Historian's Office and in the Daughters of the Utah Pioneers and the Deseret News Press. Finding the Society to be a suitable umbrella were writers with an anti-Mormon bent, like the prolific and vitriolic Charles Kelly (*Salt Desert Trails* [1930]; *Holy Murder: The Story of Porter Rockwell* [1934]; *Old Greenwood: The Story of Caleb Greenwood* [1936]; *Miles Goodyear* [1937]; *The Outlaw Trail: A History of Butch Cassidy and His Wild Bunch* [1938]). Others were people who simply had a strong interest in all aspects of Utah history. Among the most prominent was Cecil Alter, a professional meteorologist, whose name and personality were indelibly imprinted on the Society of the thirties and early forties by his long-time editorship of the *Quarterly* and by his writing, which included *Early Utah Journalism* (1938) and *Utah, The Storied Domain* (1932), a serviceable multi-volume history of the state. Also denizens of the Society in these years were Father Robert Joseph Dwyer, later Archbishop, whose *The Gentile Comes to Utah: A Study in Religious and Social Conflict, 1862–1890* had immediate impact when it appeared as a Ph.D. dissertation in 1941; Herbert Auerbach, collector and early translator of the 1776 Escalante expedition diaries; and J. Roderic Korn, whose posthumous *West from Fort Bridger* Morgan encouraged Russell Mortensen, by this time editor, to publish as Volume 19 of the *Quarterly* in 1951.

During the late forties Morgan himself had been acting editor of the *Quarterly,* which reached one of the pinnacles of its achievement. Concerned always with the primary record, he not only saw to the publication of the several pre-Mormon-era diaries edited in Korn's book, but for the 1948 and 1949 volumes of the *Quarterly* lined up a notable set of editors for the journals of the John Wesley Powell explorations, including Powell's biographer, William Culph Darrah, and Herbert E. Gregory and Charles Kelly.

But perhaps even more importantly, Morgan helped secure the appointment of Juanita Brooks to the Board of State History in 1949. With a brief break in the early 1960s when she was editing *On the Mormon Frontier: The Diary of Hosea Stout* (1964) under a grant from the Society, Brooks sat on that board for nearly thirty years, representing the interests and high standards of what proved to be a passing generation of freelance or independent historians. After 1960 the Society's board fell increasingly under the control of what may be called political appointees and of university historians who, careful training notwithstanding, were rarely as productive as the independent group of the 1930s and 1940s of which Brooks and Morgan were representative.

Indeed, in many respects Brooks' work is the best product of those years of ferment. As we have seen, she had published her first essay with *Harper's* in 1934. In 1941 articles appeared in *Harper's* again and in the *Reader's Digest.* Her interest in the Mountain Meadows Massacre dated to some time prior to 1920, when a dying participant's unrequited desire to tell "the little school teacher" his story marked it on her soul.[12] By 1933 she had begun to think about writing on the subject. As she went about her collecting role in the Utah Historical Records Survey between 1934 and 1937, she had good opportunity to observe how word of it had been repressed in the records of her own area. Simultaneously, she turned her attention to Jacob Hamblin, by all odds the best-known folk hero in southern Utah.

It was in this context that her long association with Dale Morgan was apparently initiated. Unable to get her biography of Hamblin to jell, she finally wrote Morgan in 1941, inquiring how to cope with a tendency to treat some topics fictionally and some historically. In what he called a "fatherly tone," he taught her the first of many lessons about the character of history when he warned that Utah biography was often "sticky with Mormon history, muddy in style, and fumbling in its realization" and that it demanded "a certain

---

[12]See pp. 226–229, below.

feeling, a sense of the texture of life" not often found in earlier biographies of the region.[13]

It was not long, however, before Juanita Brooks recognized that Hamblin was central neither to the Mountain Meadows Massacre nor to her own evolving sense of southern Utah's history. In this period, as later, she herself and the people closest to her remained central to the thrust of her studies. As a result, she was easily turned by her father's suggestion from the Hamblin study to the history of her grandfather, which was published in 1942 as *Dudley Leavitt: Pioneer to Southern Utah.*

After paying her respects to the Leavitt family, Brooks turned her attention to the stories that ultimately became *Quicksand and Cactus.* These she worked on extensively during 1944. In that year she sent Morgan several episodes along with a prospectus for the book. He immediately became the enthusiastic promoter or "spiritual father" of the work, recognizing in it a high order of genius. It was, he wrote, a "passionate personal book . . . ," its material "absolutely wonderful!" and its tone "warm, human, witty, and wise." "Full of sunlight," it "gives you a renewed sense of the dignity of the human soul and the worth of human living; and it also gives you a great feeling of admiration for a modest woman who is a valiant woman in all the meaning of that term."[14]

But Morgan could also be a stern taskmaster. Over the next two years he wrote numerous critiques of the manuscript and shared it with Fawn Brodie, Bernard DeVoto, and several others whose criticisms he passed on to Mrs. Brooks. Among other things he warned against "institutionalized Mormondom." He wrote: "Let your people be human beings first, people second, and only then Mormons."[15] A tendency for the book to fall into its component stories also worried him. "The book should be, when you finish, not a sort of collection of magazine articles but a homogeneous thing which continues

[13]Morgan to Brooks, 5 November 1941, Juanita Brooks Collection.

[14]Morgan to Madeline McQuown, 11 February 1944, and to Bernard DeVoto, 4 August 1944, Morgan Collection, Marriott Library.

[15]Morgan to Brooks, n.d., Juanita Brooks Collection.

to grow in the organized unity of its wholeness. In other words, it should end by being more than the sum of its parts."[16]

But particularly he emphasized her personal development as "the first condition" of the book. Become, he urged, "the critical intelligence," the "outside observer," write "like a New Yorker explaining a far-away people, . . . try to achieve an external point of view on the life and people you are writing about."[17] "You are like that outside observer, intensely aware of and interested in the distinctive life you see."[18]

Altogether the 1944–45 criticism added up to a stiff seminar in the historical method. From it Mrs. Brooks acquired knowhow that would later appear in her other historical works, but she maintained the independence of her own position. During these years she also formed close and productive friendships with Austin and Alta Fife and Wayland Hand, Mormon Country folklorists. As Austin Fife later pointed out, she "adopted many of the principles of folklore and applied them to her writing, especially where historical methods failed. But the methodology of folklore never captured her. She remained independent, true to her own marvelous sense of the people and culture about which she wrote."[19] In a real way the same thing may be said about her response to Morgan's effort to have her write history as one who has left the community about which she wrote. Indeed, a major quality of Mrs. Brooks' writing continued to be the perspective of "being there." An affinity for the whole record and a determination to have the original facts speak for themselves remained dominant.

As things developed, *Quicksand and Cactus* did not find a ready publisher in the 1940s. With Morgan and DeVoto helping, Mrs. Brooks contacted Houghton–Mifflin, Farrar and Rinehart, and Bobbs–Merrill in quick succession. Later Alfred A. Knopf and E. P. Dutton were also approached. All responses were evidently negative. The manuscript was laid aside by 1946 and thereafter revived only

[16]Morgan to Brooks, 26 April 1945, Juanita Brooks Collection.
[17]Ibid.
[18]Morgan to Brooks, n.d., Juanita Brooks Collection.
[19]Conversation with Austin and Alta Fife, March 2, 1982.

periodically during the late 1950s and 1960s. But like other undertakings to which Mrs. Brooks set her hand, it remained on her agenda and, as the present publication attests, was ultimately finished.

In the veritable flood of letters about *Quicksand and Cactus* that came in 1944 was a passing reference that heralded another major step in Juanita Brooks' movement into the "untravell'd world." She was informed that the Henry E. Huntington Library in San Marino, California, had acquired the diaries of John D. Lee. Anxious to see what they might contain on the Mountain Meadows Massacre, she contacted Leslie Edgar Bliss, librarian at the Huntington. Not only did Bliss invite her to examine the Lee diaries, but, together with Robert Glass Cleland, senior research historian at the Library, he offered her a position as "field agent." Bliss himself continued to make periodic collecting trips into Utah, but Brooks became the kingpin of a successful collection drive that ultimately acquired more than three hundred original and photostated Mormon diaries, making the Huntington an important repository for Mormon studies. Thrust once again into a wide-ranging examination of sources, Mrs. Brooks turned her attention increasingly to the Mountain Meadows Massacre.

For nearly a hundred years Mormons had presumed that the less said about the Massacre the better. To the degree that it was discussed at all it was a strained subject, particularly in southern Utah. Generations had come and gone in whispered restraint. Mormon historians regarded the subject to be "forbidden ground" and ignored it or passed it off as an Indian depredation in which the limited role of white men was justly punished by the excommunication and eventual execution of John D. Lee, one of the participants. Supported by a Rockefeller grant arranged by the Huntington Library, Brooks proceeded quietly, but with determination, to study and write between 1945 and 1948.

As it came time to line up a publisher, another of the truly significant relationships in Mrs. Brooks' life began to take form. Wallace Stegner, who was serving in an editorial role at Houghton–Mifflin, as well as standing in well with the Stanford University Press because of his position as Professor of English there, took an interest in the manuscript. Like DeVoto, whom he admired and whose biography he has written (*The Uneasy Chair* [1974]), Stegner was an extraordinarily gifted writer with a rare flair for both fiction and history as well as a deeply spiritual sense for the West as an environment and place. He also had Utah connections, but lacked DeVoto's anger as he regarded his background there. By 1948 Stegner had already proven his worth as both a literary and historical observer of Utah's culture in *Big Rock Candy Mountain*, a 1938 novel set partly in Salt Lake City, and in *Mormon Country*, an impressionistic history published in 1942 that still has no superior as a sensitive treatment of the region's full culture. Later he drew upon his Utah awarenesses for very different narratives of labor martyr Joe Hill and government surveyor John Wesley Powell. He also wrote *The Gathering of Zion: The Story of the Mormon Trail* (1964), an enthusiastically received volume in McGraw–Hill's American Trails Series, on which Mrs. Brooks helped with sources and conceptualization.

But in 1948 Stegner learned that Houghton–Mifflin was not interested in the Mountain Meadows Massacre manuscript and then helped guide it through the process of acceptance at Stanford University Press. After the usual number of difficulties, *Mountain Meadows Massacre* appeared in 1950, the fruition of a lifetime's interest and a decade's direct effort. Breaking the long silence, the book at last handled the records, allowing readers "to see each steadily" and to see them as nearly whole as possible.[20] As Weber State College's Levi Peterson has pointed out in a thoughtful essay, *Mountain Meadows Massacre* was also an expression of the "profound emotional bond between . . . this quiet little woman . . . and the people of whom she writes." She had used history for the "elemental" purpose of expressing "the tragic emotion of her region and her church" and, in the hearts of many Mormons, had worked a "paradoxical alchemy whereby affirmation and relief arise from pain and despair."[21] The book was and remains a definitive statement, a penetrating analysis that through its approach to a sore spot gets near the heart of the frontier process.

[20]Brooks, "Just a Copyin'," p. 394.

[21]Levi S. Peterson, "Juanita Brooks: Historian as Tragedian," *Journal of Mormon History*, Vol. 3 (1976), pp. 47 and 54.

Obviously her relationship with the Church was of the essence. She was of the Mormon community, born to it, steeped in its tradition, and with a keen and loving sense of what it meant to be Mormon. Unlike many other Utah intellectuals of the era, she had no desire to leave Mormon Country either for distant centers or by way of close affiliation with institutions that would redefine and redirect her life. She remained a believer, on the other side of what she called the "philosophical Great Divide" from Morgan, who felt "absolutely no necessity to postulate the existence of God." "An unshakable conviction of the reality of God," he wrote her, "is basic in your whole attitude toward Mormonism. It gives an emotional color that subtly shapes all your thinking. . . . The result is that when you contemplate Mormon history, there is a vast area of the probable and the possible that you accept without much question."[22] She replied that not only would she have to make her own "judgements in light of . . . the reality of God" but that the Church was "as much my church as it is . . . anyone elses [*sic*]" and that she was "loyal to it." Yet, in view of what she had come to know about the Mountain Meadows Massacre, she was unable to "yield unquestioning obedience" to the Church's efforts to suppress the Massacre's full and real history.[23] In short, she was convinced that "nothing but the truth is good enough for the Church to which I belong, and that God does not expect us to lie in his name." As "an honest historian," she owed it to herself and "to my readers to tell the truth, for the truth suppressed is its own kind of a lie."[24]

In her determination to examine the truth even if it was embarrassing, she met opposition in many forms. The social atmosphere itself was not inviting. In St. George few understood her passion for opening the record. Although she longed to "write openly and unashamedly," her sense that her neighbors were unsympathetic became so strong that she did much of her research and writing under the closest secrecy.[25] She also feared that premature announce-

[22]Morgan to Brooks, 15 December 1945, Juanita Brooks Collection.

[23]Brooks to Morgan, 28 December 1945, Dale Morgan Collection, Manuscripts Division, Bancroft Library, University of California, Berkeley.

[24]Brooks to Jesse Udall, 23 June 1961, Juanita Brooks Collection.

[25]Brooks to Morgan, 13 August 1944, Morgan Collection, Bancroft Library.

ment would cause the project to die aborning. As she explained in 1944, she hesitated to request materials from the Church until she could "say why and when I was to use it and what for." Inquiries, she feared, would bring "the wrath of the leaders upon me before they understood that after all, I AM a good member of the church and not an apostate."[26]

To some degree, at least, her fears appear to have been well founded. When she made efforts to use materials from the Church Historian's Office in Salt Lake City, she was rebuffed by A. William Lund, Assistant Church Historian, who on one occasion apparently told her that "the Church" had "possessory rights in all the historical documents that are preserved among the Mormon people."[27] Overtures to lay the entire undertaking before David O. McKay, then a counselor in the first presidency, were repeatedly ignored or turned over to subordinates. And J. Reuben Clark, counselor to three Church presidents during this era, passed a prior judgment he was poorly prepared to make when he rejected Brooks' request to see one particular packet on the grounds that it contained "nothing that you do not already have, nothing that will do you any good."[28]

Indeed, J. Reuben Clark, whose influence among mid-century Mormons was by all accounts vast, seemed in Brooks' eyes to symbolize a growing tendency in the Church to control all elements of Mormon life. Referring to the "dictatorship of Brother Clark," she noted that the "term 'Reubenized' has been coined and generally used to refer to the regimentation which has developed. . . . By 'Reubenized' I mean the writing out of every program, every speech, whether for Sunday School conference, Mother's Day Program, or what not — the attitude that he gave out to the Seminary teachers that 'you are not hired to think. You are hired to teach — ' and then outlining certain things which *he* considered basic and the interpretation which *he* wanted placed on them."[29]

[26]Brooks to Morgan, 15 August 1944, Morgan Collection, Bancroft Library.

[27]Morgan to Fawn Brodie, 9 December 1951, Morgan Collection, Marriott Library.

[28]Brooks to Morgan, 19 May 1946, Morgan Collection, Bancroft Library.

[29]Brooks to Morgan, 4 June 1945, Morgan Collection, Bancroft Library.

While anger may occasionally be seen in the correspondence of Mrs. Brooks, one is impressed at the moderation of her general tone. In retrospect she must be seen as a responsible thinker, not as a rebel or even a dissident. Indeed, the commanding element of her character, as well as her writing, is loyalty to what she was herself, including the Mormon community. For subject material she turned again and again to southern Utah. She worked with and through her stake president, Harold Snow in St. George, who showed her records at the St. George temple and helped lay strategy for her approach to the general authorities of the Church. She met with George Albert Smith, president of the Church from 1945 to 1951, and received from him a backhanded kind of blessing when he ended an interview with: "The Lord Bless you, Sister Brooks. I hope that you are happy, permanently happy, with what you do."[30] At all points, *Mountain Meadows Massacre* and her later books were handled carefully to avoid a breach between herself and the Church.

In some degree she doubtless pursued this policy as a matter of sentiment. To some part, however, it grew from her conviction that the history of the Massacre and John D. Lee's life could most credibly be handled by a member of the Church. To withdraw personally or to be excommunicated would impair her effort to alter the Mormon approach to its past. In characteristically homely language she explained: "When a cowboy wants to turn a herd of stampeding cattle, he doesn't run directly counter to them. If he did, he'd be run over. He rides with them, and turns them gradually. So if I don't like the stand of the church, I can do more about it by staying in."[31]

In the process of writing *Mountain Meadows Massacre*, Mrs. Brooks had become increasingly convinced that something further

[30]Brooks to Jesse Udall, 23 June 1961, Juanita Brooks Collection.

[31]Quoted in Morgan to Fawn Brodie, 22 December 1945, Morgan Collection, Marriott Library. In Bitton and Ursenbach, p. 12, Brooks elaborated as follows: "One day Dad said to me, 'My girl, if you follow this tendency to criticize I'm afraid you will talk yourself right out of the Church. I'd hate to see you do that. I'm a cowboy, and I've learned that if I ride in the herd, I am lost — totally helpless. One who rides counter to it is trampled and killed. One who only trails behind means little, because he leaves all responsibility to others. It is the cowboy who rides the edge of the herd, who sings and calls and makes himself heard

was needed to put right the terrible burden John D. Lee had borne for the Massacre. To this end she joined Robert Glass Cleland in editing *A Mormon Chronicle: The Diaries of John D. Lee, 1848–1876* (1955). When Cleland fell ill, she completed the job, but from him learned more about the historian's disciplined approach, insight she applied ably to what is widely acknowledged to be one of the foremost Mormon diaries. In addition, her wide knowledge of Mormon history and determined care for accuracy enabled her to provide an extensive set of footnotes that greatly enhance Lee's narrative. The Huntington Library itself published the two-volume work.

Once this undertaking was finished, she turned to a biography, *John Doyle Lee: Zealot, Pioneer Builder, Scapegoat*, which carried her into the pre-Utah periods of Mormon history. In 1961 it was published by the Arthur H. Clark Company. Still pursuing her broadening interest in early Mormon history, she then edited *On the Mormon Frontier: The Diary of Hosea Stout*, the two volumes of which cover from 1844 to 1861, critical years in Mormon history. This work was published in 1964 by the University of Utah Press and the Utah State Historical Society, marking in a way a shift back towards home in Mrs. Brooks' writing. In the years that followed she published numerous articles and at least nine additional books, all of which dealt with Utah and family themes and were published by Utah or regional presses.

Taken together, the early essays and biography, the great contributions of mid-life, and the work of later years show the push and pull of two great forces upon Juanita Brooks: the family and local attachments on the one hand, and the great "untravell'd world" on the other. The appeal and perspective of what lay beyond contrast with the comfort and roots of the near-at-hand. Underlying currents include commitment to what birth and heritage made her, the broadening and tempering of personal trial, the ferment of the 1930s

---

who helps direct the course. Happy sounds are generally better than cursing, but there are times when he must maybe swear a little and swing a whip or lariat to round in a stray or turn the leaders. So don't lose yourself, and don't ride away and desert the outfit. Ride the edge of the herd and be alert, but know your directions, and call out loud and clear. Chances are, you won't make any difference, but on the other hand, you just might.' "

and 1940s, and a continuing sense of obligation and responsibility. A whirlpool that gives these currents special power is the Mountain Meadows Massacre. Picked up a bit at a time, her sense for it is tragic and haunted, but dominated finally by her feelings for self, people, and place. Among these feelings may be seen respect, agony, sorrow, comic relief, and hope.

Her writings stay directly on target throughout her long career, and the target on which they stay is the culture of Mormon Country's Dixie. Her published works began there: the *Harper's* and *Reader's Digest* articles, the first edition of *Dudley Leavitt,* and the early drafts of *Quicksand and Cactus* were all done from the perspective of Dixie's Middle Years and convey, as do no other writings, the spirit and values of the era. Through the Utah Historical Records Survey and the Huntington collecting she came close to the original settlers of southern Utah and Nevada. The glory of their aspirations, the heroism of their efforts and the burden of their tragedy were hers, almost as surely as if she had experienced it all.

Yet the broader untravelled world called. Her spirit is different from Dudley Leavitt's — much broader, much more involved in continuing, complex judgments, and marked with new vistas, different slants on truth, and what they implied. Different, too, were her associates — Morgan, DeVoto, Stegner, and Brodie included — who in many ways left Mormon Country. Yet, her excursion into the world was tentative, the excursion of a true descendant of Dudley Leavitt. No nonsense. No rebellion. Perhaps more than even his and his pioneer associates', hers was a service to her people. She opted to stay in her society, if not in the sense of a compliant Mormon faith, then perhaps in a larger and better sense than one often finds among individuals narrowly committed to institutions rather than to people and their heritage. Although Mormon faith is inextricably intertwined with her roots in Mormon Country's Dixie, it was ultimately the spirit and character of that country's Middle Years that guided her. The local culture was also more important in the course her writings took than were the sentiments and conventions of scholarship, although, to be sure, these were used to get at the character of her people, and to apply the salve that a frank and public discussion of the past represented to a society long troubled by half-silence.

Quicksand and Cactus

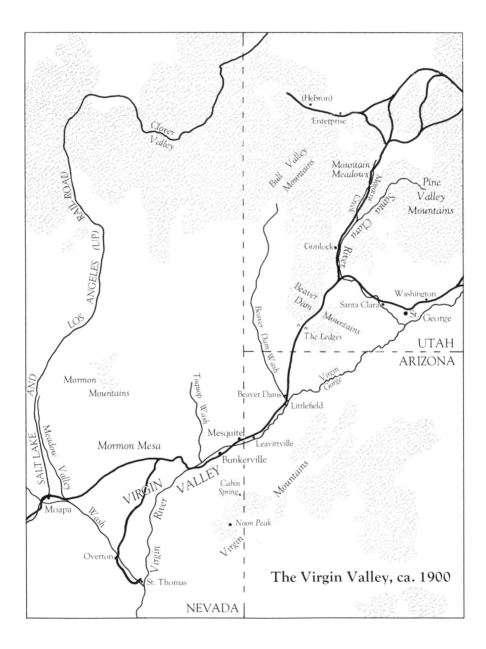

(Hebron)

Enterprise

Clover
Valley

Bull Valley
Mountains

Mountain
Meadows

Pine
Valley
Mountains

Gunlock

Beaver
Dam
Mountains

" "
The Ledges

Washington

Santa Clara

St. George

UTAH
ARIZONA

Mormon
Mountains

Toquop Wash

Beaver Dam Wash

Beaver Dams

Virgin
Gorge

Littlefield

Mesquite

Mormon Mesa

Leavittville

Bunkerville

Mountains

Cabin
Spring

Moapa

Virgin
River Valley

VIRGIN VALLEY

Noon Peak

Overton

Virgin

Virgin

St. Thomas

Wash

Meadow Valley

SALT LAKE AND

LOS ANGELES (UP) RAIL-ROAD

The Virgin Valley, ca. 1900

NEVADA

PART ONE

Wide, Wonderful World

Wide, Wonderful World

IT WAS THE SATURDAY AFTERNOON BEFORE EASTER when our Sunday School teacher took her class of six- and seven-year-olds on a hike up the hill. The crowd gathered at our place, because the only bridge across the Big Ditch was straight across the road from our gate. It really wasn't a bridge; it was a big log that had been squared off on top and settled into the banks so that it was solid. Near as it was, I had never ventured across it before. I was taught to stay away from the Big Ditch.

Our teacher went over first, and stood ready to take the hand of each of us as we arrived. After three or four had run across, it didn't seem dangerous at all, and I wondered that it was so easy. A well-beaten path went for quite a ways before it branched, one trail to go over to the windmill in the wash, the other up the hill. We took this, the left-hand road.

The hill rose before us in three tiers: an easy-to-climb one to the first level clearing; a longer climb to the second level — but not a steep climb. The third was both long and steep.

Our teacher stopped on the first level while we gathered wild flowers: Indian paint-brushes, blue-soldiers, buttercups, sand verbenas, and miniature red hollyhocks. Better than the flowers were the "Bottle Stoppers," tart and tasty. We ate them with great relish, for they are the nearest thing to satisfy the thirst that the desert offers.

At the second level we rested again. Now the scene below had broadened; we could see the homes and trees in town clearly.

"See the town? Can you find your own home in it? Look at the Meeting House, set off there by itself. Everybody comes to the Meeting House, so we will count from there."

We found the School House in the northwest edge of Bunkerville, the Store and the Post Office together, and the Bishop's house next to them. Every home had its quarter-of-a-block for corrals, garden, fruit trees or vineyard. We counted forty houses, but some had no families in them. Just old couples or one woman living alone. There were also three brand new brick houses going up — not adobe, but real, burned brick!

"Look toward the east across the river. Can you see Mesquite?"

Of course we could. Most of us had relatives living there in that brand new settlement just getting a good start. It was five miles away, with the river to cross, but we had all gone over with our families. A trip to Mesquite was for all day. We would get our morning's work done, give all the animals extra feed, ride in the wagon, and stop at one or another of our relatives', make brief calls on others, invite them to come over and see us sometime. Sometimes Ma would name a day when she would have a quilt on the frames. These trips were usually made on Saturdays, and we must be home by sundown. Yes, we knew Mesquite.

"Now look at the blue mountains far to the east. Behind them is St. George, a big city with a temple and a tabernacle. This is where our young folks go to get married, so some day you may go there, too."

None of us had been as far as that.

"Now look at the fields, up above the town and just behind it, and way down below it. They look like a quilt made of square blocks, with the cottonwood trees the stitching to hold them together. Do you know how important those trees are? They are called 'living fences,' because they have grown so large that their trunks almost touch. What else are they good for? Can some of you tell me?"

"They give us our winter wood," one called out.

"We use them to make corrals and pole gates, and some pole fences around the public square."

"The horses and cows eat the tender branches and peel off the bark for food."

"Yes, indeed, the cottonwood trees are a very important part of our lives, and we should appreciate them and take care of them. A few were here long before a white man came to settle. The Lone Tree in our pasture would be one of these.

"Now look past the fields and out to the Mormon Mesa that looks as flat as a table. I think it is called that because the Mormons made the first road to the top. Far, far down, over many days' travel, is California and the ocean, but the place we know best is Las Vegas, three or four days' travel. All of this is a desert where several people we know have died of thirst.

"People have learned that they should not travel that road in the summer months; if they do go, they must carry big barrels of water and travel in the night as much as possible. And they must be sure that their wagon tires are solid. The heat dries out the wood until sometimes the tire gets loose and runs off. That was what happened to Brother and Sister Davidson: the tire ran off, the wheel broke down, and they had water for only one day, but they all died of thirst. That was years ago; now things are much better. Still, in its own way, what we see here is beautiful. Listen to me and we will all say it together:

> Great, Wide, BEAUTIFUL, wonderful world
> With the wonderful water around you curled
> And the beautiful trees upon your breast
> World, you are beautifully dressed."

The climb ahead was long and steep. Some of us had handfuls of flowers or bottle stoppers as well as lunches to carry. Our teacher made no suggestion as to how we should manage our lunches, but she took some care with her own. She had picked no flowers, but she had several items to adjust, among them a lunch box, with a solid handle in one hand and her jug of water with its woven back and handle in the other, along with a roll of brown paper. She wisely kept a slow, even gait, for this climb was not only long, but steep. Boys who had started on the run were dragging slowly before they reached the top. The girls, for the most part, were content to keep along with the teacher, but by the time they reached the top, they too sank in exhaustion, not caring whether they looked at the scenery.

The teacher selected a clear place where she unrolled the stiff paper she had somehow managed to bring and on top of it spread a small white cloth. We all gathered around, each with his individual paper bag or box, and after the brief blessing, we ate as hungry children do. The boys had a game with their eggs, cracking them together, with the broken one surrendered; "Playing Bust," they called it. Before long one boy had almost half the eggs in the crowd. For dessert our teacher gave each one a decorated cupcake and a drink of lemonade from the bottle, one dipperful around, and then seconds as long as it lasted.

Again the teacher called us together to show how much of the wide, wonderful world we could see from this point. How changed the town looked from here! How much wider the river bed, how endless the stretches east and west! This time we all stretched our arms out at shoulder level and said in unison, twisting our bodies to right and left as far as we could:

> Great, wide, BEAUTIFUL, WONDERFUL WORLD
> With the wonderful water around you curled
> And the beautiful trees upon your breast
> World, You are beautifully dressed.

Due west of us in the valley stood the windmill, its silver wheel spinning in the wind as fast and lively as though it were actually operating a pump and bringing out water.

I knew the story of the windmill well, for Pa had put in many days working there. Our need for water — for good, cool mountain water — was very great indeed. Many of the folks had heard of "Water Witches" who could locate underground streams by means of a forked stick, so when one came to town and persuaded the Bishop and several other leading brethren to go with him to run some tests, all were pleased when the forked stick would turn and point downward at the same approximate point in the wash, indicating that there had to be an underground stream along that line. Convinced at last, the Bishop called a meeting and asked the brethren if they would support the project by their labor. Not many would be able to work at the same time, but all should work equally in turn.

[8]

The decision had hardly been made and the water witch out of town before a windmill salesman came to visit the Bishop. Again a meeting was called of all the brethren to hear his proposition. Now some were doubtful; some just plain didn't have money to invest in a windmill. Two or three walked out, wanting nothing to do with any part of it; they would do their dam and ditch work for the river water, but put in neither time nor money on this. Others, lacking money, offered to work up time for those who would prefer to have their digging done for them and pay for it.

The salesman talked of a gushing stream of clear, cool mountain water from the snows that fell high around the Noon Peak. He would not only sell them a first class windmill, but would give them a franchise on all the wind within a thirty-mile radius, which meant that if and when they tapped their underground stream, no one else could come in and sink another well on it.

How long the digging lasted, I do not know, but they went down and down until they could see the stars at midday. At last they struck mud! Such an excitement as went through the town! When the first buckets of muddy water came out, the workers told themselves that they just hadn't hit the main stream yet. But another day's work convinced them all: the water was brackish, like slough water — totally unfit to drink!

Most folks charged the whole thing up to experience — lost time and lost effort. Brother Abbott took apart the fine wooden trough he had made to hold the water for the cattle to drink from, and stacked the board for future use in building caskets or items of home furniture. But the windmill stood for years, its silver wheel spinning in the wind.

Nor would any of us venture to go near it; we had already been warned that that area was the Devil's Ground. Nothing good could come to any child who was poking around there; on the contrary, there might be serious dangers lurking there, not visible to his eyes. So we paid no attention to the windmill; we set ourselves to gathering the hill flowers to take home — plenty of buttercups, and miniature hollyhocks, blue bells, piss-a-beds, rare sego lilies. Some gathered succulent bottle stoppers instead of flowers; they would take them home for their younger brothers or sisters to eat. Cactus blossoms were the most beautiful by far, but their thorns were so numerous that it was almost impossible to get one to carry home even on the end of a long stick.

A quick run down the hill, along the trail, across the log over the Big Ditch, and I was back in our own dooryard. But the place would never be quite the same again since I had seen it in relation to the Wide, Wonderful World.

A One-Room Adobe House

MY EARLIEST MEMORIES ARE OF A ONE-ROOMED ADOBE HOUSE with a flat, shingle roof that sloped from front to back, its edges extending about a foot beyond the walls all around. The building faced south, and the door, in the exact center, told Ma the time of day almost as accurately as did the striking clock her father had given her for a wedding present. We knew that when the sun was straight in the door, it was noon, and the table must be set and ready, whether the food on the stove was cooked or not.

Ma made a sort of game with the sun, noting when it reached its point of turning at the back in mid-winter, and again when it was almost directly overhead in the summer, marked the place, and checked the calendar.

Our floor was interesting, too. They laughed about it, saying it was like Bill Bracken's, which he claimed was twelve-inch lumber put down so green that it shrank an inch a year for fourteen years! Ours wasn't quite that bad, but the cracks were so big that Ma had only to brush cross-wise and the dirt disappeared through them. When she scrubbed it with her bar of oose-root soap, she worked the sudsy water lengthwise, then threw clear water on and swept it crosswise. The floor shone, and there was little wiping up to do. Braided rugs covered most of the space in the front of the room, while a length of rag carpet filled in across the back.

[11]

The furniture? Well, the big bed filled one corner; the trundle bed on which Charity and I slept folded down and was pushed under it. The crib for the baby was across the foot.

The other front corner held a homemade clothes closet, a triangular piece of lumber fitted and braced securely enough to hold hat boxes and other items that needed to be put back out of the way. At the same time it supported curtains behind which Pa's Sunday suit and Ma's nicer dresses could hang.

At the back of the room the little stove stood on solid four-by-fours, which lifted it up about two feet. This brought it to a height where Ma could cook on top without having to stoop over too much. She would have to kneel to take out the ashes or scrape out the soot. She was proud of the little stove, though. It was hers and paid for. For now, it was adequate. It would take two loaves of bread at a time, and bake a cake or a pan of biscuits as nice as one would want. The only other item I remember was the crocheted tidy on Ma's trunk. It had a peacock design on top, and the fringe touched the floor all around.

Pa was tall and athletic, standing six-foot in his stocking feet. Ma was six years younger than he, and hardly reached to his shoulder. He called her his "Little Dutch Gal" because she was Swiss. Family genealogists said that his own ancestor came to the British Isles along with William the Conqueror in 1066; later members were among the first settlers of the Massachusetts Bay Colony in America.

Many things Ma could do. She could play the guitar and sing — it was her favorite pastime. She enjoyed working in the garden; she made her own clothes; she could do many kinds of fancywork. She was also a good cook, where special Swiss dishes were served; her yeast bread was faultless, but she couldn't make good quick breads, or said she couldn't.

Our washdish stood on a bench just outside the door. The bench was covered with oilcloth, as was the wall behind it. An extra big nail supported the towel, which hung from the strip of lumber along the top. The towel had a loop of heavy tape on each end, so that when it got dirty on one end, it could be turned to use the other.

Pa was a messy washer. He needed a bigger dish, for one thing. He'd sozzle and slosh around — hands to elbows, and head all over, often wiping long dirty streaks onto the towel. Then he'd stand straddle-legged and bent at the knee to try to see in the mirror. It was too low for him and too high for Ma. She'd have to tip it and rest the bottom on another nail in order to see herself.

One noon after an especially wet wash, Pa combed and combed at his hair, working it up and back in front and sides, and smoothing down the back, but leaving on top an upstanding lock for all the world to see, like the top-knot of a father quail. I saw it and was about to tell Pa, but Ma, with a grip on my arm, shook her head for me to be still. We talked of other things, until finally Pa wiped off his mouth, pushed back his chair, clapped on his hat, and was on his way back to ditch cleaning.

"If Pa had been going to a meeting, I'd have smoothed his hair down," Ma said, after he had gone. "But it will look just the same the minute he takes his hat off at work."

She was so right. Pa thought his hair was perfect, and he'd have been upset if we had told him. I knew Ma's way was best.

Pa became more of a hero to me after one night when a hurricane of wind came up, black clouds over the mountain, with lots of thunder and lightning. Pa roused Charity and me and told us we were going down to Aunt Rell's place, because she was always so afraid of lightning. I wondered if it wasn't that Ma was afraid to stay in our house. The roof was bobbing up and down, like it just might fly off any minute.

Pa carried Charity and me, though we were big girls and well able to walk. It was quite cool, though, and we had just been awakened from a sound sleep. Ma had Aura, the baby, well wrapped.

What a wind! Already one big limb had been torn from a tree we passed; everything seemed bending before the wind. For a while it seemed to me that even the moon was running away, but Pa assured me that it was only the clouds that were running; the moon was far and beyond anything on this little earth and its winds.

Of the rest of the night I remember nothing, but the next day Pa brought home a huge iron bucket in the wagon. It seemed almost as big as a barrel. He had also a long, heavy chain. He at once proceeded to put one end of the chain around the bottom of the pomegranate bush at the west side of the house. Close to the ground he placed it, drawing it tight, and fastening it with a big hook. To be sure that it would never break, he wired it securely with barbed wire.

Then, bringing it over the roof of the house near the front, he fastened the iron bucket on this end. Next he filled the bucket with big rocks, scrap iron, old horse shoes — anything that would add weight. The bottom of the bucket was about three feet from the ground, and we children were ordered to stay away from it.

Finally surveying the project, he said with some pride, "Now let the wind blow! Our roof will stay on!"

I must not forget to tell about the "Wire House," our summer bedroom. In all the Mormon settlements in the west, people were counseled to build their first, temporary shelters back deep in the lot, so that there would be plenty of room in front for the large, permanent home. That is why we had such a large dooryard. Toward the west, where the ditch slanted to go across to the garden spot there, four cottonwood trees had been planted some twenty-six years earlier, when the place was first surveyed. They were now large trunks which had been topped many times, and were heavy with branches about the size of a man's arm. These would be thinned and later topped again, but now they provided wonderful, deep shade.

Here the Wire House gave us a cool place, free from mosquitoes, flies, and creeping bugs of all kinds. Four cedar posts, well-barked and trimmed, formed the corners. A wide plank, one-by-fifteen inches, went all around the bottom, with soil against it on the outside. Another plank a little narrower went around the top, with three crosspieces, the middle one a little higher, to give the roof a bit of slant. A two-by-four all around the middle, and fitted in between the posts, matched neatly the width of the screen, with one strip above and one below, tacked on firmly and held with lath. With screen sides, a heavy canvas roof, a solid screen door, the place caught even the faintest whiff of a breeze, and with all four legs of the bed in cans of water, the ants and other creeping insects had not a chance. We had a full-sized, iron bed the length of the room and a small one across the bottom. On hot nights we would throw buckets of water over the yard to cool the air. How proud we were of this Wire House! Children went inside only to sleep; never to play.

Missionary's Wife

ONE REASON THAT MA COULD BE CONTENTED IN THE LITTLE HOUSE was that she knew it wouldn't be forever, though it did stretch over almost seven long years. The opening of the mines at Delamar, Nevada, made a good market for anything Ma and Pa could raise and haul in. The first peddling trip with dried fruit, molasses, and eggs convinced Pa that here was a venture to take seriously. His first profits were invested in a new freight wagon, team, and harness. As these were paid for, he began work on a new home.

He found that live chickens paid best, next eggs by the twelve-dozen crate, then dried fruit, especially figs. He used the bottom bed of his wagon for the chickens, strewing it generously with straw.

The top bed was lifted up by two-inch wooden blocks placed about a foot apart. This gave the chickens ample room to feed and drink from the tin cans which were placed on the outside. This arrangement made it possible for the birds to reach the market in prime condition.

In the top bed of the wagon Pa had crates of eggs, tomatoes, peaches, summer squash, string beans, green corn, all covered with a wet blanket and a dry canvas. Not having ice, he couldn't carry butter.

He would load in the afternoon and drive through the night, then stop in a shady place through most of the day, travel again in the night to arrive just at daybreak.

After his first trip Pa had no trouble selling his wares. People liked their chickens freshly killed and their vegetables fresh.

Ma's record book says that he cleared more than a hundred dollars on his first venture, and he soon began to turn whatever he got into the building of a new home. Compared to most, his home was modest: two large rooms, with a cellar under one, and a back porch behind the other.

Things went well with him. He paid as he went, and on his return trips hauled material for his own house and some for neighbors who were also building. Freighting both ways made double profit.

Through all this Ma worked almost harder than Pa did, for she kept the books and paid for his purchases. In addition, she had the children and the chores, the irrigating, and the fruit, grapes, and garden. But things went so well that she was more than happy, singing every night.

Ma was so proud to see this beautiful house go up. Already she had almost enough carpet rags sewed into large balls and stuffed into a gunnysack to go to the weaver. All her life she had longed for an organ. Now seemed the time to get one, while they were making money. She was very tactful, but she did make it clear that of all the things she needed, she wanted an organ most — more, even, than a big new stove. So it was ordered from a catalog to come by freight from Salt Lake City to Delamar, and Pa could bring it in. Such a rejoicing when it arrived! True, it had come early and would have to stand in the crate until the plastering and painting were done.

It was not yet safely under cover when the letter came from Box B, Salt Lake City. Pa was called on a mission! Horrors! How could he go on a mission and leave his home and family in this stage? And even before that, he must attend the Brigham Young Academy in Provo for three months and take a "Prep Course" to orient him to the new business of preaching the Gospel and quoting Scripture. This would be counted as part of the mission.

He had time for two or three more peddling trips before he must go; the house would be fully plastered and the woodwork painted. The cellar steps would be only flat rocks and the floor dirt. The family, with Pa gone, could get along well in the smaller room, and the school district would rent the other for $7.50 a month to hold the first three grades of school in.

When the time came, Pa sold his wagon, team, and harness to Uncle Wier, Pa's oldest brother; he leased his land for two years; he disposed of the few head of range cattle that he had. That would not be enough, so the mowing machine and rake went also. Someone asked gently if Ma might do well not to even uncrate the organ, but to sell it, add the freight and the trouble and make a little profit on it.

Pa's answer was a firm NO! If a mission meant sacrificing Mary's organ, he would not go. This pleased Ma above everything else, to be assured of her husband's loyalty and love. It made the organ doubly valuable to her.

Of Pa's leaving I remember only that we all went with him in a wagon as far as Leavittville, where he had to say goodbye to his parents. I ran and hid to cry out my grief alone, and would not come out at all until the buggy he went in was far out of sight, and I had slept an hour or two.

At home everything seemed empty and bleak. True, we were in the big, new house, where one room seemed twice the size of the old place. And we had a fire in the fireplace every night, and the beautiful organ, with all its fancy trimming on top, and a large mirror so high up nobody could see into it without climbing on the round stool, which was apt to turn unexpectedly.

Ma didn't play the organ often, though she shined it up every day. There were so many chores — the cows, the pigs, the chickens, the irrigating — besides the children and the housework. And she was getting heavy with another baby. She had little heart to sing, and when she did, she used the guitar.

When he arrived, the first son, our joy knew no bounds.

"Won't Pa be surprised? Let's have another one before he gets back, and surprise him again!" I suggested, and could not understand why Ma laughed so hard when she agreed that Pa most certainly *would* be surprised.

What should we name the little fellow? Ma's taste in names was past anyone's guess. I got mine because she had heard the song about the little Mexican girl who stabbed her American lover after he told her that he was going back to his old sweetheart at home.

"My Juanita, I must leave you; I have come to say farewell," was the first line. Then, after several verses in between, "There lay El Americano, with a dagger in his heart," was the end. She had picked it up by hearing it, and sang it to quite a fancy guitar accompaniment. Hence my name, *Waneta*, on the Church records. Not only that, but it was pronounced *W'neeta* and soon shortened to *W'neét*.

Charity got her name as a compromise between *Patience*, which Ma wanted in honor of a good friend, Patience Lee, and Pa's preference for a family name like *Thirza*. It became slurred into *Cherie*.

Aura's name, like mine, came from a song which Ma had not seen in print, but which began "Aura Lee, Aura Lee, maid with golden hair, She brings with her the birds and bees, and sunshine in the air." We all thought it appropriate; Aura had such beautiful golden hair.

For her first son, Ma knew that she must use his father's name, but decided to have it as only an initial. He would be Melvin Henry, in honor of Melvin Harmon, who had been her teacher in the last two grades of school at Santa Clara, Ma's happiest years. This teacher had been kind and understanding, quite in contrast to the stern one who had preceded him and used a switch or ruler to enforce his orders. She always said that she learned more under Melvin Harmon than under all the others put together. And she never outgrew her *Heimweh*, or homesickness for Santa Clara.

For the first months, life without Pa was very hard. I was old enough to know that we could not expect him back for a long, long time, but Charity wanted him NOW! She refused to be comforted, until at last Ma would cry, too. As she once said later, "each evening was a howling success!" But now with a new baby boy we could be entertained and comforted. Each day we saw something new in his development. Each evening Ma would play the guitar and sing to us happy songs or little ditties that we might join in on, or teach us little poems, one of which was set to music. We sang it often.

> Dare to do right! Dare to be true!
> You have a work that no other can do!

Do it so bravely, so kindly, so well
Angels will hasten the story to tell.
Dare! Dare! Dare to do right!
Dare to do right! Dare to do right!

She taught us the Lord's Prayer, and when she could see that I might learn more difficult things, she began on the Articles of Faith then the Ten Commandments. She knew all the time that I was a monotone when it came to singing, so she drilled me in learning poems.

Ma had two ambitions during this time: first, to train her children well, and second, to beautify this new home. The one room we lived in needed so many things — new curtains at the windows, pictures on the walls, nicnacs on the mantle, an extra large rug or two to fill in the bare strip the new rag carpet didn't cover. These were only a beginning, but Ma never lost sight of her goal. Food she could raise largely on her own lot, with the vineyard, the peach and plum trees, the almond trees, and with her skill in the vegetable garden. Milk, butter, and cottage cheese she could be sure of. But she must have more than just basic necessities; she needed beautiful things also.

It was hard for Ma to adjust socially now that she was alone. Here she was, not twenty-four years old, with four little children and no husband. And she did love to be in things, to sing and dance especially — just to be where the crowd was, to see what the other girls were wearing, and who danced with whom, and how. In the warm weather she might leave us three girls all asleep in the wire house and take Melvin with a little pillow and put him on one of the benches on the back stage, where other babies were sleeping. Then she would stay the dance out.

Though she might dance only once or twice — maybe with the floor manager, or the Bishop's counselor, or the husband of one of her good friends — it was worth it just to be there with the music, the activity, the crowd. Listening to the music from the wire house wasn't enough.

She must go to the weekly choir practice, too, for she was first soprano, and there was nothing she liked to do better than to sing. She would always tell me when she left us. Our coal oil lamp would burn low on the mantel if we were inside; from the wire house outside we could see the church lights clearly, and come over if we needed to.

Each year the choir presented a concert — a full evening of music, with perhaps two or three readings or short stunts, or special duets, trios, or quartettes, with perhaps a violin solo. But whatever it was, Ma figured in it, and would go, even if she occasionally got an older girl to sit with us.

The first holidays after Pa left they put on the play, *Ten Nights In a Barroom.* Mina Wittwer was the mother; I was the little girl. I'm not sure who the drunkard was, but I think it was Uncle List, Pa's older brother. I think they chose me because I was skinny and little and puny, like a drunkard's child might be. Then I lived so near that Ma could bring me over to say my lines and take me back again. I appeared in only one scene near the end of the play. I was to follow my mother to midstage, where she fell in a faint upon the floor. I must run to her, kneel down and cry, "Mama! Mama!" in the saddest voice, and then lean and rest my head on her knee, and sob.

The trouble she had to learn to faint! At first they put a heavy camp quilt, doubled, for her to fall on. Sometimes she would start to crumple at the ankles, then fold at the knees and go down in a lump; sometimes she tried to stand stiff and go down straight as a post. Neither seemed right; they weren't natural. I'm not sure how she finally did it; I know that each time I would run in, kneel beside her, and cry "Mama! Mama!" in a doleful voice and then actually cry, or make sounds of crying. The curtain for the third act came down on this scene.

We worked at it night after night. The prompter would be in place, the director there to supervise. Mina would stagger in as if exhausted, say her line "O, Dear Lord, what *can* I do?" and fall in her faint. I would run to her, kneel beside her, and say "Mama! Mama!" and try to shake her a little and cry.

It all seemed simple enough. I looked the part; I knew my lines. But they had never rehearsed the storm before, so I wasn't familiar with the sound effects. Whatever they made the wind out of, it was the most moaning, shrieking sound, and was actually blowing what looked like snow in. Just as Mina stumbled and fell there was a flash of lightning and a bang of thunder that petrified me there in the wing. Someone pushed me out, my fear was very real, so real that I almost forgot to say my lines. The manager from the wings facing me called crossly to me and motioned, "Down!" I said the words "Mama, Mama," all right, but with a fear so genuine that though I did fall down, I wanted to charge off before the curtain dropped. At least my crying now was very real, and the audience heard it clearly.

From that time on I have had no desire to act upon the stage.

We all soon learned that it was different to be the family of a missionary. Not only were we remembered in the prayers of many of our neighbors, but we had extra favors and attention. Early in February the priests' quorum of older teen-age boys came on a Saturday to work on our lot under the direction of two of the older brethren. They pruned and cleared out the vineyard; they hauled manure from the corral to the long garden patch and then plowed it under, all this after they had raked and burned last year's leavings.

For Ma, this was a special blessing, for she loved to work in the garden and among the vines, and this would assure her of a good crop. She said over in German that "Many hands make work light"; she also pitched in, made a big pan of fritters, baked a cake, and served a lemonade of sugar, cream of tartar, and lemon extract. For the boys, this was just a pleasant party. For us, it meant a clean corral, a vineyard which could be easily irrigated, and a garden spot almost ready to plant.

When people killed their pigs or beef, we always got some of the liver, and occasionally a bit of spareribs. Some, knowing Ma's Swiss background, and not wanting to handle the pork heads and feet themselves, offered them to her. She made a wonderful "Head-cheese" out of them.

One time we found a new sack of flour on the step; another time a half sack of potatoes. Uncle Wier would ride up on horseback, call from the sidewalk, and without getting off his horse, toss a coin or two into the dooryard — a dollar, or two or three quarters, or a couple of half dollars. Ma always called her thanks, but let the children pick up the coins. Uncle Wier's wife had been dead for a long time, and he didn't want anyone to think he was courting Ma;

and she was equally careful not to be too cordial. But for us, Uncle Wier's gifts were worth all the rest. In fact, I wondered about some of the others. "Do you think that Father-in-Heaven will bless folks for giving away stuff that they don't want themselves?" I asked one day. "Like the liver that their own kids won't eat, and the heads and pigs' feet, that they'd give to the dog — only they haven't got a dog. So they give them to us?"

"Don't you worry about what Father-in-Heaven will do," Ma told me, "and you be thankful for things that we can use, whether the neighbors can or not. Different folks have different ways, and they're not always right or wrong — they're just different."

It wasn't long before we were adjusted to being without Pa. Ma still went regularly to all her meetings, usually taking all four of us along, but sometimes getting a neighbor girl to stay with the two younger ones.

I don't remember Ma ever bearing her testimony in meeting. She sang in the church choir, which gave her a seat on the stand, and as long as Melvin nursed, she took him with her, nursed him when he was hungry, as all the other mothers did, and laid him on the bench while she sang.

Sister Snow was living in Bunkerville on the underground, that is, she was a second wife in a polygamous family and the officers were after men with more than one wife. She had a rich alto voice and could also sing by note, so that when a new song appeared in the *Juvenile Instructor*, she and Ma would get together, figure out the tune, and learn to sing it. At least twice that I remember, they bore their testimony by singing a song. They would sit together and stand all unannounced, in the middle of the meeting. The first song was "Count Your Blessings," which seemed most appropriate, sung by these two young women who were now husband-less.

The other song, rendered months later, frightened me and troubled me sorely: "Let Zion in Her Beauty Rise," it began, and then went on to describe the Last Days, the Second Coming of the Savior, and the horrible happenings which would precede it:

> . . . the moon be turn-ed into blood, the waters into gall . . .
> The sun in darkness shall be clothed, all nature look afright
> While men, rebellious, wicked men, stand trembling at the sight . . .

Worst of all, they repeated some of the awful lines two or three times, until by the end, I was almost sick. True, their voices blended well and they sang well, and the words and music were in our own publication, but I didn't like it, and told Ma so after we got home.

"I don't know how the good can be picked out, because not all the goers-to-church are too righteous, and some who never darken the door are the most kind. Uncle Wier never goes to church, but he helps us more than anyone else does. I'd hate to see him burned as stubble," I argued. I think this was my first open question regarding any of the Church preaching. "Whoever wrote that song, I don't believe it, and I never will," I declared. "I don't think Father-in-Heaven works that way."

Ma didn't press the point, though I think she was disappointed that I didn't approve of this song. It was a difficult song, and she hit the high notes true and strong, and their voices did blend. But to me, it was not a song to be sung in a meeting of Saints. Evidently no one else felt as I did, for the testimonies were more prompt and fervent after the song, and the Bishop made special thanks that these two sisters should use their lovely voices "and introduce us to the new songs that come out."

One activity I remember was the result of Brother Adams' testimony. Brother Adams was one of the best farmers in the valley, and this year he planted a large field of cotton. In the Fast Meeting where members of the congregation arose to speak as the Spirit prompted, he stood up and said, "Brothers and Sisters, when we first came into this valley we were told to raise cotton. For the first few years, every family had cotton, but now I am the only one who has followed that counsel. I planted a large field, and it has produced much better than any I have ever had before. But my boys won't pick it, and I can't pick it. It would be a shame for it to go to waste. But what can I do?"

His voice broke and he sat down in tears.

Instantly the Bishop was on his feet.

"Brothers and sisters, I understand Brother Adams' problem perfectly. Sister Viola, do you think that the women would agree to pick the field on share? We would see that your share is hauled to the Washington Factory and made into cloth or batting. What do you

[23]

say? How many sisters will volunteer to go out tomorrow morning and start to work at it? Raise your hands!"

All hands went up.

This was in September, so Melvin was nearly seven months old. Ma took us all, with a lunch, a two-quart bottle of milk wrapped in wet cloths, a pint bottle of new honey with a piece of butter in for our bread, which was in one solid loaf to be sliced off when the time came.

How enthusiastically Ma entered into her work; she hummed a little as she fairly snatched off the fluffy white bolls and put them into her sack. Several of the older women said she was worth two or three of them, she filled her sack so quickly. It was a fun day for us, too. The sand in the ditch was just damp enough to work into houses and roads and walls.

We all went home tired, but Ma was light-hearted in the fact that she had accomplished so much and that the sisters noticed and appreciated it. And she had paid just a little of her debt to Brother Adams, who had hauled a load of green cottonwood, small-sized enough that the boys could cut off stove lengths in just a few strokes.

This cotton picking experience was a good recommendation for Ma in another way. As they were emptying their sacks, Brother Adams came over to Ma and asked if she thought she might let her mother take care of the children for a day or two, and help his wife with her late fall housecleaning. Ma was happy at the prospect for several reasons. Sister Adams was Swiss; she was Mary Neagle from the wealthy Neagle family who had given almost a fortune to the Church. Mary never came to church or entered into any community activities. Her family consisted of seven stalwart sons, and she had all she could do to take care of the home, prepare meals, and keep everything as immaculate as she thought it should be. Thomas suggested that Ma drop in sometime tomorrow and tell Mary he had asked her to.

Sister Adams did need help. In general, she preferred to do her own work, but now if Ma could work Friday and Saturday of the next week, she would see how much more she would need her.

Melvin was not yet weaned, but it might be good if he were

away from her for a few hours during the day. Grandma Hafen encouraged it.

Ma came home the first night very tired, but much encouraged. She could take another day of this kind of scrubbing, but Sunday would be a welcome day of rest.

By Saturday night the long parlor room in the Adams home had been newly calsomined, the woodwork washed, the window panes washed, the floor covered with fresh clean straw, with the carpet securely tacked down. New lace curtains were at the windows.

Ma's reward? Well, there was a dollar a day in cash, and all the old curtains. At first, Ma was a little resentful, but when Grandma Hafen looked through them, she thought them a very good bargain. First, there were so many; almost the full north side of the long rock living room was windows, besides one on the east and another on the west, all a uniform yard-and-a-half long with wide hems, and a nice satin finish. True, they were faded a little, but they could be washed, dipped into a yellow dye and used as window curtains far as our kitchen needed curtains. Or they could be colored red or blue and made into dresses for the three little girls, or they could be cut into quilt blocks. Yes, indeed, Grandma Hafen could find use for the smallest scraps.

Better than either the money or the cloth was the discovery that Mary Adams also loved to sing, that she also had a rich alto voice and could read the notes perfectly. Sister Snow had moved back to the St. George area, and Ma had found no one else to sing with her.

They ran through a song that both had learned at Santa Clara, "The Whippoorwill Song," which gave both soprano and alto a chance to star. They hummed it a little at their work, and decided to really take time to practice it seriously to the guitar accompaniment.

Thus it was that these two Marys began to sing together, Ma coming down occasionally in the late evening, until they had several numbers that they would do on call. They never were asked to participate on any program, partly, perhaps, because Mary Adams seldom went out anywhere.

As the holidays drew near, they practiced more often, for every year there was one evening set aside especially for adults and married folks. Soon the Committee announced that the Christmas program this year would be called "The Fruit Basket Tipped Over," and each lady should bring a dish that would serve at least five people. It was suggested that the sisters cooperate to see that the menu would be balanced, and that each should be prepared for some small part on the program, in case she might be called.

The Fruit Basket Tipped Over

MA MADE A LARGE DISHPAN OF FRITTERS, TIMING THEM SO THAT THEY WOULD STILL BE FRESH AND CRISP, and ran across to take them, coming back for her guitar and the baby. The other two girls didn't really know about the party, but had gone to bed tired after an active afternoon. The baby was too heavy for me, and Ma wouldn't trust the guitar to me, so I carried a pillow and shawl out of which to make a bed for Melvin on the back of the stage. I would go to watch him, but I must stay behind the scenery, and never even peek out. I was very much relieved to find Vinda Waite when I got there. Her reason for coming was the same as mine, and her instructions the same. We could talk to each other in whispers, and maybe play a game or two of jacks.

The committee had arranged the dance hall with the benches pulled into a square which covered only the front half of the floor. On a low platform was the organ, and a very high chair for the Judge. All the food was covered up on a table at the front side of the circle. As each person came in he had pinned on him a strip of paper more than an inch wide and four or five inches long upon which a name was printed in heavy black ink, clear enough to be easily read.

The officials were the Narrator, the Teamster, and the Judge. Several people helped in pinning on the names, so that she could be conscious of those who wore different names.

At last the crowd had gathered, the Judge came and sat in the big chair, the Teamster in a big hat, with vest and boots, and a whip for show. He stood beside the chair, and the Narrator stepped forward to explain the game.

This was the story of a family who had been called to move to a different town — a procedure with which many in the room were familiar — and of their adventures en route.

"You have your names in plain sight, so whenever you are mentioned in the story, you must jump up, bow, turn around, and sit down. You must act quickly, so that the story will not be delayed. The sheriff will collect a forfeit from everyone who fails to respond."

So the story began by naming the members of the Slattery family which was moving in search of better climate. The Mother, the Father, Slow-foot, the son, and Tangle-locks, the daughter, were all duly introduced, along with Bouncer, the dog, Scratchem, the cat, Crump, the cow. In addition, there were parts of the harness and wagon to be mentioned, and each horse had his own name.

The adventures of this family were hilarious: the tire ran off, they must prop up the wheel and repair it; the dog ran away with a part of the harness; the endgate was loose and spilled out some items on the climb up the hill. Parts of the harness broke; the various members had been snitching from the grub box and the fruit basket. When it came time to camp and each had to take over his particular chores, the fruit basket tipped over! At this signal every person in the room had to scurry to a new seat.

In the meantime, the Teamster had collected a boxfull of forfeits from people who had failed to jump up promptly enough. Each of these must redeem the forfeit that the Sheriff held by obeying the orders of the Judge.

The court was set up and proceeded with the Judge in the chair and the Teamster selecting an object out of the box and holding it high so that the audience could see it, although the Judge could not.

"Heavy, heavy hangs over your poor head," he would say.

"Fine or Superfine?" (Male or female?) the Judge would ask.

"Fine. What shall the owner do to redeem it?"

For the first penalty the culprit must entertain the crowd for five to ten minutes by reciting a poem, or by giving a series of jokes or conundrums for the crowd to guess. We two girls, listening behind the scenes, were much interested in these.

A house-full, a hole-full, can't catch a bowlfull. (Smoke.)

Round the house and round the house, and leaves only one track. (Wheelbarrow.)

Little Nanny Etticoat in a white petticoat — and a red nose
The longer she stands, the shorter she grows. (A candle.)

As I was passing London Hall
I heard a Fellow so loudly call.
His lips were bone, his toes were horn
And this Fellow was never born. (A rooster. He was hatched.)

The next culprit was to do a turn of athletic feats, or do a step-dance.

Several others who had been called up before the Teamster held up Mary Adams' bright red neckerchief. As it was pulled out, she gave such a loud outcry that the Judge immediately recognized her.

"The culprit must entertain the house by singing a song, but if she wishes she may choose one other person to assist her."

That meant that Ma would accompany her on the guitar and sing the lead. Naturally, they did the Whippoorwill Song which they had just learned, and which had never been sung in Bunkerville before. It was a real love song:

> Oh meet me when daylight is fading
> And is darkening into the night
> When the song-birds are singing their Vespers
> And the sun has long vanished from sight.
> And then I shall tell to you, darling,
> All the love I have cherished so long
> If you will but meet me this evening
> When you hear the first whippoorwill song.

The chorus consisted of Ma's repeating the whippoorwill calls on the high notes, while Mary Adams sang "Oh meet me, yes, meet me, when you hear the first whippoorwill, hear the first whippoorwill song," repeated twice.

The second verse was equally passionate, and the girls did justice to both, so that the audience clapped and stomped and called for more, but the Judge ruled them out, saying that there were many other nice things ahead.

The Judge was right. There were several other numbers, clever and well-prepared. At last the final one was called: Uncle Jim Barnum, our best entertainer. Not only did he have a rare, rich singing voice, but he was a good actor as well, light on his feet, and wearing a smart pointed mustache.

Addressing the Judge, he said, "May it please Your Honor to permit me to choose an assistant for this number?"

Permission was gladly given, and he walked straight across the floor to my mother, bowed and held out his hand. Ma stood up promptly. No, he didn't need her guitar; his son Cal would accompany on his banjo. He needed only herself and her voice, and a few minutes in which to instruct her. Would she step aside a little while? She soon stepped out on the stage wearing a long skirt with a bit of a train, a flower-covered hat and beads, and took her place in the middle of the stage, while Cal began playing a right interesting prelude on the banjo.

Enter the gentleman, his hat tilted, a cane in his hand. He stopped a moment to look her over, and then approached, took off his hat, bowed low and sang:

> Dear Madam, I will give you a pocket full of pins
> To pin up your dress, or do many other things
> If you'll WALK with me anywhere, anywhere;
> If you'll WALK with me anywhere.

With a toss of her head and a voice full of scorn, Ma answered,

> I WILL NOT accept of your pocket full of pins
> To pin up my dress or do many other things
> And I'll NOT walk with you anywhere, anywhere
> And I'll NOT walk with you anywhere.

She sang as she walked to the edge of the stage to the west, where after a little hesitation, he followed her with a new proposition:

> Dear Madam, I will give you jewels bright and rings
> And flowers for your hat, and many other things,
> If you'll WALK with me anywhere, anywhere
> If you'll WALK with me anywhere.

[30]

Ma was pert and pretty in her scorn as she sang her "I Will Not" to this offer, and came back to center stage where he followed her with still another proposition — "Fine, silken gowns." She seemed to grow only more disgusted in each refusal, as she moved to the east end of the stage, where he offered her "silver and gold." By now she had grown so emphatic that she stamped her foot, whirled and came back to center stage again.

Now her lover took another tack:

> Dear Madam, I will give you the keys to my heart
> And my heart and your heart will never, never part
> If you'll walk with me anywhere, anywhere
> If you'll walk with me anywhere!

Now she melted, and sang with what sounded like true love in her voice,

> I will accept the keys to your heart
> And your heart and my heart shall never, never part
> And I'll walk with you Anywhere, Anywhere,
> And I WILL walk with you ANYWHERE,

at which his arms encircled her and she lifted her face for a kiss that looked like the real thing, a sure-enough lover's kiss.

I confess that I didn't like it, but the crowd clapped and stomped and cheered. I had expected her to turn quickly, so that he'd just peck her cheek.

The noise woke Melvin, who began to cry lustily. If Ma heard, she made no sign. She had brought me especially for this, and I'd just have to wear it out. She must change her costume, adjust her hair, and wipe a little make-up on or off her face before she went down to the dance floor to greet her friends, and receive their congratulations.

Uncle Jim came to say that he had never had that part done better. It would be a great favor to him if she'd finish this dance with him. To me, struggling with a spunky baby, the thing seemed endless. No one else seemed concerned about Melvin as I had him out of sight behind the stage; so he just cried himself tired, finally taking the bottle I had been offering all along.

That dance ended at last, and Ma came up back stage, gathered things together, and we slipped out the back door. She bundled

Melvin heavily, gave me the pillow and the empty dishpan, and walked so fast I could hardly keep up. With Melvin quiet, I also dropped into bed and asleep instantly.

I had no idea that Ma would go back to the dance, but she did, for a few days later the word came back to her that a neighbor had said "If Mary Hen can carry on in that fashion in public when her husband hadn't been gone even one year, she will have forgotten him entirely before his two years are up. Maybe they'd do better to release him so that he could come back and take care of his own family and let someone else preach to unbelievers." This really troubled Ma for a while.

I must explain how it was that Ma was called "Mary Hen." Everyone called her Aunt Mary Hen. This came from the fact that there were so many Marys in our town: Mary Adams, Mary Bunker, Mary Ellen, Mary Jane, Mary Josephine, Mary Elizabeth, Mary Liz, and Mary Em. Since there were two other just plain Mary Leavitts, each took the name of her husband and became Mary Hen and Mary Will. Some of Ma's best friends said that she should change it to "Merry Hen" because she liked to work in the garden so well. Ma talked to the Bishop about this slanderous remark and he comforted her, saying that the Dear Lord knew her heart, and she herself knew it, and such false, undeserved insinuations should be forgotten.

It did make some difference, though. Ma didn't bear her testimony in song again that I remember, maybe just because she couldn't get anyone to sing the alto, maybe because of this remark.

The next spring and summer was much like the first, with the young men of the ward plowing the garden spot and cleaning ditches and chopping wood. Ma pruned her own vines and cleared out the runners before they knew that it was time. She really wanted to be as independent as she could, and always served those who worked with good treats of pies or cakes or both, and with lemonade or punch. Her garden meant a great part of her living, and she appreciated this preparation.

Although I was far too young to go to school that first year after Pa left, I was happy to see it start, for it was being held in the large room of our house, and Aunt Selena was the teacher. Aunt Selena had always been a very special person to me. So during the long, warm fall days, I would sit on the door step and listen to the classes. Aunt Selena didn't send me away, as I wasn't disturbing anyone, and I liked to do this very much.

After the weather became cold enough to shut the door and start a fire in the stove, she would let me slip into a spare seat at the back of the room. But she never called on me to take part; I was just a visitor, though she knew that I was doing the same work as the others, and reading the same books. Actually, I was reading more than most of the others.

Ma did the janitor work, so that I could take books into our house for the evening, and put them back into their place before school opened in the morning.

It was about this time that I learned that I was a monotone. I was playing on the floor with a little box of "doll-rags" when Aunt Lovina and two of her girl friends — all young ladies in long skirts and tall hair styles — came in. I was singing to myself as contented as you please, when one girl said to another, "Listen to that kid there! She's just like Selena; she couldn't carry a tune if you put it into a sack for her!"

So — I couldn't carry a tune! Not even if it was put into a sack! I didn't know that Aunt Selena couldn't sing! We all sang in her school room, with her leading us. I thought all of Ma's family could play the guitar and sing. They had two guitars, and both the boys, Uncle Albert and Uncle Roy, had violins and played them well. I supposed that I myself was singing. But I would not try any more. I took after Pa, I thought, for I had heard several references to the fact that Mary's only fault to find with her husband was that he had no ear for music: he couldn't sing and didn't know it.

Now that I knew it, I'd not try to sing any more. I'd learn to play the organ and let the others do the singing.

As I started my first formal year of schooling, the new school house was not yet finished; Pa's mission wouldn't be up until March or April. That meant that the school would stay in our house until the holidays. But this year Miss Lois Earl was the teacher.

On the very first day she put me in the first grade, for she could see that I was reading as well as any of the others in that class, and

I was happy and eager. But when she announced that we would sing "America" for our first song, I sat with my mouth firmly closed. I hadn't forgotten that I couldn't carry a tune even if it was put in a sack for me.

Evidently I wasn't the only one who was not singing, for she rapped for all to stop.

"You must all join in the singing," she said. "Sing out! Be proud of your Country! Every person in this land should know this song and sing it through from beginning to end. Those who don't want to sing with the class may come to the front and sing by themselves."

Now this was something that I did not want to do, so I learned to "mouth" the words without making a sound, and to sit up straight and try to look pleased and interested. And I resolved that if I couldn't sing, I could learn to play the organ, so that when I was old enough, I could play while others sang. I asked Ma about it, and she was glad that I should show an interest, so she went to Lillian Bunker's, where the only piano in town was. Yes, she would be glad to give me lessons at fifty cents each.

Now fifty cents an hour seemed a lot of money. Ma would wash all day for a fifty-cent piece. If I must pay all that much, I must spend at least an hour a day at the organ, one-half hour before school, and one-half hour in the evening. But after eight lessons I had to quit. We just could not afford music lessons.

The new school building was finished by the middle of December, at which time the trustees moved all the benches and school gear out of our large room. Now Ma could get at the business of fixing things up before Pa should arrive — or at least be released — in mid-March.

She would begin with this large empty room. A fresh coat of calsomine was applied, the windows washed, and the new yellow curtains hung. She had long ago ordered linoleum for the floor, and it arrived early. She had been making payments out of her butter and egg money; then it occurred to her that the sack of dried figs in the cellar might be processed and boxed and sold to good advantage. With that, she was able to almost clear the debt. So Bishop Bunker, learning of her eagerness to have it, sent the roll up and told her to not worry about the balance. How wonderful!

Now the kitchen floor could be covered, and the areas at the front and on the sides of the fireplace in the Other Room could also be filled in.

Best of all, she was able to trade the little stove for one twice as large, without much difference. A young couple moving away from Bunkerville hadn't space enough for the large one in their wagon, and were glad for the exchange. Surely the Lord must have had His hand in it all. She just couldn't be that lucky!

Almost a year ago she had set out to get pictures for her home. She had read an advertisement in a magazine offering ten beautiful, classical pictures, all mounted on heavy cardboard, for the sale of a certain number of cans of Cloverine Salve, a wonderful, healing remedy good for so many things, an essential in every family medicine chest. She got the salve and we visited every home in Bunkerville and Mesquite trying to sell it for fifteen cents a can. We did not sell many, but we let folks know we had more when those were gone. Ma made up the extra money and sent it in. In due time the pictures arrived, and we each picked one that we could claim for our own and put wherever we wanted it.

The lace curtains in the Other Room were still as good as new; they needed only to be washed, starched, and put onto quilting frames to be stretched and dried in the sun. These, with the new pictures, almost satisfied her, but Aunt 'Ress also made her a beautiful "What-Not," a set of three shelves with colored spools between them, and threaded with special rope. They fit into the corner of the wall, and served as a display case for any little beautiful item: figurines, fancy little dishes, handmade pincushions.

With a new embroidered bedspread for her bed, a fancy little quilt in Melvin's crib, her polished and shining beautiful organ, and the Swiss striking clock on the mantel, she was pleased with the Other Room.

The family would live in the kitchen. With this fine, large stove, the table with the dropleaves, her nice dish cupboard for the better dishes, and the one made by Uncle Heber Hardy for storage, stove dishes, and milk pans, she had things handy. Then, instead of a bed, she had the drop-leaf cot for a couch. This cot was different: one leaf folded up against the wall, so by throwing a heavy camp quilt over it and covering that with a fancy cover, she had a sofa of sorts — at least a place to sit on in the daytime, and for three little girls to sleep on at night.

Some of the best of Mary Adams' curtains, which were not only dyed yellow but trimmed with appliqued green leaves and red flowers and tied back with red bands, gave color to the whole room.

Yes, Ma had worked almost around the clock to have her home clean and attractive for her husband's return.

The Returned Missionary

MA WAS ALMOST READY FOR PA'S RETURN, BUT SHE MUST GIVE THIS NEW STOVE A BIT OF SHINING UP. Having made the trade herself, she wanted Pa to feel that she had a good bargain. Pa had written her his plans, at least the date of his release, and his expected route. But he was ahead of the letter. He came by train to Delamar, and on home by buggy. Our telephone system went only as far as Littlefield, which his route missed, too.

As the buggy came up the lane east of our lot, Pa saw Melvin playing with a little wooden wagon that Uncle Roy had made for him out of spools and a thread box.

"That's my boy!" Pa said, jumped from the moving buggy to take the little fellow in his arms, wagon and all, and carried him home. Melvin regarded him with wonder, but didn't cry.

I caught sight of them just as they came to the gate, and ran into the house calling, "Pa's come! Pa's come!"

"For the Land's sake!" Ma cried, all in a dither. She jerked off her soiled apron, wiping her sooty hands on it as it fell, and came hurrying outside between laughter and tears.

"Why didn't you let me know?"

It seemed that Pa would break her ribs with his hug, and never get through kissing her. She freed herself and went in to wash up and straighten her hair before a mirror, while Pa turned to Charity and me, one in each arm. Word got to Aura a little late, for she was playing with her little dollrag ladies under the pomegranate trees. She raced to him as if she had been waiting all this time to be caught up in his arms.

Pa went through the house and praised all Ma's attempts to beautify it, noticing all the new items: the pretty curtains, the pictures, the new stove and utility cupboard, and was pleased with it all.

But he was more impressed with the outside: the ricked stack of chopped wood piled in an orderly row against the back wall, the pruned and growing grape vines, the clean ditches, the west strip all spread with manure from the corral, and ready to be plowed under. He could hardly believe that things could be kept up so well by a woman and four little children.

Here were pea vines in bloom, radishes and young onions ready to eat, potato vines pushing through the ground. Ma was really planning to feed her family out of her own garden.

We really didn't need a fire in the fireplace that night, but we had one, anyway. Visiting is easier before an open fire. Pa told us some of his experiences, and sang us some songs. Before he left for his mission, he would never try to sing, and Ma didn't encourage him. Now he needed no urging. He thought that one song had been instrumental in bringing some families into the Church. So he sang it all the way through — all four verses. It had a rollicking tune, and he sang it full strength.

It went like this:

NONE CAN PREACH THE GOSPEL LIKE THE MORMONS DO

> We're going to preach the Gospel
> To all who want to hear
> A Message of Salvation
> Unto the meek we bear
> Jehovah has commanded us
> and therefore we must go
> For none can preach the Gospel
> Like the Mormons do; like the Mormons do!
>
> Faith in God and Jesus
> The first thing that we teach

A genuine repentance
The next thing that we preach
Baptism by Immersion
And this you all must know
That none do preach the Gospel
Like the Mormons do; like the Mormons do!

How to obtain the Spirit
The next thing that we say
As in the days of Peter
The same as in our day
'Tis by the laying on of Hands
And this will plainly show
That none can preach the gospel
Like the Mormons do; like the Mormons do!

The old time religion
Is what we want you to know
With Prophets and Apostles
As in days long ago
Read Acts the second Chapter;
Ephesians four and two
For none do preach the gospel
Like the Mormons do, like the Mormons do!

Pa may have been a monotone, but there was a tune to this, and what he lacked in pitch he made up for in volume. He sang as if he enjoyed it and expected you to.

The second song was quite different. It began on a slow, deliberate tempo, with the words of the last line drawn out so long that they seemed almost a wail, ending in a minor key:

When first that band of pioneers did look upon the scene
They thought they never saw a land so barren and so mean
Their hearts were filled with nameless fear
And O! Their spirits sank!
There was quick-sand in the river-bed, and CACTUS ON THE BANK!

Sing rol di riddle, di riddle, di ray
Sing rol de riddle di ray!

The refrain might last through several repeats, as Pa bounced Aura or Melvin on his knee. We older ones didn't remember that Pa used to sing so many songs — nursery rhymes, most of them, before he had been encouraged to sing. "All around the mulberry bush" and

"Yankee Doodle Went to Town" and many, many others Pa sang now to entertain the little ones. It really pleased us all that Father-in-Heaven had helped Pa to find and develop his voice. Still, he and Ma never sang together with the guitar. Their voices didn't "blend." Pa just seemed so glad to be home that he sang anyway, and we loved it.

Pa's first errand the next morning was to walk down to Uncle Wier's place at the very end of town. Since Pa had "sold" his team, harness, and wagon to Uncle Wier during his mission, Uncle Wier had advanced some money on it, which Pa would return. It seemed to us that Pa was a long time gone, but we knew he'd have to call in at Aunt Mary Ellen's — Aunt Rell, we called her — and greet anyone else he met, so we weren't surprised at his being gone so long. Ma was genuinely relieved; it gave her time to get things organized.

Pa came driving back as proud as a peacock in his own wagon behind his own team.

Pa made no explanations of whatever business he and Uncle Wier had transacted; he only said that he was going to Leavittville to visit his parents before he did anything else. He had been gone two years; they were all getting older; he must not wait. From what he could learn, no other members of the family here had been to visit them, either.

Pa went at once to call on the Bishop. Today was Thursday. Pa would stay and report his mission in church on Sunday. But he expected to leave on Monday to go visit his family in Mesquite and on up the river to Beaver Dams and Leavittville. He didn't know their situation, but he wondered if it wouldn't be appropriate to take some items from the Fast Offerings along. Grandpa had grown older, and could no longer work, and there were the four wives, each living alone or with one of her children. Grandma Mary had been living with her son Frank for many years, so there was no worry about her. He wasn't just sure about some of the others; a few items from the Fast Offerings might be most welcome.

The Bishop took kindly to the idea, but suggested that Pa wait until Tuesday to leave, as that would give them Monday in which to make preparations. Pa consented, but remarked in an aside to Ma that he almost wished he had taken out tomorrow. That would have given him plenty of time to be back on Saturday night to report on Sunday. But he knew that some Bishops like to be recognized and given a chance to alter a man's plans in order to show authority.

Pa kept his own counsel, but made a long visit with Sammy Reber on his way back from calling on Grandma Hafen, who lived next to him. He also spent some time with Aunt Annie and Uncle Ithamar Sprague, who lived just across the lane from us. Aunt Annie was Pa's sister, the oldest daughter of Grandma Janet, the Indian wife. Her husband, Ithamar Sprague, was the stone mason who had laid up the walls of the big rock church near where we lived. They now had a family of five sons.

We were all so proud of our Pa when he made his report in the meeting the next day. He spoke clearly, without hesitation or reference to notes. He quoted Scripture from memory, giving chapter and verse. He related two stories of times when he and his companion were welcomed into homes by people who said that they were expecting them. One had seen him in a dream, he said; the other had been searching the Scriptures and was impressed with the feeling that someone would come who would be able to help him interpret the meaning. In the area where Pa worked, the backwoods section of Arkansas, the field seemed ripe for the harvest.

And he bore a strong testimony of the truth of the Gospel as it had been restored in these, the last days, and the Kingdom set up which would never be taken down or given to another people. Naturally, he was glad to be back again to his home and loved ones. He thanked the Bishop and all those who had been so helpful to his family in his absence — who had cleaned his corrals, plowed his land, cleaned the ditches, and especially those who had seen to it that his family had fuel during the cold weather. He would not attempt to repay them, except by helping other families in the ward when the father was filling a mission.

In my secret heart I wondered if he had heard of Ma's part on the program in which she sang with Uncle Jim Barnum, so I was relieved to see the warmth of their handshake.

When the Bishop suggested that they could find a place in the ward where they could use him, he said, "Give me three months, and I'll accept any assignment you give me."

On Tuesday morning early we were on our way. Pa had taken the top bed off the wagon box, put the spring seat in place, and stretched the small wagon cover over only the front four bows, with the sides all around rolled up so the air could circulate. A heavy camp quilt was doubled on the floor just behind the spring seat, where we children could sit, and the younger ones could sleep during the ride.

In the space next to this were two bales of hay across, with some grain in a sack just in front of them. In the far back were the items for the widows that Pa and the Bishop had taken from the Fast Offerings: two sacks of flour — fifty-pound — a big box which held several five-pound buckets of lard, ten-pound sacks of cereal, boxes of matches, soap, and one box of bottles of honey, quart size. This was the new honey, even though it might be a year old, for it was that gathered from the wild flowers in the hills, before the clover and lucerne and fruit trees in town came in bloom. It was darker, much darker, than the later honey, but it was extra sweet, it seemed, and had a delicious flavor for those who liked it.

In the cool of the morning we made good time, getting across the river and to Uncle Frank's place just as they were eating breakfast. Uncle Frank was an early riser and a hard worker, putting in two or three hours before breakfast. Aunt Selena, his wife and my favorite school teacher, was now married to a family, and hoping for children of her own.

Pa told Uncle Frank that he wanted to spend what little time he had with Grandma Mary, his mother, so Frank went on with the business of irrigating his lucerne field, while Pa went in to Grandma Mary's room.

Ma and Aunt Selena were in the kitchen washing dishes and talking women talk; the younger children were involved with toys in the dooryard. I followed Pa to Grandma Mary's room, where she sat in a large rocking chair, which she filled comfortably. I slipped in quietly and settled myself on the floor at the foot of the bed, where she couldn't see me, and Pa didn't even notice me for a while.

Pa kissed her and told her how fine she looked all cleaned up; it looked like she had put away a good breakfast, too.

"Here, you," Pa said to me, "Come and take these dishes down to the kitchen. See if there is something you can do there to help."

I soon came back with a small pitcher of water and a glass that Aunt Selena sent up. I set them down on the stand beside her chair, and again sat down on the floor where Grandma Mary couldn't see me.

"The family of Uncle Jacob Hamblin tell everywhere that he never married an Indian girl. They know better, but just don't want it mentioned. All the folks in the fort knowed that he took two girls, Susie and Ellen, in to Salt Lake to marry them. But Ellen — she was the prettiest one — hung back and didn't want to even go into the room. Jacob didn't force her. But Susie, the other one, did marry him and they both came back to Santa Clara. I think it was Susie that was with them when Young George A. Smith was killed. Soon after that, Susie left and went back to her own people. She married Old Poinkum. Ellen got sick and died; the Indians didn't have any resistance to white men's diseases."

This seemed to be important to Grandma Mary. It seemed that she still resented the fact that her husband was called a "Squaw Man." Then she began talking about life at Clover Valley. "Here the Indians were always a threat. And the plague of black canker which took every baby under the age of two years; Aunt Mary Ellen, Sam Gentry, and a Syphus baby were all that were saved. Eleven little graves in one summer!"

"Hebron wasn't exactly a paradise, though we did all have pretty good health there," Pa reminded her. "The main fault there is that it was so cold, too cold to raise fruit and garden stuff."

"Well, about the prettiest girl in the whole family died there. There's mighty few girls as beautiful as Maria's Elsie, and she went at age seventeen. But that place was not intended to be for human beings, only cattle and sheep." Here Grandma made a long pause, as if trying to remember something special, or make up her mind.

"From the time I first married I have been dragged from pillar to post, with every place harder than the last. From the coldest to the hottest and driest. So when Lindy died, and I moved in to help Frank raise his two boys, I decided that I'd made my last move. And I have. I don't intend to leave this room until I'm carried out."

Pa finally told her he'd have to leave; we had quite a way to go before night. I think they left several items for Aunt Selena, for after all, Grandma Mary deserved as much help from the Church as any of the others. The lard would come in handy, and the honey was special.

Pa didn't take the harness off the horses here, but he did unfasten the tugs and take out their bridle bits, and let them feed at the manger. Uncle Frank had large stacks of alfalfa hay.

Uncle Frank's place was about three miles below the Big Wash that marked the western border of the village. Pa seemed surprised and happy at the growth that had taken place here in just two years.

Grandma Martha's house was almost in the center of town. I had never seen Grandma Martha; I had just heard that she had been married young to Father Zera Pulsipher, and had several children by him. After he died, she married Grandpa Dudley, and had three or four births, but only one who grew to maturity. This was Aunt Lydia, now married to Uncle Walt Hughes.

Pa told us all to stay in the wagon; we wouldn't be here long. Grandma Martha came out to the wagon with Pa. She was a tall lady, almost as tall as Pa. She greeted us loudly and in great good humor, and accepted Pa's gifts with loud and hearty thanks.

"It's not hard to see why you wuz always the family pet," she said. "Remember the time when Mariar was sputtering about something, and you handed her a handful of cotton seed and said, 'Here. Take these and crack 'em. They're good for what ails you!' "

Pa grinned. "Your memory must be bad. That must-a been List. That couldn't-a been me. Aunt Mariar was always my friend; she'd protect me against the older kids."

"Many's the time you'd need protectin'. You could think of the most things to do."

"Now, now, Aunt Marthie, you mustn't poison the minds of my little children, making them think their father was a naughty boy!"

"No! No, you wasn't exactly naughty! Just full of mischief. And your Father's pet. The fav'rite son of the fav'rite wife,' I used t' say. But never mind. Looks like you're really goin' t' be a Joseph to your Father."

Around the corner and down two blocks we found Grandma Maria's house beside the home of her son Jeremy. Uncle Ira, as yet unmarried, was living here with her; though her work as a midwife took her so often away for ten-day periods. She was midwife for all the area, the distant ranches as well as the homes in town.

Ever since she was eighteen years old, Grandma Maria had been delivering babies, and in all this long career, she never lost a mother, and very few babies.

When we were here last, Grandma Maria was living in one-half of the house at Leavittville, with Grandma Thirza in the other, Aunt Nora staying with Grandma Maria, and Aunt Theresa with Grandma Thirza. But so great was the need of her services in the young, growing town of Mesquite that she was "called" to set up headquarters here.

The Bishop explained this in the Sacrament Meeting one Sunday. Brothers Arthur Hughes and Edgar Leavitt, friends and neighbors living across the street from each other, were given a special mission call to last for one year. They were to see that Aunt Maria was taken to wherever she was needed.

First, women who were expecting babies should notify her well in advance, at least three months. At the first sign of labor, the husband should send a messenger to tell her. He should go from her house to the homes of Arth and Edgar to give them word. They should stop whatever they were doing and see that Aunt Maria got to her destination with all speed. If it was within a few blocks, they should make a "chair" with their arms and carry her to the door. Both men had sons old enough to carry her satchel; they might arrange between them who would take which turn.

If a team was sent for her, Arth and Edgar must go and help her into the wagon, by removing the endgate, seating her on her rawhide-bottomed chair and lifting her into the back of the wagon and pushing the chair up to fasten securely to the spring seat, so that she would be safe, even if the horses had to run. If she went by wagon, only one of the two young men would need to go. The husband would help unload her, and get her into the house.

When the subject was open for discussion from the floor, several points were brought out. The problem was not that simple. Suppose a woman at the Big Bend needed to be delivered at the same time, or even near the same time one was due here in town. The area that Aunt Maria was expected to take care of was just too large; she would have to know much earlier than just two or three months ahead. If each woman would report as soon as she felt life, it might be that we could work out something. It just might be that we would have to set aside a room here in town, where husbands could bring their wives, in case Aunt Maria was tied here with one.

Then another thing: If there was any evidence during the pregnancy that all was not well or normal, Aunt Maria should be consulted. It's hard to write it out in letters, and hard to get answers to problems. But Aunt Maria should be aware of it. You went to her.

Finally it was decided that during the following two or three weeks Aunt Maria should be visited by every woman who expected to have her services later, and work out such plans as they could, and when she learned just what the immediate situation was, perhaps we could work out plans for the best good of all concerned.

One other thing: we all knew our financial situations. If no complications arose and the birth was a normal one, we need not worry. But a government bulletin had come in, put together for frontier women. We should pass out the two copies we received, and ask those who were interested to read them, sign their name, and pass it on to another pregnant woman. By signing it and putting the approximate time of delivery, we could all cooperate more easily.

Aunt Maria's standard fee was three dollars, and while she would prefer it in cash, she would settle for some in produce: wheat or cured meat, butter, eggs, garden vegetables, or molasses. It was the husband's business to return her safely home after ten days, with something more than just "thanks" for her labor.

Aunt Maria was home when we pulled up in front of her place, and she came out to greet us. She seemed right happy to see Pa. Maybe she was a little relieved to see that he had come just to visit with her. After he had picked her up off her feet in a big hug and kiss, she patted him and had him turn around like she was going to examine him, and then said, "My goodness, but that mission has done so much for you! Maybe we should send you right back out on another one!"

We all got out of the wagon, and were told to play around outside in the sunshine. From the sound of laughter inside, it seemed that Pa and Aunt Maria were really enjoying this little game of "Do you remember when?"

This grandma also accepted the little items Pa brought with a fine show of gratitude: "Just what I needed!" or "I was almost out of flour!" or, "How long it has been since I tasted honey like this! It's my very favorite; it reminds me of the first hill flowers in the spring."

But we must not tarry; we had almost ten miles still to go. We were traveling up the river bottom, which meant deep sand for most of the way. We girls all walked, wading the shallow stream some twelve or thirteen times. After an hour's traveling, we stopped at a little green place on the bank, rested, ate our lunch, and fed the horses from the bale of hay in the back of the wagon.

Pa stretched out on his back, covered his face with his hat, and slept a while, during which time Ma entertained Melvin and us girls in the shade of some tamarack bushes on the bank, far enough away that we would not disturb him.

The sun was getting low when we pulled up out of the riverbed to travel along the foothills. Uncle Clarence had a home and farm near here, but Pa didn't take that road. Instead, he stopped after a short distance, and called all of us up to the front where he could talk to us.

"Listen, all of you! Remember what I tell you! We are going to Grandmother Janet's house to stay tonight," he said. "Grandma Janet is an Indian lady. Don't gawp and stare at her with your mouths open! She looks like an Indian because she IS an Indian. But she is a fine lady; she is one of your Grandpa's wives, and her children are all your cousins. They're all very fine people, some of them smarter than some of the all-white cousins. Just remember this!"

Grandma Janet's home was one large lumber room with a lean-to on one side, and a willow shed on the other side. The house faced north and this shed on the west was filled all along that side with upright willows, until it made almost a solid wall. During the summer she used it as a kitchen and dining room and a parlor all combined. Her stove was here, and her table, and a cot along the bush wall was a fine place to rest during the long afternoons.

[47]

"Oh, it's Henry!" Grandma Janet cried with delight. She put down her milk bucket, as she was starting out to milk her cow, and came back toward the wagon.

Pa gave her the same hearty hug and kiss that he had given the others.

"I'm so glad to see you!" she said. "I've thought of you so much while you've been gone. I didn't have any money to send you, but I remembered you in my prayers every night. You must have had a good mission. You must tell us about it after supper; we've all been so concerned about you. You will stay for supper, of course! I don't have much, but what I have is fit for a king!"

"I'm sure of that," Pa told her. "I've fed at your table before. But first I must take care of my team. Visit with Mary awhile, and I'll be right with you."

With the horses unharnessed and eating from their nosebags, Pa would have time to walk to the corral with Grandma Janet while she milked her cow. He didn't offer to milk; he understood these old "one-person" cows, but he pulled some fodder and cleaned up around the haystack. Our horses would eat our own hay; that's what he had brought it for.

Grandma Janet was proud of her garden. Clarence had prepared the ground and planted it for her, but she kept the weeds down. Her early radishes and lettuce were gone, the potatoes not quite ready. But always she had onions, young or old.

Soon she called us to supper. What did she serve? Little hot biscuits that would melt in your mouth, with butter, molasses, young onions from the garden, and fresh new milk. That was all, but in all my life I have never tasted anything better. And I wasn't alone. Everyone there said the same; they cleared up that pan of biscuits entirely.

There was an early moon, so they had no need to light the lamp. Ma fixed the beds for us youngsters in the wagon box — a pillow for each and a light blanket spread over all three, with me, as always, in the middle. Later she would bring Melvin and put him close to Charity.

Pa would likely tell Grandma Janet some of the missionary experiences that he had told in meeting or at home before, but mostly it seemed that his errand was to persuade her to let him and her sons move her down to Bunkerville. It wasn't good for her to be here alone so far from help if she should have an accident or get sick. She could be more comfortable nearer some of the family and in a town. He planned to get his father and mother moved down, too.

We children didn't even rouse when the wagon started the next morning. Pa had pulled into the yard of Grandpa Dudley's home just before sunrise, and we were all sound asleep until Aunt 'Ress came out to milk the cow. Then Pa gave a big whoop which brought us all up. Pa jumped from the wagon and Runt 'Ress dropped her bucket. It was easy to see that these two thought a great deal of each other; they were pals and friends as well as brother and sister.

Grandpa Dudley's two-story adobe house with its two front doors and windows upstairs and downstairs both, seemed large to us. We knew that Grandma Maria had lived in one half of the house before she was "called" to live in Mesquite. Here Aunt Nora had lived with her, but now Aunt Nora was married to Nephi Hunt and they had moved away, which left only three in the house. Some of the grandsons were working the farm, though. There was a big patch of cane, and a lucerne field that we could see, hay in the barn, and horses and a cow besides the one that Aunt 'Ress milked.

But most interesting of all was an old mother duck and her flock of ducklings. We had never seen a duck in all our lives before. The wide canal that ran across the top of the lot under very, very old cottonwood trees made a perfect place for them. How beautiful they were! What fun it would be to hold one! Melvin held out his hands and coaxed, but when I tried to reach one, the mother duck was quick to show her displeasure. Her real place was in a small slough at the bottom of the field.

We could hardly stay inside to eat breakfast, we were so eager to watch the duck. Then we found a big turtle — we thought it must be the grandfather of all turtles, it was so large. We held Melvin's hands and stood him on the turtle to see if it would carry him away, but it just closed up shop and wouldn't move at all.

It seemed no time until Pa came out and told us to load into the wagon; to reach home before dark tonight, we'd have to make haste. We knew that we couldn't take the duck home; we didn't have any water for a duck to swim in. But the turtle was different. Might we put it into a box and take it along? We'd like to know more about turtles.

"Do you think the turtle would like that?" Pa said. "What could you do with it if you had it?" So we gave up on both counts: the turtle would be better off if left here, and we needed nothing less than we needed a turtle. But we would try to learn if turtles laid eggs, or if their young were born alive.

The trip home was faster; it was downhill most of the way, and we didn't even pull out of the river bed to go through Mesquite. That put us to the Bunkerville crossing much earlier, and in just no time we were home.

"Here we are!" Pa called. "All out!"

Later, as we sat at the supper table, he remarked quite seriously, "I can't remember when I ever spent two more profitable days. We certainly did accomplish a lot on this little short trip."

We children didn't understand the exchanges of land and property that had been made, or the movings that would take place. But we now knew all our Grandmothers on the Leavitt side of the family: Grandma Thirza, Grandma Martha, Grandma Maria, Grandma Janet, as well as our own Grandma Mary. While the first three would think of our visit as just an incident, Grandma Janet and Grandma Thirza would find their whole lives very much improved by it. Both would be moved to Bunkerville and each would be set up in a comfortable home, with a daughter to be near enough to answer any call, but with her own private things and her own schedule. Old age they would have, and senility, yes, but not aloneness.

Pa Goes Freighting

THE NEXT AFTERNOON PA LEFT TO GO FREIGHTING FOR THE BULLFROG MINING COMPANY with headquarters located at the fast-growing new town of Las Vegas. We knew nothing about it, so that if anyone asked about Pa, we could say only, "He's at the Bull Frog." Nor did he write any letters; he would be home about the middle of June. We could depend on that.

Nor did he talk much about his experiences after he got home except to say that it did seem that the Lord was on his side.

In the first place, he was last to load, which meant that he started from the mine to the mill in mid- or late afternoon and would do most of his traveling at night. This was good for his team; he could load heavier and with less trouble. Then with two fifty-gallon barrels, he could always have water to spare, and water on the road would sell for anything from a dollar-a-bucket up, depending on the supply.

The Company had developed a place near a high cliff about mid-way on the haul, where they kept a young man employed. He had a small stock of necessities: axle grease, horseshoe nails, chewing gum, candy and crackers, and some canned stuff. Many drivers left barrels of water there in the shade. With only two horses, Pa would always have extra water. He left a full barrel there with instructions for the boy to sell it at the going price. He would use what he needed on the way to that point, and then with a hose he would

[51]

siphon out often more than a half barrel into the barrel on the ground. He would always find his barrel "sold out" when he came back again.

Pa was very friendly with the boy, visiting with him, giving him a generous cut in what money he collected, and sharing his midnight snack. The boy, in turn, told Pa much of the news of the road.

For example, one driver who had no water of his own either forced the boy, or in defiance of him, stole water from several barrels. The boy took the numbers of the barrels which had been tampered with — Pa's wasn't one because Pa had the cork in real tight and the boy said it was locked. Anyway, the lad got the man's number in the line, a description of his outfit, the identification of the barrels from which he had taken any water at all, and the amount of each.

Whenever or however, later there was a lynching; the man was hanged on the uplifted end of a wagon tongue, the argument being that a man who steals another's water on the desert dooms him to death. This was near mid-June; the weather for the next two or three months would get increasingly hotter. How they disposed of the man's body, who took his team, Pa evidently didn't know. The wagon and a new harness were left at the station and Pa bought them and brought them home with him. At least Ma wrote it in her record book as one of the bonus blessings he received. Details of the bargaining or price were never mentioned, so far as any of us knew. The man himself had just disappeared; only those involved in the matter would know what happened to his body or to the team.

Not only did Pa earn more cash than he had spent to get himself into the mission field, but on his way home he got another bonus. A cloudburst out in Nevada had sent a flood down the Meadow Valley Wash which took out several miles of the railroad track. A whole train was derailed, tipped over, and broken open.

Company guards were there, but they encouraged Pa to take as much as his team could pull of damaged canned goods by the case, and bolts of damaged heavy blue cloth, as heavy as denim, with the right side smooth, and with a fine white line running through it. Since he got this all gratis, Pa was liberal in sharing it. Every family in town received some canned goods and a generous amount of the blue cloth. They tried to make the amount given in proportion to the size and needs of the family. For example, Uncle Wier didn't get any of the cloth, but he had a box of assorted canned goods: salmon, tuna, tomatoes, coffee, peaches, and applesauce. Families with many children got ten yards or more cloth, as much as the mother would estimate she would need, either for shirts for the men folks or linings for camp quilts.

At first Pa thought they could just go along in the wagon and give out as they went, but after two stops, he decided to consult with Ma and select boxes of canned goods in advance, and let the family come to our house and get them. This was announced on Sunday the day after Pa got home. The Bishop called on him to speak, which he did very fluently, we children all thought, and then at the end he told about this train wreck, and actually advised some of the brethren to go at once and get this merchandise which the company couldn't handle. Several teams went.

The result was that when school started that fall, every boy in town had a new blue shirt; indeed, the teachers all commented on the sea of blue that they faced daily; almost like Navy uniforms. The cloth was colorfast and had no wearout to it. Those shirts lasted all winter.

Probably the edge of the storm that took out the railroad tracks reached near enough to us to take out our dam, so Pa came home to a dry ditch. This meant that right after church, we must go to the river for water. After he had changed his clothes, Pa proceeded to see what barrels to take. The two fifty-gallon ones were already in the wagon, well toward the front to balance the load.

What a motley collection of barrels we had! In the cellar there were small barrels for pickles or sauerkraut, and a brine barrel for treating the side pork and hams. At the back of the house, just off the porch, was the swill barrel into which all dishwater was poured, and into which all potato peelings and vegetable waste, and extra clabber milk that we didn't want for cottage cheese, made their way. This barrel had a lid to cover it, but at times it stank to high heaven, and collected flies without number. It was really the worst single item of all our lives, but so essential, for it was our pig feed, and pigs were important in our economy.

Down by the fig trees where we had our washing setup was the lye barrel. This was always kept full, first to keep the barrel from drying out, and second to give the water time to settle. On Saturday we would boil up a big kettle of cottonwood ashes which we would pour into the lye barrel — this was indeed the lye itself, these ashes. But on Monday morning the water would be clear and soft, so that we could have a rich soap suds to clean our white clothes. But right now this barrel was dry, and was first to be put into the wagon. Since it had no lid, Ma turned a tin tub upside down over it to keep in the splashings.

Last to be loaded was our little, twenty-five gallon drinking barrel, which was set on a wooden block under the big cottonwood tree close to the ditch bank. Swathed in burlap gunnysacks kept in place by row upon row of baling wire, this barrel held for the family some of the sentiment of "The Old Oaken Bucket." Men, wringing wet from work in the fields, drank deeply from the dipper which dangled on a string; young people lingered over its coolness, children reached and coaxed for a drink. Always, always, any water left in the dipper was thrown on the burlap to help keep it damp. This barrel was emptied and filled fresh every morning before six o'clock in the summer and seven o'clock in the winter, as those were the hours at which the cattle were turned out to drink.

For a cover, Ma brought out a square of oilcloth, to be held into place by a tight-fitting hoop.

"Now turn out all the stock, and let's be on our way," Pa ordered, unwrapping the lines.

A block down from our place Aunt Rell came out to stop Pa and ask if he thought he could crowd on her little drinking barrel, too.

"Sure. Sure. One that small won't make much difference." With it she brought a small brass bucket half the size of Pa's big one, and also an old broom handle to suspend the bucket in the barrel, after it was filled.

"They say that will keep the water from splashing out on the road," she explained.

"That's a new one on me, but we'll try it," Pa assured her.

Charity, young Gladys, and I walked ahead, after the cows in the general procession, as all the town went for its evening drink. Dust billowed up in clouds, which spread themselves and dissolved over the fields. The evening air was rent by the clamor of rattling wagons, the bawling of anxious cows after bewildered baby calves, the barking of dogs ordered to "sic 'em" after stragglers, and the calls of boys on horseback to the little folks on the spring seats, just along for the ride.

Tomorrow morning the cows would come over this same road on their way to the field, following the stream down past the Adams and Con Neagle fields to go through the salt grass pasture into our own.

The horses, pigs, chickens, and calves would all be watered from the fifty-gallon barrels, siphoned out into buckets and tubs.

When we reached the stream, Pa scorned to stop way back on the bank and carry every bucketful up, as some of the more cautious neighbors were doing. Instead, he drove down the roadway that had been cut through the caved-off ledge to let the cattle down to drink. Above the herd he found a place where he thought the riverbed would be gravelly and safe. While we girls played on the bank, he filled the barrels, standing with one foot on the brake block and dipping with the big, three-gallon bucket. With expert accuracy he poured the water into the bungholes of the two closed-headed barrels, and pounded in the corks securely when they were filled. The lye barrel and the little drinking barrels he attacked with a great flourish, dumping the bucketfuls in single, great splashes. After these were filled and covered, Pa picked up the lines and spoke to the team.

The horses strained into their collars, but the hind wheels had sunk into the sand and they couldn't budge the wagon. To get stuck anywhere would be bad enough, but to get fast into a stream was a predicament indeed. Pa swung the team first to one side and then the other in an attempt to loosen the wheels. Finally he stepped down onto the tongue, wetting his feet, and began to yell at the horses and to strap them with the lines. With a quick jerk they loosened the wagon, hurried through the water on a trot, and took the bank with a lunge.

Safe on the top, Pa stopped them, and turned to get back from the tongue into the wagon box. His face took on the expression of mingled shock and disgust, much as if he had swallowed a fly. All five barrels were tipped over; the two corked ones safe enough and the tin tub still secure on top of the lye barrel, but the hoop and oilcloth were on the ground, as were also the little brass bucket and the broom Both little barrels were empty.

I wanted to laugh or to say Ma's favorite, "More haste, less speed," but a glance at Pa's face made me think better of it. Besides, the getting of those big fifty-gallon barrels upright seemed almost a task for a Hercules, they were so heavy.

With everything upright again, Pa pulled the wagon over close to the bank in a place just being vacated by a neighbor.

"Here, you girls!" he called. "Come and fill these barrels again." And he walked away to visit with someone he hadn't seen at church.

We looked the situation over and tried to work out a plan. We finally divided the work into three parts, all about equally hard, and agreed to change places every eight bucketfuls. Charity had fixed a secure footing near the running stream, and three steps from the top of the bank; Gladys would take the bucket from her and bring it to me, standing on the brake block. I must step over the wagon box and pour the water into Aunt Rell's barrel, which was farthest away, then bring the bucket back to Gladys — and so on.

After eight trips, we decided to rest and see actually how long it would take us to fill these two little barrels. Now I went to the water's edge to dip my allotted number, while Charity carried the bucket on the level, and Gladys poured the water into the barrel.

We each had a turn at all three positions before Aunt Rell's barrel was filled, and ours was a little larger. Maybe we should each take ten trips before we changed; were we spilling too much; we'd be more careful. Eventually, the barrels were filled — the oilcloth secure over the top of ours, and the broomstick with the brass bucket suspended in Aunt Rell's.

At last we called Pa to say we had finished and could go home now.

"You made quite a job of it," Pa said. "I didn't have any idea it would take so long."

"We hurried as fast as we could," I answered. "We had quite a ways to carry it and the bucket was heavy. We didn't just fool around." I was a little nettled that he didn't give us a word of praise. As for me, I was tired — bone tired. And it was after sundown.

At Aunt Rell's house Pa had to angle the horses until they had the back of the wagon against her front gate. Then he called for her to bring some dishes to dip out some of the water; we'd hauled it this far, we didn't want to spill it now. First, the little brass bucketfull was carried in, put into the teakettle, and returned. Aunt Rell brought her dishpan, a large preserving kettle, and another bucket, each of which was filled and carried in. Then Pa angled the barrel until it was right on the edge of the wagon — the endgate was out. Now Charity and I must hang back on the barrel so it would not tip out before Pa could get out and around to steady it to the ground.

Everything worked out just fine. Pa let the barrel down easy, worked it into place inside the fence, and called Aunt Rell to say that she might do well to get a lid of some kind over it to keep it clean.

At home we drove the outfit up near the front gate and left the barrels in place. We would siphon the water from the big barrels out for the horses, pigs, and chickens; Ma would put ashes in the lye barrel, and we'd carry drinking water and dishwater out of the little drinking barrel. This load should last two days — maybe three.

The next morning early Pa was out stepping off the west part of the dooryard between the wire house and the fence. My guess was right! Pa was going to dig a cistern! That very day two men came to measure and figure and estimate as to size and materials. Of one thing Pa was sure — it must be BIG! — Bigger than any of the others in town! There were now three, some of which would hardly hold enough for even one season.

They should make their estimates as soon as possible, so we could begin digging right away. On the other hand, we didn't want a great hole there until it could be properly completed.

In the meantime, he'd hire Aunt Rell's son Elmer or someone else to haul the water. He was through with that business.

The Mail Contract

I WAS EIGHT YEARS OLD WHEN PA GOT THE CONTRACT TO RUN THE MAIL FROM BUNKERVILLE TO MOAPA, and this made a great difference in the social pattern of our town. Now the mail left at five o'clock in the morning on Monday, Wednesday, and Friday, and returned at five o'clock in the afternoon of the alternate days. There was no mail on Sunday.

It seemed that the very first day after Pa returned from the Bull Frog haul, things began to happen. Somewhere, sometime, Pa had some dealings with Sammy Reber, who lived just one house from us up the sidewalk. Sam had a sturdy rock house behind a five-foot rock wall, and his lot ran through the entire block. His corrals were across the street, up near the Big Ditch.

Grandpa Dudley held the deeds to a large field on the Mesquite Flat, just below Uncle Frank's farm, which Pa traded for Sammy's house, lot, and corrals here in Bunkerville. The papers were all signed, and some of the boys were moving Grandpa, Grandma Thirza, and Aunt 'Ress into the house, while Pa was taking possession of the corrals. With the mail contract and so many horses, he'd need a large corral, and this one just seemed built to fit.

As I went over them first, I could see why Ma often said that she wished Pa was more like Sammy Reber, and not so slipshod in his building. Here every little item was designed for the best care of the animals. The whole covered half a block: the stackyards with ample room for a long haystack big enough to last a whole season, a derrick or "stackerpole," as we called it, was in place. There was also room for stacks of wheat and barley, and for the thresher. For most of the way, the Big Ditch was fenced between the trees on the bank, but there was a space of two or three rods where the horses had access to the stream.

The mangers were long enough to accommodate six to eight head at a time, and the whole length was covered with a long shed of bagasse covered with straw, so thick that neither sun nor rain could penetrate it. The log pigpen was also covered, that is, the "Waller-hole" was covered, and a little ditch ran from a low area on the bank of the Big Ditch, where water could be dipped and poured in to run down and go under the bottom log for the waller-hole. The feeding area was dry; the trough a hewn-out stone that couldn't be tipped over or pushed around; a feeding spout between the logs which made it possible to pour all the slops in without danger of losing half of them. The cow corral was spacious, but it had no shed. Evidently the cows would be taken to pasture or turned into the hills during the day. The calfpen did have a shed cover over one corner, and a feeding manger. Strange to me was the door, which lifted up instead of swinging out. The whole area was designed for five to six cows and calves, and was quite clear of manure.

The whole was so carefully planned and executed that it was a great contrast to our corrals at the bottom of the lot. Of course, Pa had not built these, but neither had he improved upon them.

Pa brought the mail ponies as he secured them here to the new corral for a while, until we could get somewhat acquainted with them. The cows — three of them now — and the calves were moved. He would leave the pigs where they were until slaughtering time, and bring only young ones here.

Sammy's chicken coop and run were on the lot just behind and to the east of the house; Aunt Theresa and Grandma Thirza would bring their chickens here, and Ma would keep hers where they were.

Our old corral at the bottom of the lot was soon reduced to a pile of poles, the mangers knocked apart into rough lumber. The only thing of interest in all this was the discovery of a milking stool wedged in between the manger and the fence. Ma thought it was so beautiful that she wanted to take it to the house and put a cushion on it for a footstool for Pa. She didn't tell Pa this. She didn't talk to him about it; she just hauled it up in the express wagon and hid it back in her closet.

The coming in of the mail was the occasion for people to gather at the Post Office. Windy Bill, with two or three of his pals, would always be seated on the ledge under the store window. Each time, as the mail rig pulled in, Windy would look at his big, open-faced watch and announce whether it was on time or early or late, and step forward to meet it as if he were an official delegate assigned to that duty. The other men snapped their pocketknives shut, too, standing and brushing off the backs of their levis. Three times each week they waited in the same place at the same time.

It was not that they expected any mail. They didn't. Except Windy, who got his weekly newspaper on Thursday. Still he was in his place just as faithfully on Tuesday and Saturday. It was just that the arrival of the mail was a diversion; there might be a passenger, and there was sure to be something interesting for someone in the mail bags. The trotting ponies and the rattling buckboard were our only link with the outside world.

Since the Post Office was an annex to the general store, women delayed their shopping to the cool of the afternoon. Just at mail time they came carrying pans of eggs or pounds of butter to exchange for household necessities, and then visited while the mail was being put into the boxes, though most folks just called for theirs at the general delivery window. Often several people from one family would be there, though they all knew that there would be no mail.

But what if you didn't get any yourself? You could be with the crowd; you might hear bits of news that Windy reported from his paper, *The Las Vegas Age*. You must take these with a grain of salt, though, for sometimes Windy made up local items that he pretended were printed. You'd know whether Elzina got a letter from her beau who was off working for a wedding stake, or whether Aunt Mary Josephine heard from her son who was on a mission, or whether Annie Cox got her order from Sears. If a young girl snatched her letter and walked away quickly, you could be sure it was personal and precious; if her younger sister received it from the window, her friends gathered to see the return on the envelope and the postmark and make guesses about it. Occasionally someone would open a letter and read it aloud, after it had been hastily scanned. These were usually from missionaries, and sharing their contents with the neighbors was much the same as passing a box of candy might have been.

The fact that the Post Office window opened directly onto the sidewalk, and that it was shady and pleasant at this time of day, invited people to loiter. Besides, there was choir practice on Tuesday night and a dance on Saturday, so that young folks could quite easily make social arrangements.

For me, the arrival of the mail meant that I should be at home, though I sometimes was at the Post Office early, and rode back in the buckboard. It was my business to take over the ponies as soon as they were unharnessed and had time to roll and get a drink at the trough. I put on the nosesack with four doublehandfuls of grain. When they had finished I would ride one and lead the other to the pasture, where they would stay until their next run. I would bring back the team for the next morning's run, and give them grain and hay. We had eight of these mustang ponies, a team for each of the three trips and two extra, just in case. No team could make the trip more than once a week.

Of course, we had the farm team besides, but my special care was the mail horses. I soon learned the art of catching these ponies, and I had genuine pleasure in taming them. Pa would hobble them always, because he just didn't have time to run after one when he needed to catch it. I always talked to these hobbled ones, coaxed them with a bit of grain, and finally I could get close enough to rub their necks and shoulders. After about a week of "getting acquainted" with one, I'd take his hobbles off. If he gave me trouble catching him, I'd put them back on. I learned to hold out a little grain in a pan and keep the telltale rope behind me until I could get close enough to put it on. The outcome was that I could catch any of them without a bit of trouble, while Pa would have to corner even the hobbled ones.

Folks started calling me "Hen Leavitt's boy," for they saw me so regularly on a horse, trotting or loping along bareback, hatless and shoeless.

[61]

One morning Pa came to my bed, shook me a little and called me by name. When I didn't rouse, he pulled me out and stood me on my feet.

"Here, you, WAKE UP!" he was saying. "You'll have to go to the field and get me a horse. Old Jeff is lame, and I can't start over that road with a lame animal. You go down and bring one of the extras — I don't care which one, any that you can catch — and bring it out to the road to meet me. Jeff can make it that far, and you can ride him back. That way the mail will leave on time."

"You don't mean Old Flax?" I asked. Flax was Pa's own special horse.

"You know better than to ask that! Of course I don't mean Flax; you stay away from Flax. And you'd better walk out and lead the mustang, too, if it's one of the last ones I bought. But get a move on; the mail must leave on time."

It was still pitch dark outside. This was the first time in my life I had been sent to the field before daylight. I found, as Pa said, that the darkness wasn't really so dark once you were out in it, and the road was familiar as it was in daytime.

At the field I caught one of the mustang ponies, and followed Pa's suggestion. I didn't try to mount; I led him out the road that divided Uncle Tom's field and Brother Adams'. I could hear the buckboard way up the line, and managed to get to the road first.

"Good work!" Pa said heartily. I could see that he was pleased with my promptness, and glad, too, that I hadn't risked riding this new horse. He shifted Old Jeff's harness onto the new pony, and was ready to be on his way. He held Jeff while I mounted, without offering to help at all, for he knew that I would resent that. I didn't need help. Then, as he handed me the reins, he slipped something into my hand, gave Jeff a smart slap on the rump, and turned to climb into the buckboard.

I opened my hand. Glory Hallelujah!!!! A QUARTER! A whole twenty-five cents! Never in all my life had I owned so much money! When we were little kids, we took eggs to the store for candy, one egg for two sticks. Then on holidays I sometimes had a nickel to spend, and a few times, a dime. I had earned thirty-five cents gleaning wheat last summer, but I didn't get it in cash. It went to help pay for my new slippers.

Now here I was with all this for my very own. I didn't have to divide with anybody; I didn't even have to tell anybody. I'd keep it until I should see something very special that I wanted. Never in all my life, before or since, have I felt so wealthy. I didn't want to break it into dimes and nickels; I wanted it all in one precious piece.

But my resolution didn't hold. It wasn't any fun unless I could tell Charity, and it wouldn't be unless she shared it. So I decided to not break it for a while. Maybe we could make a trip with Pa on the mail sometime, all the way out to Moapa. Then we would have some money to spend. That one piece of money conjured up so many plans and projects! As I rode home on the limping horse, facing the crimson and yellow sunrise, I knew that the world was wide and wonderful and beautiful, and I was a part of all the nice things in it.

On that very trip Pa brought home a dog — really only a puppy — that he found almost dead near his noon camping place. He called the dog Griz, and said that he would likely grow to be a large animal. Our only fault to find with him: his eyes weren't the same color. One was blue and one was yellow, but he was so sharp and friendly, and a self-appointed guard for baby Francis, who was just learning to walk, that he was loved by us all.

The Cistern

By the end of August Pa had the mail run working smoothly. The worst of the summer heat was past, and he turned his attention to the matter of the cistern. The circle on the ground was outlined with a scalloped ring of shovelfuls of soil taken out. When he told Grandpa about it that evening, Grandpa said, "Why don't you hire me to do that digging? I'm pretty handy with a shovel."

"I'll be more than glad to let you do it, if you think it won't be too hard on you. Would you work for three dollars a day?"

"No, that's too much. I'd be glad to work for two dollars a day and my noon meal. I could come early in the morning and take a long rest at noon on that bed there in the wire house, and then work again three hours in the later afternoon. But I'd want to be paid every night in silver coin."

It was evident to Pa that his father had this all figured out from the time he had first learned of the cistern project. So he was glad to accept the terms. The very next day Grandpa began in earnest. He was on the ground early with his chair and cane. Pa brought the shovel, and told him to take it easy and not overdo until he got more used to the pace, and not to be afraid to take time out to rest.

A little before noon Grandma Thirza and Aunt 'Ress came down to see how he was getting along, and to bring a midmorning snack. It was only a short walk, and it broke the monotony for them. As the work progressed only one would come at a time, but they were both very concerned for Grandpa's welfare. It was surprising, though, how much earth he did move, as every two or three days Pa would have a team and scraper push the soil away onto the sterile strip at the west side of the lot. This made it easier for Grandpa; he didn't have to throw the dirt over so high a bank.

As the hole became deeper, Aunt 'Ress came to help Grandpa out at noon; help him to the wire house, where she would take off his shoes, bring a washdish of water, washrag, and towel, and help him freshen up. Sometimes she'd take off his shirt, pull back his underwear, and massage his shoulders. After his meal, served there on a little stand, he would take time out for two or three hours, stretching out and sleeping.

Every night his money was ready for him. Pa would count it out to him, sometimes in two silver dollars, sometimes one silver dollar and the rest in halves or quarters, seldom in anything smaller.

"Once a man and twice a child," I heard Pa comment to a neighbor who happened to be present when Grandpa was being paid. I thought about this a lot; I couldn't believe that Pa would say anything disrespectful about Grandpa. Maybe he was just stating a well-established fact. I could see the logic, though. A man would have taken his pay at the end of the week in a single check or in greenbacks.

For a while, Grandpa went up and down the ladder, pulling his weight with his arms, and filling the big bucket of earth that was lifted up by a horse and a pulley. Finally, he decided that he must quit, to the great relief of everybody concerned. They all thought that the experience hadn't really hurt him, and he took such pride in his earnings.

Now younger men went on with the digging and with scraping the earth down onto the lot. Already some rock was being hauled to lay up the sides, and cement mixed to finish everything off. What a happy, proud family just a week before Christmas when it was finally all ready for the water! Pa said that they should put a big red ribbon bow on top of the crosspiece that supported the pulley and label it as a Christmas gift for the whole family. The little people wouldn't be satisfied with only that, of course, nor would their elders.

Pa had quite a complicated setup for filling the cistern. The water left the Big Ditch to run through a wooden pipe with a coarse screen over it to hold out sticks and trash. Every half-hour or so while the water was running, he would clear the trash away. From there across the road in our irrigation ditch, across the head of the lot to the cistern pipe, the water ran in an open ditch, newly cleaned. The entrance to the cistern was a pipe, covered with a much finer screen, which stopped small sticks and trash that had gone through the coarse one.

The first water was turned in on Christmas Eve, as a part of our Christmas celebration, but Pa wouldn't let much in. He wanted to wait for the January thaw and catch the snow water, which he thought would carry less mineral than the regular river water.

What a great blessing this cistern was! Clear, cold water on hand all the time, enough for ourselves and animals, enough for our neighbors, many of whom would carry their drinking water in big buckets or pour it into a couple of regular water sacks to hang in the shade.

All the sacrament water at the church came from our cistern, the boys waiting until the meeting was ready to start so that the water would stay cool. It wasn't that our water was better than other people's; it was that it was nearer the church.

In January the cistern was filled right up almost to the very top, and with all that we used for household use, for watering the animals when the water was out, and for whatever the neighbors wanted, we didn't quite empty it in a year. Henceforth Pa wouldn't fill it so full; he thought the water was cooler farther beneath the surface. Grandpa Dudley was proud of the part he played in building the cistern, for it proved that there was some good in the old man yet. The little tasks which followed seemed trivial compared to this.

Across the Mesa

I KNEW WHAT THE MAIL RUN WAS LIKE ON THIS END, but couldn't guess what it was like on the other. Charity and I were talking about it one day when we didn't know that Ma was listening, so she decided that the right thing would be to let us go and see. I don't think Pa was very anxious about it, but she usually got her way in the end. It was mid-June, and hot, but it would only get hotter for the next several months. Then the fruit time would be on, and she'd need us more than ever.

"There ain't much to see, but I guess they'd as well go first as last," Pa finally said.

It was Friday. Before daylight we were on our way, perched on the seat beside Pa, our bare feet dangling. We wished some of our friends could see us ride away, but it was too early, of course. The road past the field gates was all new and the land mysterious in this early morning haze. It was daylight when we came to the river. It looked the same here, with the red bar and the stream all running against the bank. Here Pa pulled out and stopped, got the brass bucket from the back and gave each of the horses a small bucket of water. He didn't even unhitch, but took the bit out of each one's mouth while he drank, and then replaced it.

From here the Mesa looked close, but so high. It was like a broad belt that held together the billows of land like a belt on a stiff organdie skirt. Our hardest part would be to get on top of this Mesa. We had no idea the road would wind around — across wash and gully, always climbing, so that even though we had no load, the horses must stop once in a while to puff.

At one of these stops Pa said, "This is Toquapp Wash. When I used to take peddling loads out to Delamar, I followed this wash a long ways. *Toquapp* is the Indian word for tobacco. They gather the leaves and smoke them," and he climbed out to walk a little and to get some branches.

"Toquapp, toquapp," I kept saying to myself. Where had I heard the word before? Then suddenly, as Pa climbed back into the buckboard, I remembered.

"Is this the place where Grandpa Dudley and the other boys helped the Indians stampede the cattle?" I asked. "They scattered them so far in a half an hour that it took three weeks to gather them up again."

"Where did you get that?" Pa's voice was almost sharp.

"Wasn't you there? I thought he was telling it to you, but maybe it was just to Grandma Thirza and Aunt 'Ress. But that's what he said — that he blacked his face some and tied a red handkerchief around his head, and with a mighty WHOOP led out in it."

Pa sat silent for a while. Then he said quietly, "Grandpa is a very old man. He has had many experiences in his life. Sometimes he gets mixed up. You should not repeat what he says. It could as well have happened during the Indian troubles at Tooele, or out at Hebron, either." But I knew it was Toquapp. I also knew better than to contradict my father or press the point, especially right now.

The road twisted and turned, until as we neared the top I could well understand how they would have to double teams on loaded wagons, and at the last pitch have everybody help. Then suddenly we were there, to the top! We didn't stop long to look back at the scene behind us, the river so low and far away and all the rolling land between. Now we must make up for lost time. Pa had a saying about horses: "Uphill, let him walk; downhill, let him trot; on the level, spare him not!"

What we had heard of the Mesa was all true: it was, indeed, level and flat as a table, covered with a dotting of scrubby little bushes in a white, chalk-like formation with dust much finer than sand.

As we set out now on a swinging trot, this dust billowed up until we looked like an earthbound comet trailing a white tail that extended for miles before it settled. Any traveler on this mesa would be seen from his dust, if he were moving fast enough to stir it up.

Then, without any warning, Pa slowed down and pulled off the road, made a sharp back turn, and pulled down into an arroyo, one steep, foot-high drop, and down an incline into a wash that was deep enough to hide our outfit from any other travelers. Here Pa stopped the buckboard and unharnessed the team, turning them loose to urinate and roll. They shook themselves and came back for the nose-sack with a half-feed of grain and the bucket of water, this time from the keg.

We had sandwiches and cookies from the grub box, with a bottle of peaches for the dessert. The water in the canvas waterbag was wet, but not cool. Milk would not carry at all. Then Pa relaxed on a camp quilt on the ground, while we followed the arroyo down to "The Pockets," a stone formation where water would be stored for a while after a rain. They were stone dry now, though.

Out on the flat again, we took the same trotting speed, for we must be on schedule — thirty-five miles in seven hours, with an extra hour thrown in for resting the team! That was a record speed, and maintained only because every team was fresh for the trip. The sun was now directly overhead and heat seemed to reflect back from the ground.

Suddenly Charity pointed and cried, "Look! There's Moapa!"

"I didn't think there would be so many trees," I said. "I thought it would be just a common little place like Bunkerville, but there are such big houses. And a lake, even."

"That ain't Moapa," Pa said, pushing back his hat. "That's a mirage. Don't ask me what made it or how it comes to be there, but quite often it is there at this time of day. It's sometimes a little to one side or the other, and I don't know how long it lasts. I only know that I have seen it a number of times. A man who didn't know better would start to find it, but it's like the rainbow with the pot of gold. No one ever got that, either."

"But it does look real," I insisted. "With trees and water there, and buildings, most anyone would want to go to it."

"That's the Devil's way," Pa answered. "He tries to cover sin and deceit and wicked things with a cloak of beauty. That way he can get the silly and the weak."

After the mirage, Moapa was a disappointment. Pa had told us not to expect anything much, but we weren't prepared for this. We knew that Moapa was the Indian word for *swampy land — Pah* in Paiute is always *water —* so we thought there would be a stream somewhere, with grass and tules and trees. But this was stark, barren desert, with a black line of railroad tracks running through. A sorry little row of houses stood facing the sun on one side of the track — the station house, a general store, two saloons, an eating house, a rooming house, and one or two plank buildings that seemed to be homes. Two anemic, stunted little cottonwood trees struggled for existence in front of the station house; a morning-glory vine clung to a bit of chicken wire between them. There was not another green thing in the place; everything was burned to a blister.

Pa's headquarters, a shack for grain and baled hay, a shed with a corrugated tin roof, and a watering trough with a dripping tap, was on a little elevation on the opposite side, the only bit of a human habitation — poor as it was — in that vicinity. Besides the storage place for the horse feed, there was a bit of a kitchen attached, with a small, two-hole wood stove, a table, and a box with a shelf in for a cupboard. Clearly Pa's cooking amounted to boiling water for his tea, or maybe frying an egg. His single cot was outside under the shed, the bedroll tied securely and locked in with the hay and grain. A tramp might lie on the bare cot on Pa's off nights here, but Pa didn't leave any bedding where it could be carried away.

We didn't come to the shack at all until we had delivered the mail at the station house, for it must be there by one o'clock. That was the first consideration; the next was the team. They must not only be watered and fed, they must be rubbed down after they had rolled. This had been a strenuous trip; tomorrow would be another.

We girls washed up in water from the trough, and slicked our hair back a little with the broken comb — Ma had braided it up tight before we left, and we were not to undo it until we got back home. We would wear our bonnets, freshly starched and kept in a box. In this sun, we would really need them. But first we changed our dresses and buttoned each other down the back. We would explore a little while Pa was busy with the horses.

We started toward the east end of town, where we had noticed three lumber shacks and a big trash pile that looked interesting — there were so many different bottles, some still unbroken. At each house the broom was brush side up in a holder outside the door, and tied around each was a red ribbon with a big bow and streamers.

"Hey, you two! Get back here!" Pa's voice was sharp and cross. "What you doin' poking around there?"

We hadn't meant any harm; we didn't think it would be stealing to get things out of a trash pile. But we came back and started in the opposite direction toward the station house. As we came onto the platform, a strange voice called out, "Hello! Hello! Ha! Ha! Ha!"

We soon discovered the parrot in a cage, and I wondered why it should laugh at us like that. We tried to start a conversation, but it told us to "Get home, you brats!"

We didn't like that, even though it came from only a bird, so we went back to the shack again. By now Pa was ready to go with us to the store. We had heard talk of the owner, Mrs. McKinney, and knew that she lived up above the store. A very large lady, she more than filled the rocking chair. Her hair was skinned back into a large bob, and she just kept rocking, except when she started to talk.

"Well, well!" she exclaimed, "What have you got here? Twins, I'll bet!"

"Oh, no," Pa said. "Not twins."

"Not twins! Which is the oldest?"

I expected Pa to say some fool thing like, "Well, I'm not just sure which *is* the oldest," so I said with what dignity I could, "I'm fifteen months older."

Her mouth opened in a shriek that was more than human. "Lordy, Lordy! Can you beat that! The little one here says she is fifteen whole months older! Whoooooeee!!! Who ever heard tell of such a thing!"

Her whole body, even her fat forearms, shook like jelly with her laughter.

I didn't see anything very funny about two sisters being the same size and wearing identical dresses, even if they weren't twins, and

I didn't quite get the reason for all this fuss. Charity was as uncomfortable as I was, so we slipped outside.

We saw a Chinese with a long queue and a loose coat dodge out of a door and toss some waste into a barrel near the step, and then dodge back in quickly. I would have waited for him to come out again, but we heard the whistle of the freight train, and hurried to get by Pa. It whistled and puffed and steamed, and finally came to a stop, and Pa showed us that it was getting a drink from the high black tank at the upper end of town, while men were unloading goods from the caboose onto the station platform. Its whole panting length seemed almost alive.

Then right in front of us a door opened and a colored man stepped out. He seemed amused at our open-mouthed wonder; at least he rolled his eyes and showed his white teeth in a broad grin, did a bit of a dance step, and grimaced for our entertainment.

We went back to the camp for supper, which we ate out of the grub box, with sardines for a special treat. Pa had paid Mrs. McKinney for our room for the night, and we had the key, but we wanted to wait for the Limited, which passed at ten o'clock.

At the first faint whistle we started toward the tracks. When the big, glaring eye rounded the bend, we both clutched at Pa, for this monster was coming right at us. The long-drawn whistle raised the hair on the back of your neck; the clatter was deafening. Like a monstrous black dragon with a light in every segment, it dashed by at such speed that we hardly had time for more than a fleeting glimpse of people inside, relaxed or visiting. We had no time to say anything or point out anything; we could only look as hard as we could and see as much as we could. It came and went that fast.

Now Pa took us to our room in Mrs. McKinney's rooming house. It was the front one on the right as we went in, with a double bed, a wash stand with a big earthen pitcher, a wash dish, and a bucket on the floor for the slops. The toilets were outside and placed according to the general rule: "Gents to the right; Ladies to the left." We ran out there together before Pa left. We had no need to worry about getting up; Pa couldn't get the mail until nine o'clock, anyway.

"How do you suppose we go about to put out this light? One sure thing—we can't sleep with it on. It's too bright," Charity said.

The light was attached to the ceiling and came by a long cord to the dresser, where it was in a coil like Pa's lariat, and tied by the side of the mirror. I untied it. There was enough cord there to take it to the end of the hall. The light was fastened permanently into the end; there was no gadget to push or pull or turn. I tried to loosen the globe, but it was in so solid that I thought it had been built together that way. We had no idea what to do with it.

"Shall I break it?" Cherie asked. "We can't sleep with that strong light in our eyes. We've got to put it out some way."

"Yes, but if you break it and turn all that electricity loose in the room, it might kill us," I argued.

We tried to adjust ourselves to it, to turn our faces to the wall, or cover our heads, but it was no use. How could we endure a whole night of this? I'd rather take a quilt and pillow and go out and sleep on the ground. But then I had an idea! I opened the top bureau drawer, put the light inside, and shut the drawer as tight as it would go. Success! There was a little streak of light across the ceiling, but that was fine; it helped us remember where we were. We both slept so sound that we didn't need it.

I took the light out of the drawer the first thing in the morning — I was troubled a little because there was a small burned place, but I couldn't help that. I wound the cord just like it was and tied it back where it was, and left it burning. We never said a word about it, either of us, but waited for several months before we learned how to turn off an electric light.

We had breakfast with Pa at the shack, and put on our other dresses, because we'd not be going anywhere this morning. Our new ones were put back into the box, but we kept our bonnets out. Before nine o'clock we had all of our own things loaded, and some boxes of freight for Bunkerville, and were waiting at the station house for the mail. The trip home would not be so strenuous for the horses, because we wouldn't have such a long climb out, and at the end it would be downhill off the mesa.

We stood waiting for the train when Mrs. McKinney came to the door and motioned for Pa to come over. She handed him an empty candy bucket, the size that would hold about twenty-five pounds of candy or five gallons of liquid.

"Maybe you can find some use for this," she said.

"Indeed we can," Pa said. "Thank you very much. It's a beautiful thing."

It was indeed beautiful, all varnished and with two inch-wide copper bands around it. Maybe Ma could plant a young oleander tree or a climbing vine in it.

Now we had plenty to talk about: the parrot and its training and regular line of talk (here Pa filled in with other expressions used by this remarkable bird: "Go to Hell," "You're Crazy," "Close Your Trap," among them); the clicking of the telegraph that we should have seen more of; and Mrs. McKinney's son, Barney, who was found dead-drunk by a tamarack bush near the tracks — from a distance we had seen two men supporting him and walking him home.

Our stop at The Pockets was shorter this time, for the team was not so tired. Pa drove them down into the place, unhooked the tugs and let down the tongue, but did not take off the harness. With the bits out, the horses could eat their "bait" of grain and drink the water. It was near this place that Pa had found our puppy, "Griz," not long before. It seemed such a miraculous, wonderful thing to us that we wanted to know just where and how it all happened.

"You found him on your way out, just as you turned to pull down into The Pockets, you told Uncle Herb at the time," I reminded him. "So this is The Pockets, and it must be near here."

"It was last August," Pa said. "Nearly a year ago, and about the hottest day I ever lived through. I don't know how I happened to see him, but just as I made the turn I got a glimpse of something; I didn't know what it was, but I stopped the team and backed a little and there he was kind-a wadded up under a bush. I jumped right out and went to him, sure that he must be dead from the way he looked. He didn't seem conscious, but the body was not stiff. I climbed back into the buckboard and reached for the canteen. I poured out a lidful of water into his mouth by holding him on his back and forcing it open. Then I wet my handkerchief and patted it onto his lips and then soaked it again and put it over his eyes and head. There were quivers in his body that made me know there was life there."

"Did you forget your team all this time?" I prompted him, for he had made a point of that when he first told the story.

"I sure did," Pa agreed, "but I made it up to them. I gave them their grain and water and some extra time to rest while I worked with the puppy. He seemed so young, I couldn't imagine anyone losing him. Certainly no one would leave him on purpose."

"I wish I knew how he got there myself. I think the Lord let him stay and led you to him and helped you save him."

"Well, I guess the Lord directs more things than we know about, but anyway Griz did get well fast, and the whole family seems glad that I found him."

As usual, Pa drove into town on a smart trot and right to the Post Office without stopping. He always made it a point to trot out and back into town, no matter how he traveled on the road between. We were so proud to climb out there in the crowd, all dusty, as the passengers always were, shake ourselves, and answer the questions of our friends. Yes, we had been all the way to Moapa, and it was a long, long way, and we had seen many things. Though later we might become tiresome to our friends, we had much to talk about between ourselves, for our world had now a new dimension. Moapa was not beautiful, but it was a part of the wide, wonderful world, with strange people and with trains running back and forth every single day.

For me, the ten-o'clock Flyer was the most important event of all. Night after night it passed in my dreams, heralded by whistles and bells and then gliding by so fast that it was gone before I had time to really see it. I remembered the beautiful women in the windows, and the dressed-up men, all so matter-of-fact in the midst of the hurry. Where were they going? I wondered. Some day, I told myself, I would ride in one of those Flyer trains and I'd go all the way in it, and not be afraid, either, but just go along like I was as good as any of them!

The Outside Comes In

"And he's got a music box with a great big horn like a morning-glory, and it sings songs and says pieces and plays band music and everything! He's going to play it tonight for everybody, FREE!"

We carried the word around until every family in town knew about it. It made us feel very important and like community benefactors to be thus sponsoring so great an event. It all happened because the night before a strange man had come to our house to see about getting hay for his donkeys. He had stopped his outfit at the bottom of our lot, where a row of tall cottonwoods made a heavy shade. When we lined up to gawp at it Ma called us back sternly, but not a detail had missed us. Here was a covered wagon like none we had seen before. Ours had round bows and a separate cover tied more or less securely, while this had a square, permanent top of thin boards, with a regular door and steps to go up, and a window with a glass pane — not a very big window, but a window, just the same.

That night as we lay across our beds in the back dooryard, we heard the strains of "See That Chicken Pie" from the bottom of the lot. We all sat up, ready to go investigate.

"You stay right where you are," Pa ordered. "I'll go down myself. You can hear all you need to from where you are."

It seemed to us that he was gone a long time, for we heard several

[76]

musical numbers — a band piece with such a marked rhythm that we beat the time out on the side of the spring cot; then a wailing guitar number that tied me all up inside, like there was something I really wanted and couldn't have. Then there was a talking number — "Uncle Josh" — but it was not clear enough to understand.

When at last Pa came back, he told us that the man and his wife would stay another night and play their phonograph free, and we could invite all the town to come and hear it. Pa would feed their mules in exchange for this entertainment; this would be our first concert by outside talent.

The next evening as soon as the chores were done, people began to gather. There were married couples carrying babies and leading young children; there were giggling girls in groups, keeping a weather eye out for the young men who would saunter up later. Aunt Sade hobbled up the middle of the road carrying her rawhide-bottomed chair in one hand and her cane in the other, while a grandchild trailed behind carrying a cushion.

The moon was in its first quarter, high and bright; the night was warm. Pa and the Wagon Man had improvised seats out of boxes and planks for the older people to sit on, while children climbed onto the big cottonwood logs that had lain there all season, too heavy to be dragged away and too big to cut up. Young folks, mostly paired off by now, were content to listen from a distance and hold hands over by the pole bars. The older ones visited and looked at the unusual wagon with its window of light and its open door where the music box with its gorgeous morning-glory horn rested on a stand. The lady of the wagon, obviously middle-aged in spite of heavy makeup and long earrings and frizzy red hair, held a mite of a dog and talked a line of baby talk to it to keep it from barking.

"Whoever heard of keeping a dog like that?" someone behind me whispered. "Not good for an earthly thing but an ornament. And she talks to it like it was human!"

Now was beginning the ritual of getting ready to start. The Wagon Man picked up one after another of the black cylinders, studying them and putting them back into place, as though in search of an extra good one with which to begin the program. Finally he found one to his liking, slipped it onto the shining shaft, lifted up the contraption at the foot of the horn, blew at the needle and turned the crank.

"That needle is a diamond," he explained, and the audible intake of breath from the crowd showed that they were duly impressed. "Never have to change a needle on this machine, but you do have to keep it clean."

A click and it started. No audience at grand opera was ever more attentive or appreciative. The program was varied. There were many songs, among them "On a Bicycle Built for Two," "On the Banks of the Wabash, Far Away," and "See That Chicken Pie." There were band numbers and Hawaiian guitar pieces. And Uncle Josh in the city told about the bathroom with a big bath tub to get in all over, and one place to wash your hands and face, another for your feet. How he wished it was Saturday night, so he could use them all!

About eleven o'clock Pa and the Wagon Man held another brief consultation, after which the man announced that this would be the last number for tonight, but if the crowd wanted to come again tomorrow night he would be glad to play the phonograph again. Since he and his wife had a long trip ahead, if anyone felt like bringing some little thing, like butter or eggs or a bit of garden stuff, they would be glad to get it. They were not charging tickets, understand, but would take whatever the people cared to bring.

So the next night there was another concert. People came carrying a loaf of bread, a dish of eggs or a roll of butter, a bottle of jam or an armful of green corn. Although he was feeding the mules, Pa felt that we should make a further contribution, as there were so many of us to listen. So he brought a live hen. Ma said she didn't have time to scald and pick and clean it, and Pa thought they might prefer it alive, anyway. He tied it by a heavy cord string to the wagon wheel. Now the lady had a real reason to hold her dog and keep him from barking.

The Wagon Man outdid himself trying to make this program interesting. He announced each piece, telling who was performing and giving bits of information to help us enjoy it. When the crowd laughed heartily at Uncle Josh in the city and on the elevator, and ordering his dinner, he bowed slightly as though the applause was meant for him.

The moon passed the meridian and filled all the scene with honey-colored light, falling full into the faces of sleeping babies and turning Aunt Sade's hair into a halo. Only the pole bars where the young people whispered and giggled softly lay in dappled twilight. A few older folks shifted on the backless benches, yet were reluctant to leave.

"Let's have that Uncle Josh piece again," Lem called out.

"Play 'Shine On, Harvest Moon' again," Cal Barnum called out, after the laugh following Uncle Josh had died down. Now Cal led out and the young people all joined in the chorus. "Daisy, Daisy, . . ." followed, again, with the crowd joining in as they could.

"It's getting late," the Bishop said in an aside to Pa. "Don't you think we should bring this to a close?"

Pa didn't want the party to just peter out, with some going and others staying, so he talked again to the Wagon Man, who then made a little speech, saying that the next number would be the last. It didn't seem appropriate to close such a gathering with prayer. Instead, Pa thanked the visitors for these two evenings of entertainment. He didn't suggest that they stay another night, because it was Saturday, and nothing — not anything — could interfere with the Saturday night dance. And whoever heard-tell of a concert on Sunday? So the Wagon Man and his wife left with their little toy-like dog and their phonograph with the gorgeous morning-glory horn. But the live hen either escaped or was turned loose, for we found her the next morning in the yard, still dragging her bit of rope. Ma guessed that the lady didn't know how to pick and dress a chicken; Pa thought maybe the man didn't have the heart to kill it, and they had no way to carry it. At any rate, the string was taken off, and the hen scratched happily among her fellows; Pa allowed that the feed for the mules for an extra night more than paid for our tickets to the entertainment. And the townspeople had set them up with food enough for weeks. The town was never quite the same, though.

During the next week the crowd of young people gathered at the molasses mill to eat cane and visit and court. It was just a short distance away, and we could hear Cal Barnum's voice lead out in "Shine On, Harvest Moon," with others harmonizing with alto or bass. Often, in other places, the two nights' concert were referred to, as though another dimension had been added to our entertainment.

Whatever it did to anyone else, the phonograph did something to me. It made me dissatisfied with myself and with things about me. Here I was, teaching myself to play the organ — that is, to play songs from the hymn book, songs like "Silent Night," "Catch the Sunshine," and others in the key of C, thinking I was really doing something when I could go through without having to stop once to find my place. Of course, I could play only the bass with my left hand. The tenor notes were too complicated. And this fellow brings in an instrument which gave a whole evening's concert with only turning a crank and placing a needle. But the needle had to be a diamond!

Surely there must be many things on the Outside that we were missing here. I had heard talk of a new road soon to be made between Los Angeles and Salt Lake City, a road over which cars would pass. Some people here had seen cars; some had ridden in them, but not even on our trip to Moapa had we seen an automobile.

At school I sat behind Chuck. Pa had bought himself a pair of new shoes in Moapa, and in the box with them as a sort of prize was a little tin beetle that would pop and crack when you bent the tin at the bottom. I brought it to school that morning expecting to show it off at recess and maybe trade it for something, but I had to run the last half-block, and then barely got to march in with the class, so the beetle was still a secret.

In getting settled, adjusting slate and books and slipping my dried figs and raisins into the back of the shelf underneath, I let the beetle fall to the floor. Our teacher was small and nervous, always tense, as though she expected something dreadful to happen at any moment. Now she was looking so hard at me that I didn't dare stoop and pick the beetle up; I just reached out my bare foot, covered it, and pulled it back to safety under the desk. Later, when the teacher became occupied with something else, I would get it and put it inside the desk.

I got out my geography book and set to work. I liked geography because I enjoyed reading about strange people in different lands; I liked the book because it was big enough that I could put *Under the Lilacs* inside and slide way down on the end of my spine and enjoy myself behind its covers. Life this morning had just begun to be interesting; the story was so good that unconsciously my big toe began to move, like a little lamb's tail works when he is enjoying his breakfast.

Click! Click! Click!

"What is that?" the teacher asked, stopping the reading class in the other side of the room and listening intently.

Without looking up or pretending to hear, I stopped the noise, thinking absently that I must be more careful. In the seat in front of me Chuck was trying to untangle a string and to watch a doodlebug push backwards through a little pile of sand. His activities were also screened by his geography book.

I really didn't intend to click the beetle any more. I didn't want to attract attention in school; I meant to demonstrate during recess. But just as when you have a chew of gum in your mouth, you will chaunk once in a while, so there were times when my toe worked by itself just once or twice at a time — not more than that at a time. I did not know the teacher was listening and watching, trying to locate this noise. I had not noticed that she had gone to the back of the room. I was in a faraway land with Bab and Betty.

She passed with a swish as she strode up the aisle like descending Vengeance, passed me, and grabbed Chuck. She lifted him out of his seat, shook him till his freckles rattled, and jammed him down hard enough to drive his spine right up into his head.

"Click that thing, will you!" she screamed in rage. "Click it and keep on clicking it after I have told you again and again to stop that noise! If I hear that thing click again, I'll give you something to remember the rest of your life!"

She was all breathless with her exertion and flushed with anger.

Poor Chuck! I was honestly sorry, for I had no idea that there would be such a violent outburst. I wouldn't have gotten him into trouble on purpose; he had a hard enough time to study. The words didn't mean much when he read them, and his fingers were awkward with a pencil. School for him was hard enough at best.

For the rest of the time until recess there was perfect order in the room, but there was also a tension that made it hard for the reading class to get back any interest in their story. I put the beetle into my desk and left it there.

"Golly, Chuck," I said, running to him as soon as we were safely out. "I'm sorry. I didn't mean to get you in Dutch. Look, this is what I had. You can have it if you want."

"Oh, was that what the old gal was fuming about? I thought it was the doodlebugs on my desk. I hadn't noticed any click. I guess she just figures I got it coming, one way or another."

"I wondered maybe if you'd think I was mad on account of yesterday, but I'm not. I wrote another story, and it's better than the one you took. I sure didn't want to make you any trouble today."

After recess we all went back to work until the room fairly hummed with the work of arithmetic problems or composition writing. The teacher was giving out the spelling words to the third grade, pronouncing each slowly and clearly two times.

All at once Eldon Leavitt lifted his head listening, for all the world like an old gander sensing something new and different. A strange *thug-thug* pulsed through the air. Like a flock of geese waiting for the signal, we all listened. Even the teacher paused.

"Gee-hos-i-phat!! Look a-comin'!" Eldon's vibrant whisper went through the room like an electric current. As of one mind, we all raised up to look; Eldon leaped to his feet and scrambled out the window.

A complete stampede followed. The whole room rose and bolted, some boys through the windows, the main crowd out the door.

For a half-hearted minute the teacher tried to protest, but she could as well have stopped the wind. Small wonder, too, for there was a real automobile, the first we had ever seen, coming up the street. I was among the first out, landing at the street just as the car was pulling out of the ditch and turning to go up the other street. Eldon was far ahead of any of the others, so he had caught onto the upright that supported the top, stood on the running board, and waved his free arm.

No one else caught up with it. We all ran through the dust and gravel, hoping that when it turned again and had to slow up to get across the ditch, we could climb on, too. But none ever made it.

The driver was a stranger, a thin man with a long neck and a big Adam's apple, smoking a pipe. He looked neither to the right or the left, he neither encouraged us nor ordered us to keep off nor admonished us to be careful. He kept his eyes straight ahead and puffed steadily at his pipe. (This was new to us, too. No one in our town used tobacco but Con Neagle and Uncle Andy, but they used Bull Durham and rolled their own. That is why some of the younger kids thought that the pipe in the driver's mouth was in some way a part of the machinery, the puffs of smoke there related to those that came from the exhaust at the back.)

The car stopped in front of the store, and we all swarmed around it until Uncle Jess, the constable, walked around and ordered us all back onto the sidewalk, where we could see all we needed to see.

There was no more school that day. At night there was a meeting and dance to celebrate this occasion, and to hear the men talk about a new "Arrowhead Trail" road that would connect Los Angeles and Salt Lake City. No longer would Bunkerville be isolated. But the outside did not come in — it passed by, and we were hardly an eddy in the stream.

Simon and the Magic Sack

I WAS BUSY WITH MY DOLL RAGS WHEN A STRANGE VOICE SAID BEHIND ME, "Hen live here?"

I jumped with surprise, and turned to see an Indian man standing behind me, a middle-aged man about Pa's age, dressed in regular white man's clothing.

"Yes," I said, "He lives here, but he hasn't come up from the field yet. He should be here before long."

"I wait." He settled himself on the corner of the porch, and at the rumble of the wagon got up and started toward the gate. Pa recognized him and pulled out to stop. Wrapping the lines around the brake, he jumped down, and came to meet him. They came together with a real impact. They did not shake hands; they gave each other a genuine hug.

"Simon, you old rascal you, where you been all this long time?"

"Where you been, too, Hen? Long time me no see!"

"Come on out with me to take care of the team," Pa said, and then turning to me, "Go tell your Mother to set an extra plate at the table. We're having company."

By the time they finished unloading the squash and came back to the house, Pa found supper waiting.

"Mary, this is Simon. He has been my friend for a long time. And, Simon, this is my squaw, and these all my papooses. Purty

[84]

plenty, don't you think." Simon acknowledged the whole thing with a smile.

After the blessing was asked and the food passed around, Pa told us all: "I've eat at Simon's house lots-a times. He was my best friend. We used to herd cows together. We would rastle and run and chase chipmunks and lizards. We never quarreled."

Simon looked pleased, but said nothing, so Pa went right on to explain, "You see there at Hebron there were more Indians than white men. I played with other Indian children, but Simon was special. He stuck up for me, and I stuck up for him."

When they left the table, the two men went to sit together on the porch. We all felt that there was more to this visit than just a friendly call.

"You got a rifle?" Simon asked after a little while.

"Yes, Simon. I got a good 30–30. Want to see it?"

Simon nodded yes, so Pa got up and went to the closet for the gun. That was one thing no child ever touched – that rifle. It was Pa's pride and joy — the one thing we all thought he would never lend. He brought it back, sat down beside Simon, and began to demonstrate the workings, putting in the cartridges, throwing them from the magazine into the chamber, feigning a shot, and then ejecting the shell. Then he let Simon take the gun and sight along the shining barrel.

"Purty nice gun," he said, handing it back. After a slight hesitation, he went on, "I go up to top of mountain purty soon. High up. By Noon Peak. Maybe see mountain sheep up there. You know, big sheep with crooked horn."

"You bet, I know," Pa said. "I was only up there once, a long time ago, but I had no good gun along. You can't kill a mountain sheep with arrows or little gun. Would you like to take my gun, Simon? You're welcome to it."

Simon's affirmative was instant. "Sure enough. Sure enough."

"OK so you take it. I'll get some bullets."

Simon was ready to go. He left without much in the way of thanks, and with no word of when he would bring the gun back. He just took it and left.

"That's the last Hen Leavitt will ever see of that gun," one of the neighbors said when I had told the story of having an Indian for dinner at the table with us, and of Pa's letting him take the rifle. "Imagine giving a gun like that to an Indian!"

Later that night when I repeated this comment to Pa, he sat for a while as silent as his Indian friend. "I only wish that I could trust all my white neighbors as well as I can Simon," he said at last.

It was nearly a month before Simon came again to the house. This time it was evening, and I answered the door. I recognized him at once and said, "Come in, Simon. Pa is here."

Simon nodded and grinned, but he said only, "I wait out here."

Pa went outside, but he left the door open and the children all crowded up. They must not miss seeing Simon!

"Did you have any luck on your hunt?" Pa asked.

"Purty good luck."

"Did you get your mountain sheep? How did you like the gun?"

Simon grinned a wide smile which showed his white teeth.

"Purty dam' good gun. Yeh, I got mountain sheep. Horns so big!" and his smile was still wide as he held out his arms to show how big. He handed Pa the gun and the box of bullets, and waited for him to set them down. Then he lifted the gunnysack at his feet.

"Pine nuts for the papooses," he said.

"Oh, Thank you! Thank you," Pa said, hefting the sack. "You brought too many! You must keep more for yourself. My papooses not know to eat pine nuts very good. They had no practice. I think I'll keep them all for myself. I *know* pine nuts."

Simon left, evidently pleased at Pa's enthusiasm over his gift.

"I'd pay ten dollars for these nuts at the store! Yes, I'd pay double that for nuts this size! Look at them! I wonder where he went to get nuts like that. They're roasted besides. No white man yet has ever learned how to roast pine nuts."

Pa twisted the sack shut and picked up the gun. He opened the box of cartridges.

"Well, he's been careful enough of the gun, looks like. And he has used only three bullets. And brought all these nuts for that! But you children must remember that Simon gave them to *me*. I think I'll eat them all myself."

We all laughed at this joke, for already we had our hands full and were cracking and munching. Certainly we had never tasted nuts quite like these before, and might never again, for nuts that we parched on top of the stove or baked in the oven lost much of their moistness and flavor. These had been slow-cooked in the cone, in a pit and left covered to steam. We learned to think of them as coming from a Magic Sack, because the older folks who ate them at once began to remember stories from the past, and how it was when they were young.

One of the best of all the storytellers was Grandma Maria, Grandpa's second wife. She had come with him and Grandma Mary and baby Hannah to Santa Clara, and her story of Old Agarapoots went about like this:

"Well, the men folks had been on the Santa Clara for a year or more before they brought the families down. President Young ordered a fort to be built before any women and children were brought down. It was made of rock and looked like the fort that still stands at Cove Fort. This one was washed away by the flood of 1862 — just wiped out completely. Actually some of us had been there the year before — as I said, but those of us that came to the fort were Jacob and Oscar Hamblin, Zadoc Judd, Dudley Leavitt, Thales Haskell, and Sam Knight. Jacob and Rachel were the oldest couple — He was 34 and Rachel, 32. Dudley was 26 and Mary 20, while I was just past 16. Minerva Dart Judd was only 18 and she had two children.

"Thales Haskell's wife, Maria Woodbury, was one of the sweetest girls that ever lived: so cheerful, so helpful, so sharp. She had a melodeon, which is a sort of small-sized accordion, and in the evenings she would sit outside and start to play it and sing. Sam Knight's wife didn't know much English, but she had the most beautiful alto voice you ever heard. Those two would have almost carried a program alone, but we all liked to join in the singing, and she encouraged even the children. Sometimes we would spend almost the whole evening singing.

"But I was going to tell you about Old Agarapoots. He was a mean Old Devil, mad all the time, it seemed like. Tutsegavit was our friend, and he told Uncle Jacob to watch out, because there might be trouble. So the men folks thought the women and children should stay inside the fort all day for safety. But it was hot as an oven in the

[87]

fort; no Indians were in sight, so we all decided to take the children out to the creek where there was water and shade. We had a wonderful time until Lyman — we had set him on watch because he was an older boy — Yelled out, 'Git for the fort! Here comes Agarapoots!'

"Sure enough, there he was with a half-dozen other warriors on horseback, loping down the hill. Did we ever gather up those young ones and get for the fort! Just about made it, too. But Agarapoots got his shoulder against the gate and pushed himself and one other in before Aunt Rachel could lock the gate — which she did, locking them inside.

"Well, all the other warriors were at the gate, so we helped Lyman climb up on the roof of one of the rooms and over the wall to the other side. As soon as the Indians outside saw him get on the horse and start up the valley, and heard him blow that whistle — (I'll have to tell you about that whistle: it was an empty 45–60 brass bullet shell that he could press against his lower lip and blow into. It gave out the most unearthly screaming noise you ever heard, and it carried for miles) . . .

"Well, as I said before, Old Agarapoots didn't want the men to catch him inside of the fort, but now Aunt Rachel pretended that she dare not open the gate for fear all the other warriors would come in. But she did open it just enough for them to squeeze through, and they were off in a cloud of dust.

"After a while Old Agarapoots got sick, and Tutsegavit came and asked Uncle Jacob to pray him dead. Of course, Uncle Jacob wouldn't do that, but when the old chief did die, the others thought it was Uncle Jacob's bad medicine that killed him."

Aunt Maria told of making the first cotton cloth, of how they had to save the contents of chamber pots in every home to set the indigo blue, and how they boiled madder root, some for bright yellow and others for red dye. That madder root — the red kind — could be anything from light pink to deep, dark wine. Oh, yes, and about making straw hats, and coloring part of the straw for trimming.

We already knew about madder root, both the red and yellow. We used it to color our own Easter eggs.

One story we could hardly bear to have told: the death of Maria Haskell. How the Indian boy in the home was handling the gun and shot her accidentally, and her little baby was born prematurely and they both died. It seemed hard to us that the Father in Heaven couldn't have saved her. But that's the way it was.

That Magic Sack of pine nuts opened a whole world of the past to us.

Flax

PA WOULD NEVER LET ME RIDE FLAX. When I asked, he usually said, "You stay away from Flax. I don't have time to go to a funeral this week."

I didn't see why. Flax was a large horse and a high-spirited one, but he didn't appear to be mean. He let me put the nosesack on and take it off again without any show of temper, but he didn't let me pet him as the others did.

One afternoon when Pa was at Moapa, I was to take the horses to the pasture. I could have waited another day to let the field dry out better after its watering, but the hay was practically gone in the stackyard. This time I would ride Flax, and Pa wouldn't need to know.

I got a rope around his neck, led him to the stump outside by the corner of the corral, and put the bridle on without a bit of trouble. I took care to fasten it solidly under his throat. It took me a while to get onto his back, for he wouldn't stand while I climbed up, holding onto his mane. I was quiet and patient; I patted his shoulder and tried to rub his back — none of which he seemed to appreciate. Finally, I took the chance and jumped, pulling myself up astride and in position, with the reins tight.

The other four or five horses started down the road on a trot. Flax insisted on being among them and in the lead in spite of how I tried to hold him back. So it was all the way through the town.

Flax pranced and fretted and pulled at the reins. Then just as we crossed the ankle-deep Mill ditch and the road stretched without a turn ahead, he broke into a full gallop, as heedless of my "Whoa! Whoa!" as if I were a fly on his back. He just stretched out and ran as if in a race, past Uncle Dud's place, and Uncle Lon's, and Uncle Weir's, with all the other horses trotting leisurely along far behind.

All this time I was pulling back on the reins with all my strength and saying, "Whoa, Flax! Whoa!" I sensed that he knew I was frightened, and I thought meant to rid himself of me. One thing sure, I meant to ride him out. Then something happened to change everything.

"You can't stop him, but you *can* turn him," flashed into my mind as if it had been said audibly. Instantly I was calm and confident. I gave him more rein; I started to talk to him in quiet tones. I knew that in another quarter of a mile the road forked, the right fork skirting the fields and ending in the river bottom; the left turning uphill on the road to St. Thomas, a clear wagon road amid low scrub brush, but all the time a steady upgrade. This would be safe.

"OK, old boy, so you want to run," I said. "Let's take this left-hand road, just for a change. Shall we?"

He responded to my pull to the left, and I relaxed. I had won; I could now afford to be confident and affable.

"Just you keep on running, Flax. You just run as long as you want to. I'll not try to stop you again. You can decide when it's time to stop."

It wasn't long before the gallop had become a trot, which very soon changed to a walk. He was dripping wet and all a-tremble with the exertion.

I turned him around and let him walk back, for I was afraid now that maybe the run had "winded him." I had heard of horses who had been pushed until they never could run again. They were called *winded*. Now as we went back, I patted his shoulder, and talked to him all the way, and prayed in my heart that I had not ruined this fine animal.

Then it became clear to me. Flax was running because he was bred to run and trained to run, and he had been cooped up in the corral for a week.

The other horses were waiting at the gate. As I approached, I saw that a wagonload of hay had just gone by, and not far behind it, another wagon carrying squash and melons. If Flax had been on this lower road, we would have had to pass both these outfits or run out into thickets of thorny mesquite or mescrew trees that grew in the broken land between. At best, I would have been scraped off as Flax charged wildly on. My blood ran cold to think how it would have been had we taken this, the regular road to the field.

I had to dismount to open the gate. The horses would go the width of Uncle Tom's forty through a tree-lined lane and enter our field through another gate. I held Flax by the bit until all the others had passed in. Should I get back on and ride the rest of the way, or should I turn him loose to run with the others? Suddenly I didn't want to ride him; I was in a way sorry that I had taken the chance at all. I didn't want to ever ride him again.

Pa evidently learned of my escapade before he even got to the house. Had someone who had seen me riding so wildly through the lower end of town stopped to give him the details? Or had he, himself, observed the tracks where Flax left the main road to go onto the St. Thomas road? I knew that he knew. I understood very well that he knew that I knew that he knew. He waited for me to open the subject and make a confession. I waited for him to ask me about it. So the evening passed without anything said on either side; I slipped off to bed early.

It was about a week before I opened the subject. Pa was sitting on the porch in the dusk and I went and sat close beside him, locking my arm in his.

"Do you know what saved my life when Flax was running away with me?" I asked, and then without waiting for his answer: "It was something that said to me, 'You can't stop him, but you *can* turn him.' After that I knew I was safe."

That closed the subject between Pa and me, but again and again it was mentioned where one or the other of us was reminded of how that little bare-headed, bare-footed girl was riding that race horse that thought he was in a national contest of some kind, and just had to win.

"Never seen the like of it before in all my life," Uncle Andy

Pulsipher said. He had been a professional jockey in his early days. "That horse has been on the track more times than once, or I'll eat my hat. Where did Hen Leavitt pick that animal up, anyway? Must-a stole him, for he'd never have money enough to pay for him."

Flax continued to be Pa's favorite mount, and never again did I suggest that I should like to ride him.

Now that Pa was in the Bishopric, and quite newly home from his mission, it was decided that he should represent the ward at the Fall Conference.

A trip to St. George would be exciting, for wasn't that the big city on the other side of the Wide Wonderful World? The very suggestion that we might go set me afire. Ma would take Charity, Aura, Melvin, and me, and we would be gone ten whole days!

Aunt Theresa would take care of baby Laurel, for he was a husky, good-natured child just weaned, and too young to remember anything about the trip. Melvin was pretty young, too, but Ma thought he just might carry through his life some impressions of the president of the Church, who would be there to preach in the great tabernacle.

How could Pa get away? Uncle Herb took over the mail for two weeks, and Uncle Roy could take care of the chores for that long.

Then Pa decided to fill the bottom bed of the wagon with rock salt to help pay the expense of it all. It would slow up the team, but it would be worth it. On top of the false floor he loaded hay and grain for the team, our grub box, bedding, and suitcases of clothing, along with some dried figs and melons. Last of all, the wagon cover was pulled on tight over a full set of bows.

We got on the road before noon on Wednesday, but moved at a slow walk, pausing only a few minutes at Mesquite to let the folks know that we were on our way, and followed the riverbed all the way up to Beaver Dams. We children walked most of the way — at least, we three girls did — playing in the damp sand when the horses stopped to rest.

We had relatives at Beaver Dams who insisted that we put our teams up in their yard for feed and water. They had accepted many favors from our folks in the past, and expected to get more in the future: a bit of credit ahead would be a good thing, anyway.

[93]

We had a campfire supper and bedded down early, all of the children in the wagon, and Pa and Ma with a bed on the McKnight hay stack — that is, the low, lean-to stack beside the big one. Long before light we knew that the wagon was moving, rumbling slowly along, stopping often. We must get up this long, steep slope during the cool of the day, but the sun was quite high before we reached the Ledges. Here must be another long feed stop for the horses, with the water a quarter of a mile from the road.

It was a good place to camp. The high ledges gave heavy shade, and there were so many caves and crannies to explore. But since we had still a long climb to the Summit we must start as soon as the horses could travel. Such a joy to finally go over the top! Now it would be down and down the twisting, winding road, often with Pa's foot heavy on the brake, to arrive in late afternoon at the Santa Clara Creek, a fine dashing stream with cottonwood trees and grass on the bank. It was early, but our team could take no more. It was just as well, for now Ma would have a chance to wash out the clothes we had on and take us in to Aunt Rosina's house in the morning all clean.

It was evident that Aunt Rosina hadn't been warned that we were coming, for as we pulled down the lane into her yard, we found her out picking up apples. Her joy at seeing my parents was genuine, though, and she included us all in her welcome. Her oldest boy, Archie, just my age, was on crutches from a long battle to save his leg. Clem, the younger brother, was the picture of health and vigor.

Pa would leave us here at Santa Clara while he took the salt over to St. George and delivered it. The fair would be opening today, but we'd have to be content to see it all in one day, Saturday.

Aunt Rosina's house seemed wonderful to me, so immaculate, everything so shining clean, and she didn't know we were coming, so she couldn't have done a special cleaning on that account. I noticed that she had electric lights, but I said not a word. I would wait until evening to find out how they worked — like those we had seen in Moapa would have, I guessed. But she had such pretty "pillow shams" over the standing-up-high-against-the-head-of-the-bed pillows. At home, we did well to have clean, plain, ironed pillow cases on our pillows. It was this extra touch, along with the frilly curtains and the

[94]

many nicknacks on the mantel that made these three large rooms seem like aristocracy to me.

I think Ma and Aunt Rosina didn't mind Pa's leaving at all; they could talk all afternoon and most of the night about things that wouldn't interest him, and he probably had friends of his own in St. George. But he was back early in the morning, before we were awake. After all, we had come all this way to see the fair, and we'd better get over there. Already we had missed the opening on Friday afternoon. Even more than the fair, we must visit the temple grounds and take time at that holy place.

In no time we were on our way, with Pa and Ma and Aunt Rosina in the seat, and all of the children in the back. The wagon wasn't loaded, and the team could trot, and did a great part of the way, as though they enjoyed being free of that heavy load. Pa made no comments and asked no opinions; he drove straight through town to the temple block far to the south. Here he stopped in the shade on the north side and lifted us out one by one from the back of the wagon.

"Stay right here until we can all go in together," he said, "and don't go racing and chasing around. Remember that you are in a holy place, before the temple of the Lord." He needn't have said that, for it was almost like entering the gates of heaven. Green grass, thick and springy, stretched to the far corners, with flowers lining the walks and edges worked into designs of circle and star; large trees here and there offered shade. Surely there could be no more beautiful spot than this. As we stood at this distance, Ma said, "Look at the spire and the gold ball on top, and when you go up town, look especially at the balls on the tabernacle spire and the Court House. Your great-grandfather, Christopher Lister Riding, made every one of those balls. He is Grandma Thirza's own father, and they came from England. Remember how she told you about crossing the plains?"

Yes, we did remember. And we would look especially at the balls on top of the buildings, for we had already heard of our grandfather and his "Tinker's Dam," which wasn't swearing at all. It only meant the wad of dough he held on the bottom of the hole so the solder wouldn't run through and form a lump on the outside.

I was so overwhelmed by the temple that I was almost afraid to go near. I felt that if I looked close, I might see angels hovering near the spire. But I did touch the wall at last, and I did climb up the steps to the eastern door where Aunt Rosina said the Savior would enter when He came.

All around the building we walked, and every part seemed so perfectly beautiful that coming back to the wagon seemed like entering a new world. Yet we were eager to get back to the tabernacle by ten o'clock, when the doors would be opened to view the displays.

The beauty in the basement of the tabernacle was just as impressive in its own way as that of the temple had been. Such beautiful fruit, such an abundance of everything, artfully arranged. Ma and Aunt Rosina went at once to the handwork and sewing department; Pa found the corn, squash, melon section and the farm gadget display.

Such a full, happy day! Things new and strange everywhere, experiences to talk over and relive for a long time to come. One only I *never* mentioned, but tried hard to put it into the back of my mind and forget it. It happened like this: I had a dime and three nickels tied into the corner of my handkerchief, and I had seen a sign advertising ice cream just a little way east of the tabernacle. So I slipped away by myself and hurried to get out of sight before anyone started to check on me. I found the place and stepped inside. To my right, on tall stools by a counter, three young ladies were sipping something out of tall goblets with straws. They were beautifully dressed, these girls, with sheer white blouses and dark skirts and high-heeled shoes. This almost stopped me, but gathering courage I started to walk right in. To my surprise, a little, funny-looking girl came forward to meet me, her hair braided, her red calico dress trimmed with white braid, her too-large stogie shoes — HORRORS!!! It was me myself in a full-length mirror coming to meet me! Did I look like that??? I was so embarrassed that I could hardly answer the clerk when she came to say, "May I help you?"

"No, not right now. Let me look around a little," I managed.

But I didn't stop to look around; I fled the place, for now the girls at the counter were in on it. They had seen my confusion and were laughing at me; I'm sure I heard one mention my shoes, and another my "purse" — the soiled handkerchief with the coins in the corner.

Outside the door, I was so weak that I could hardly stand upright. This funny face, with the hair pulled back into tight braids; this calico dress gathered in at the belt and trimmed with white braid, these SHOES! Ma always bought our shoes in the fall, and since we had only one pair a year, she got them large and serviceable. On my skinny legs these looked like — Well, I couldn't think of a good comparison. Later, Con Adams gave me one. Seeing me pass, he said: "*Shoes*, where are you taking this kid?"

My day was ruined. Maybe my whole life was ruined. But I had nowhere to go except back to the Tabernacle to join the crowd. No matter how I felt, I'd have to keep a bold front and remember all the encouraging lines that I knew, like: "You can't tell from the looks of a frog how high he can jump"; "Diamonds are often encased in the roughest stone"; "The Ugly Duckling became the Swan." I was forced to be cheerful and happy, for if I didn't, I'd have to explain what was the matter. And that I would NEVER do! I'd do whatever I could to look better — like throwing my shoulders back and trying to walk tall — but I'd not reveal the suffering of these few minutes to anyone. And I didn't. Nor did I make any great reformation because of it.

When, many years later, I came to St. George to teach at Dixie College, I could still not force myself to go into the Dixie Drug Store. Now that I do trade there and enjoy the association, I still remember the experience of "seeing myself as others see me" for the first time.

The afternoon was really a pleasant one, with all the new things to see and the abundance of melons and fruit so freely distributed. Back to Santa Clara for overnight; out bright and early Sunday morning to get a good seat in the tabernacle. We had come all this long trip to hear the Prophet of the Lord and Ma meant that we should have a good seat. So very early, as soon as the doors were opened, we were there and up in the gallery. We must have time to see this wonderful building, the ceiling decorations, the elaborate frieze, and the All-seeing Eye which followed you wherever you went and could watch everyone else at the same time.

We had agreed that all would stay through the opening songs and prayer, and then three of us should go out quietly, one of us two older girls to take the two youngsters to the wagon, which was home base, with food in the grub box and quilts to relax on. That way Pa and Ma could enjoy the meeting in peace and each of us older girls would get one full session. Mine was in the afternoon, and I must confess that I wasn't much stirred, except by the choir. They did have good music, and as I listened, I remembered that at one time Ma was the soloist for the Santa Clara ward choir when they furnished the music for conference.

The opening prayer seemed far, far too long, like the brother was determined to get in his bit of sermonizing in spite of everything. Then the business of "sustaining" the Authorities, from the top down to the least- and last-ordained deacon, took a lot of time.

I knew that this kindly, long-bearded man, Joseph F. Smith, was the Prophet of God, and my heart went out to him, but I had heard other sermons that stirred me more, that had more in the way of illustration and anecdote and every-day application. Still, it was a privilege to listen to him.

Now that conference was over, we had no reason to linger; in fact, we should get ourselves back home to the mail run and the baby and all the other responsibilities. So we slept at Santa Clara, but were out and on our way by daylight. The difference that it made to go home in a relatively empty wagon! The horses could trot and enjoy it; no uphill climb going this direction was steep enough to have to rest on, and the long slope that was such a trial coming up was a trotting road most of the way back. We were at Beaver Dams before dark, and this time we had both supper and breakfast with relatives there, for they always made our place headquarters when they came to Bunkerville.

At home, we had talking material for a long time, both among ourselves and with the neighbors. Only one incident I *never* told.

The Christmas Tree

THIS YEAR THE BISHOP ANNOUNCED THAT THERE WOULD BE no public program, no community Christmas tree, and no Santa in Bunkerville. Parents must make their own celebration at home.

This was something new! How come?

Always before we had gone to the Rock Church there near our home, where there would be a large pine tree all decorated, and a program of recitations, pantomimes with tableaux, followed by community singing of the carols. At last Santa would arrive with jingling bells and make-believe snow, laughing and calling "Merry Christmas!" as he passed out toys to all the children under twelve.

This year Christmas Eve came on Saturday. Charity and I had talked it over. We simply must have a Christmas Tree. We had that beautiful candy bucket to put it in, and Jimmy Cragun's milking stool to put the bucket on. That would get the tree out of reach of the baby. But a tree we must have.

On Saturday morning we took the ax and started down the lane toward the fields, determined that we would not come back without a tree.

But we found nothing. Absolutely nothing!

Discouraged, we cut across to come home by the Hill Road, and there, just almost on the edge of town, we found one! A beautiful little mescrew — not a mesquite with heavy dark thorns — but a young, perfect mescrew, just the right size for us to handle.

Strange that I had never noticed this little gravelly wash before, but riding on horseback or on the wagon, I had not. Here were many mescrew bushes growing in it. We both walked up and down to come back to the very one that we had seen first, the one nearest the road. This was IT!

I knew all about the Mesquite Flat on the river bottom, where giant, sprawling mesquite trees grew, but they had such large, dark thorns. Even the young trees would never do for Christmas trees. We both knew of the mesquite bean pods and how succulent and juicy and sweet they were when they were yellow with just a blush of red, but it was worth your life to get them because of the big, wicked thorns. By fall they would be as stiff as boards, the seed inside hard as rocks.

The mescrew, on the other hand, often grew in a thicket of thorns. Its branches were delicate, the thorns smaller and snow-white. The tiny cluster of blooms hardened into a screwed-up little pod so tight and with such tiny seeds inside that the small rodents who depended on them for food ate the whole little pod.

How to cut it down? That was the question.

Our shoes were sturdy and they came up well over our ankles, so we were safe so far as the undergrowth was concerned. But the branches grew so low that we couldn't get at the main trunk at all. It grew horizontally, with two branches close together enough to fill out a tree.

I had seen a long, straight stick — it was hardly big enough to be called a pole — lying right by the road. Someone had cleared and trimmed it as though they had some use for it. Just the thing to help knock off some of those thorns.

The idea was all right, but it didn't work. Nothing that we tried worked. The stick was long and smooth and strong, but it was just no good for knocking off thorns. We were about to abandon the whole project when we heard a wagon coming up the road. It was Uncle Parley Hunt, good old Uncle Parley, with his red hair and quiet voice.

"Having some trouble?" he asked, pulling his team to a stop.

"We're trying to get a Christmas Tree," we said almost in one voice. We were near tears, both of us, with frustration.

"Let's see what we can do about it." And Uncle Parley tied the lines and got off the wagon. With his heavy gloves and denim jumper, he had no fear of thorns. Within a matter of minutes he had the trunk cleared; within a dozen strokes, the tree was down.

"Now how do you figure to handle it?" he wanted to know.

"We'll put this long pole through the main crotch there, and we'll take hold of the two ends, and carry it upside down between us."

"Not a bad idea at that. Let's see if you can carry it from here to the wagon that way."

And he turned and went on ahead.

"Okay. Okay. Put it down. Wait a minute."

He trimmed off another low branch and cut off a long, straggling one. Then he squared off the bottom.

"How do you aim to make it stand up? That's the fifty-dollar question."

"We think we've got that figured out," I told him. "You see, Pa's on the mail run and won't be back until five o'clock this afternoon. He's not too good at this kind of thing anyway. We're going to use the big wooden candy bucket that old Lady McKinney put out for us when we went to Moapa last summer. We've kept it in the cellar all this time, with enough water in to keep it from drying out. We'll fill it with rocks and gravel and sand."

"Sounds fine! You really expected to find a tree, then?"

"Oh, yes. We didn't know what kind it would be, but we sure thought we could get something. We even cleared out the place for it and got the bucket there. We promised the young ones that they could help fill it."

Uncle Parley tossed the tree into the back of the wagon; we both climbed up and sat in the spring seat beside him, and told him all our plans.

"Did you ever see Jimmy Cragun's milking stool?" I asked.

"Well, now, I can't say that I have. What about it?"

"Jimmy Cragun must have lived in our house for a while long ago; or kept his cow in our corral. Anyway, when the deacons were cleaning out the corral last spring they found this milking stool in between the manger and the outside fence. No one knew whose it was or how it came there, but after they got to talking with the older people they learned that it was Jimmy Cragun's. He never was married; he was a good man when it came to working with wood, so when one of his cherry trees died, he sawed a section out of the trunk for the stool, and cut three pieces from the branches to brace it. The bark is so red and shiny and smooth!

"The old folks said that he kept it in the same place all the time and trained the cow to come to him to be milked. After he left, nobody noticed it stuck in there behind the manger, and when the boys brought it out, Ma thought it was just beautiful; she wondered how it could still be so nice after all that long time, but it was protected from the rain and sun. Anyway, she had the boys put it into the little express wagon and bring it up to the house — gave them a good treat of molasses taffy for doing it. She wants to get a piece of nice velvet, and put a cushion, and make it into a footstool for Pa's birthday. But for now, we are putting the candy bucket on top of it to keep it out of reach of the baby. It fits just right."

"We are so glad that you stopped to help us," I told him. "It would be terrible to have Christmas without any tree at all. But I don't blame the committee one bit. They had served four years; they couldn't see why the job wasn't passed around just a little, like changing two men each year, and give some of the Bishop's sons and sons-in-law a chance for part of the blessing." I was only repeating what I had heard one member of the committee say.

"Next year maybe we can plan way ahead and get real Christmas trees, I mean green ones. But we figured that we could find something today. Doesn't the Father-in-Heaven want people to celebrate his birthday with a Christmas tree? And won't He help folks if they really try?"

At the gate Uncle Parley unloaded the tree, took it to the chopping block, and trimmed a few more straggling branches, and helped us get the stick through the crotch so that we could carry it into the house.

"Thank you!"

"Thank you very much," we both said. I'd like to have given him a big bear hug and kiss. Such a fine man!

We engineered the tree through the door, and finally got it upright in the bucket. This took some doing! Now one of us kept the tree in place while the other directed the sand crew. Our three younger ones, with some neighborhood kids, worked like a busy stream of ants, each with his little load.

With the bucket full, the tree was solid.

Yes, the youngsters spilled some gravel and drizzled sand, but we kept them off the rag carpet and across the hearth. This end of the room was covered with linoleum like that in the kitchen. It was easily swept and wiped up, while the braided rugs that went here were out on the bermuda grass lawn, ready to come back.

We had just finished cleaning up when one of our cousins came in, staggering under the weight of a heavy slab of pitch pine.

"That's heavier than rock, I do believe!" he said panting. "Almost like cutting at rock, too, it's so full of rosin and pitch. It'll burn all night, that's for sure."

We knew all about this. Every year and after every flood, Pa kept his eye out for a Yule Log. His mother had been born in England, and she thought a Yule Log was the most important item for a perfect Christmas.

Last spring the floodwater had brought down this enormous pine log. The smaller end was all round with the bark still on, and all the little branches had worn off, but the large part where the giant limb had split from the parent tree was flat and seamed and full of amber and pitch. It had lodged on a big pile of trash against our fence on the salt grass pasture. It looked so precious to Pa that he worked at once to get it over onto our land, where he could claim it. It was so big and heavy that he couldn't lift it, so he broke off the top of one of the cedar posts in the fence and cut the top strand of barbed wire, and with quite a struggle he rolled it over onto our land.

He had brought his brother Ab down to see it, and they agreed that there was enough wood in that great branch to serve many families for one year, and enough for just their two for several years.

They had agreed that they should start at the big end, and since Ab had big boys who could chop wood, and a good saw where two might cut off a length, that he should have as large a piece as he could use in his fireplace, if he would see that the boys cut off one of the same length for ours. They must bring it to the house before Pa got home with the mail. So here it was!

We all helped to get paper and kindling under the andirons before he placed the log. It filled the whole fireplace perfectly, its flat surface out, facing the room.

We agreed not to tell Pa about the tree. It would be our surprise for him.

He was in fine humor, maybe because Ma had supper on the table, the chores were done, and we were all slicked up and shining. We children were just a little unsure, though. We saw no sign of gifts anywhere — not a parcel of any kind in the buckboard.

Supper over, we trooped into the other room to light the fire. The big log was on the andirons, paper and kindling all set. Pa let the littlest one strike the match; instantly the fire blazed up and Pa saw the tree!

"What's this? What IS this?" Pa said in amazement.

"How did you get this tree? What a beautiful tree!"

And he was right.

I have seen many Christmas trees since, trees of every shape and kind, but never one so lovely as this. Without electric light bulbs or candles, without tinsel or colored balls, it stood a shining, elegant white filigree, breath-taking in its symmetry and beauty. Every thorn was a pearl around which all the colors of the rainbow played: coral, pink, flame, red, blue, green, yellow — a symphony of color against illuminated white.

"It's the Yule Log," Pa said. "But it's just heavenly!"

A transfiguration indeed! A little desert thorn bush made suddenly divine! A vision of heavenly beauty in our little house! Even the copper bands on the varnished candy bucket, and the cherry tree legs of Jimmy Cragun's milking stool shone with new luster.

I studied about it after I went to bed. I have pondered on it in my mature years. This Yule Log and its story from a tall pine on a distant mountain, through all the millennia of its life and death and transportation to our pasture — it was beyond our comprehension. Yet here was the log! And here was our tree! Together they had produced a miracle! Was it only by chance? I wondered.

Ma played the guitar and led us in singing the carols, until we were all tired. After we were sound asleep, they would bring out our gifts, and after that Ma would go to serenade at Grandma Hafen's and at Grandpa Dudley's, and the Bishop's, and Aunt Rell's. This was her Christmas card, and she used it every year:

> Wish you Merry Christmas, Merry Christmas all,
> May the richest blessings ever on you fall
> Every year be brighter than the one before
> And your Christmas mornings many, many more.
>
> Let your sweetest numbers flow
> Wake the heavenly song again
> Sung by angels long ago
> "Peace on earth, Good-will to men!"
>
> Wish you Merry Christmas, Merry Christmas all,
> May the richest blessings ever on you fall
> Every year be brighter than the one before
> And your Christmas mornings many, many more.
>
> Merry, merry, merry, merry, merry, merry,
> merry, merry, merry, merry Christmas all!

The next morning in the surprise of our presents we almost forgot our tree. Neighbors who came in saw only a bare little thorn bush. In the morning it had not the splendor of the night before; the cottonwood log in the fireplace had no "pitch." Still, Pa studied it, content in his chair, as though he wanted to unravel the mystery of the night before, our Christmas miracle.

What we children did not guess at the time, was that it would be indirectly responsible for a minor rift between our parents. It happened like this: Pa was relaxing before the fire when one of Ma's friends came in. She explained that in the difficulties following the resignation of all the Recreation Committee, nobody had taken time to plan for the two elderly people in our ward who had no relatives here: Sister Freely on one corner of the block and Uncle Wilber on the other. She and her friend had collected a box of goodies for each and some small, useful presents, and were taking them even though it was a day late. Would Ma come and bring her guitar? They would sing some carols at each house, and be back in just a few minutes.

Pa seemed so relaxed in his chair before the fireplace that Ma just picked up her guitar, and saying, "I'll not be gone long," left him sitting there.

She was gone much longer than she had expected to be, so that when she came back home she thought she would find Pa in bed. Instead, he still sat in the rocking chair before the fire, just as she had left him. But he had been busy. He had the Christmas tree all burned, by snipping off the branches and burning them a few at a time, until at last he just pulled it all out and stuffed it in. While it blazed brightly, he took the candy bucket out, dumped the rocks and sand against the bottom of a pomegranate tree, and left the bucket just outside the door to stay until morning, when he would wash it out and put it back into the cellar.

Next came the milking stool. The cottonwood log was just smoldering; the stool was dry, so Pa poked it down behind into the coals. Instantly it burst into flame, almost as bright as the pitch pine log the night before. He was enjoying it thoroughly when Ma opened the door.

"Oh, Henry!" she cried as soon as she saw it, "You wouldn't burn up that lovely little stool!" Her tears were very genuine, for she had doted so on this.

Pa was completely taken aback. "Why didn't you say something about it?" he wanted to know. "It didn't look like anything worth saving to me. And a man left alone to entertain himself for a full evening must find something to do. Since I'm not good enough to be with your friends, I had to find some way to pass the time. You've been gone a long time, you know."

"It was so beautiful, and I wanted to surprise you. How could you burn it?"

Now Pa really took over. He must have set her straight, from the way she told it to Aunt Selena the next day.

Anyway, Pa gave her to understand that he did not want to sing with her and spoil the harmony, but he did want to be along for the company, the fellowship. He could hold the light and turn the pages. Or if the crowd wanted to go in a wagon, he could drive the team. But he didn't mean to stay at home while she went out singing.

We children, all unconscious of this, remembered this Christmas only as having a miracle tree.

[106]

Over the Shovel Handles

WE CALLED IT "WORKING WATER-DITCH." Of course, being a ditch, it would have to be for water, but we called it *water-ditch*. It bore the same relation to our town that the circulatory system does to the body: the Big Ditch was the main artery from which all the laterals ran out, dividing and subdividing until the water reached the roots of every plant in the valley, every plant that was to survive.

The Big Ditch was cleaned once a year. Near the head of the ditch the Watermaster could sluice out much of the sand through head-gates at places where there was a steep fall, but there was no substitute for the annual shoveling out of the sand. This was usually done in the late fall after most of the crops had been harvested, and each man worked out his assessments in proportion to the land he cultivated.

Pa had been hiring a couple of boys to do his, while he took the mail, but after he had been made Counselor to the Bishop, he thought that he could get acquainted with the young men in the Elders' Quorum better here than in any other place. Two years' growth had changed some of them into young men; this would be a good way to establish friendly relations.

Before work began each morning, the Watermaster stepped off the stints and drove in a peg to mark the place of each man. At eight o'clock each was in his place and did his stint, going ahead to do another at the head of the line as soon as he finished. The specifications were quite definite as to depth and width, and each was paid in proportion to the number of stints he completed.

What discussions developed during the noon hour! Men who would shrink from speaking from the pulpit would wax eloquent over the shovel handle; men who turned to stone if asked to address the meeting could entertain the crowd with ease. Here the cloak of sanctity was torn off, tainted jokes were told, testimonies of the over-zealous were repeated amid hilarity that was suppressed in church. Here, too, originated tall tales that became legend.

Ma had not known of Pa's change of plan; she had the grub box for the mail ready at five o'clock in the morning, but had not bread to make another at eight o'clock. She'd have to send me with it at noon. Lunch would be eaten in the shade at the top of Uncle Andy's field.

As I came up, I didn't at once see Pa; he was leaning against a tree almost with his back to me, and Pinkey was just getting into a story. Not wanting to interrupt it, I stood still.

"Well," Pinkey said, "The other night Chris's wife woke him up and said, 'Chris, there's someone in this room. Listen!' He listened, but couldn't hear anything. Their bed is in that lean-to porch that's got a dirt floor. To please his wife, he called out, 'Who's there?' a time or two. No answer. His wife knew something was there; from her feeling it was evil; she could hear it breathe. Finally she gave him no peace till he got out of bed.

"There was nobody there, nobody that he could either see or hear, but now he felt a presence, too. He was sure something was there. It must be an Evil Spirit, he decided, and there's only one way to handle an Evil Spirit."

Pinkey now stood up and assumed a pose. "I can't look like him without any whiskers and with my pants on, but you get the idea. Chris was in his shirttail and bagging underwear. He planted his toes in the sand of that kitchen floor and lifted his arm to the square, and put on his best preaching voice and said: *Spirit of Evil, whatever your name or nature, I command you to depart from this household! Depart at once and do not return to disturb us! I COMMAND you to depart! This I do by the Power of the Priesthood in me vested and in the Name . . .*

[108]

"He didn't get to finish. His wife had got out the back of the bed and run the broom handle around under it. The Spirit of Evil gave a squeal and came out so fast it knocked Chris down, tipped the table over, and scattered tinware from hell to breakfast!"

Pinkey sat down to let this soak in before he added, "It was a big black pig that had got out and was rooting around for breadcrumbs."

In the laugh that followed, I handed Pa his lunch bucket.

"Where you been all this time?" Pa asked.

"I just got here. Ma said for me to bring the bucket back."

The Danish brother did not want this story to pass off so lightly. "When people feel the power of the Evil One, it is usually real. You remember that in the olden days, Jesus cast out Devils that went into swine.

"They ran into the sea and were drowned; ain't that the story? Well, this one just run cross-lots to its own pen."

Before the laughter had died away, Nephi Hunt was talking.

"Speaking of Chris reminds me. Did you ever hear how Chris Lingo got his second wife? His name ain't really Chris Lingo, but everybody calls him that because he talks so much. He lives down in San Juan country now, I believe. Have you heard about it?"

Nobody had.

"He come down this part of the country one fall and stopped over by the cotton factory just at noon. They had between fifty and sixty girls working there then. They brought their lunches and spread them out under the trees, and Chris thought this would be a good time to look the material over. He was out in search of a second. Well, he wanted to get acquainted, and didn't know a better way, so he went and stood on a big rock not far from their table and took off his hat. You know he was tall and good looking and had a fine head of curly hair.

"'Give me your attention,' he called. 'I have just come from Sanpete County in search of a second wife. Will you young ladies please look me over and if any of you think you would be interested, I would like to talk to you when you finish your dinner.'

"Well, the girls did look him over. They joked among themselves and dared each other to go talk to him. Finally, quite a crowd did go. He picked out Serenie, and later he married her!"

[109]

The crowd began bantering some of the unmarried fellows about using the same tactics in securing wives for themselves, and in the joking, Pa became conscious that I was still there. I was ready to leave, in fact, but hardly knew how to just walk off without saying anything.

"What are you doing here?" he asked impatiently. "I thought you had gone home long ago."

"I waited to take the dinner bucket back," I explained lamely, and the crowd laughed at my embarrassment.

"I'll bet you'd like a piece of bread and honey," Uncle Jess said to me. "Here, have a piece. That's some of the famous Hewlett honey. Ever heard-tell of it?"

I hadn't, and neither had anyone else.

"Well, when the Saints was drove from Nauvoo, Brother Brigham wanted them to bring everything they had, especially livestock. One brother had a lot of bees that was going to be left, but Brother Brigham said they must be brung. So he appointed a couple of brethren to drive them across the plains. They got along pretty well after they once got on to how to handle them. They would drive them along and find a place where they could corral them at night and take turns night-herding 'em.

"By the time they got to Emigration Canyon, they thought they had them pretty well under control; in fact, they figgered that driving bees was maybe easier than driving sheep. Whether they got excited at the thought that they were nearly to the Valley, or whether they was just plain careless, I don't know, but the night they got to the top of Emigration Canyon they corraled the bees, all right, but someone forgot to put up the bars.

"The next morning there wasn't a single bee to be found. They hunted and hunted, but couldn't find a trace, and bad as they hated to, they had to go into the Valley without them bees.

"Well, it went on for a long time and a feller named Hewlett staked off a mining claim at the head of Emigration Canyon and started to drill for oil. He got a spouter, all right, but it wuz honey. All them bees had disappeared into a hole in the side of the mountain . . . So now you can say that you have tasted the famous Hewlett honey."

I had my bucket and the piece of bread and honey, and had started when Windy Bill came up.

"What's yer hurry?" he asked. "Don't let it be said that I frightened away a fair lady."

Since I was only a little girl, I knew he was trying to be funny. I had no ready answer, so I was relieved to have Uncle Jess say, "With that old pipe, and the plug in your shirt pocket, you'd scare away a skunk."

"Now, now," Windy protested good-naturedly. "You wouldn't deny me the privileges that you used to give to Brigham Young, would you?"

"What you talking about?"

"Brigham Young chewed the same brand that I do, but he had a little silver box to keep it in and a pearl-handled knife to cut it off with. He used only the Horseshoe brand, so that's the one I get. Ain't you ever heard about the time when he went to Old Man Adams, who had a little shop, and asked if he had any good chewing tobacco? Adams said no, but Brother Brigham glanced over the shelves and said, 'Here is some Horseshoe brand of chewing tobacco. How come you told me you didn't have any?' 'Brother Brigham,' Adams said, 'There ain't no such thing as GOOD chewing tobacco.'" Windy spoke with surety.

I walked on, eating my bread and honey, but sorely troubled about the idea that Brigham Young used chewing tobacco. If this was true, how come we made such a fuss because Uncle Andy smoked? Chewing was sure as bad as smoking — worse, I thought. I'd ask Pa about it.

As I walked along, I thought of the stories I had heard of Brigham Young, of how when he visited St. George and the other settlements of the south, the people lined the roads and put out banners of welcome and had the children strew flowers in his path. This last seemed hardly fitting to me, with flowers as scarce as they were in this part of the country, to throw them down on a dry, hot road for horses to walk over, even if they were Brother Brigham's team.

I remembered Grandma Maria telling about one of President Young's visits. She was in the group that was out to greet him.

"It was a hot day," she said, "and we stood in the sun waiting, all of us dressed in our best, the children with the branches and flowers to put down. Jim Andrus rode up and down on his fine horse, keeping us back of the line, and telling us about where Brother Brigham's carriage was to. I've forgot which one of mine was a baby then, but I remember how heavy he got and how tired and fretful. Well, finally the word came that they were nearly there and we could see the dust way over by the ridge. It seemed an hour after that before they got there, and when they did, Brother Brigham just lifted his hat and bowed to the left and right and went on — didn't even slow up, let alone stop. 'Well,' I said, 'That is a lot to stand in the hot sun all that time for.' Old Sister Keate heard me, and she set me right in a hurry. 'My girl,' she said, and shook her finger at me, 'Don't you know that you have just looked upon the face of the Prophet of the Living God?' I'll never forget it."

And I thought of what Grandma Mary had said once about the visit of some of the wives of President Young. "They came down to establish the Retrenchment Society. They told us how it was the wish of the President that we should do away with all our extravagances in dress and habits. I looked around at the women in the audience. We were all in homespun, coarse and faded-looking because we hadn't learned yet how to set the indigo. And the speaker wore a silk dress with wide bands of velvet ribbon and lace edging. I sat there and listened as long as I could stand it, and then I said, 'Which do you want us to retrench from, Sister Young, the bread or the molasses?' "

Much as we loved and respected our leaders, it was easy to see that many of our folk were a little jealous or resentful of the fact that the people of the north lived so much better than we and at less effort. And yet the Church was everything to us. It was for the Church that we were all here; it was the Church that had drawn our parents from all the far countries. Even the building of the ditch and the dam, the graveling of the sidewalks, the planting of cotton or cane had its inception in the Church, for ours was a temporal gospel as well as a spiritual one.

All this was reflected in our services. There were discussions of plantings and harvesting; there were stories of the hardships our parents had endured which made ours seem tame indeed; there were incidents of God's love and care. Since the speakers were drawn from the audience, often without previous notification, they could only speak according to their interests and abilities. While many of the talks were dull, many were so full of faith and devotion that they left a permanent impression.

Sometimes, especially on the monthly testimony day, overzealous brethren became almost ludicrous and some of the foreign converts brought involuntary smiles by their unusual use of the English language. There was one time when the Scandinavian brother, in his inimitable brogue, bore testimony to the marvelous barrel of molasses. "We used from it all winter," he said, "and our married children used from it, and our neighbors used from it. And I am sure that the Lord had His hand in it, too." We knew that he didn't mean it like it sounded, but we couldn't resist repeating it.

Perhaps the favorite, the one that has lived the longest, was the short talk that was given by the Danish brother. It grew out of our very unity, for our unitedness was of the kind that shut all others out. Strangers were looked upon with suspicion. At our dances a stranger must be sponsored by someone, properly presented to the Floormanager and by him properly presented to the ladies, or he had no more chance to dance than a walrus.

One time when two "drummers," or traveling salesmen, were in town with such notions as fascinators, ribbons, buttons, laces and yardage to sell, they attended a dance. Since they had been in town two or three days and had talked to some of the girls who came to shop at Mary Adams' house where they had their things, they made free to ask two girls to dance with them. The girls, excited and thrilled by the adventure, accepted and danced a two-step. At the end of the set, the Floormanager quietly informed the men that they might look on if they cared to, but they were not to participate in our social activities. The next day in testimony meeting the Danish brother took occasion to admonish the young ladies.

"Brothers and sisters," he said, "there is one thing which I would like to call to your attention, and that is how our young girls take up with these strange drummers who come here, men of the world who would only lead them astray. It is not right. It is not wise. It is not pleasing in the sight of the Lord." And turning to the row of girls on the back bench, he shook a warning finger. "Beware of them, young women! They are as dangerous as rattlesnakes! They are more dangerous, for the rattlesnake does have a rattle on its tail which he can shake as a warning to you, but they do not!"

I never did get around to asking Pa about Brigham Young, partly because I got so mad at him myself, and for other reasons. Not long after this Pa brought a passenger in on the mail, a young man from Littlefield. He had been working at the mines in Pioche for a while, and was going on to Littlefield, and Uncle Herb would take the little buckboard. We guessed privately that he had got his "wedding stake" and was coming home to get married, for that was the general procedure when a young man went to the mines to work. Brother Brigham had advised against this, but in these little towns an ambitious young man could usually get a piece of land, a farm animal or two, and adobes for a house. But he simply must have some cash to go with it, which meant from six months to a year in the mines.

Ma was away on some Relief Society business, the other girls not in.

"Fix us a bite to eat, will you?" Pa said. "This man is going on to Littlefield, and he's had precious little to eat since morning."

Seeing my expression and knowing that I hadn't been working in the kitchen, he added, "Just fry a couple of eggs apiece, and warm up anything left over from dinner, and make a cup of tea. There's fruit and preserves in the cellar. You can stir up something."

In all my life I had never prepared a meal before; I was always busy with the outside chores. But I started a fire in the stove and put the teakettle on to boil. It seemed such a long time between a cold stove and boiling water. I sliced some bacon in the frying pan and waited until the last minute to put the eggs in. I'd heard so much about overdone eggs or eggs cooked in too hot a pan. Pa said they were like shoe leather. There were two boiled potatoes with their jackets on, so I skinned them and put them with some more bacon in another pan. To this I added a sliced onion. Then there were preserved figs and currant jelly, and Ma always had good yeast bread.

I had put just a little water in the teakettle; I'd heard Ma say that

[114]

it seemed an age before she could get boiling water, especially if she was in a hurry, and the kettle was full. My concern had been for the eggs, because cooked right, they were Pa's favorite, but done too hard they weren't fit to eat. This time they were done exactly right.

Finally I had the table set and everything ready. Pa seemed pleased with it all; both men enjoyed large helpings of the potato-onion dish, and I felt sure the meal was a success. Then Pa said, "Give us another cup of tea."

Horrors! there was no more tea. I hadn't counted on tea for the visitor, too.

"I'm sorry, but there isn't any more. But maybe I could make some more in a few minutes."

We all knew that would be impossible, for the fire had gone out.

"You needn't bother. Maybe I should bind the tea leaves on my belly — it would do just as well."

Why didn't I see that it was only one of his silly jokes? I should have known, of course. But I was so eager to please him that I went to the dishtowel drawer and found a clean washed flour sack; if I split it down the two sides, it should reach around him all right. I got the scissors and cut it carefully, folded it, got three or four large safety pins and handed it all to him. He had finished eating, and was sitting back in his chair picking his teeth.

"What's this?" he asked, as I held out the long strip and the pins.

"You asked for a cloth to bind the tea leaves on your stomach," I answered soberly. "I think this will fit."

He threw back his head in such a sudden loud laugh that I knew at once how foolish I had been. The stranger laughed, too, but I thought Pa would choke himself. He tried to talk, but he could only hold up the long strip of flour sack and burst into another paroxysm.

The more they laughed, the angrier I became. Bursting into tears, I stamped my foot.

"I'll never make another cup of tea for you again as long as I live," I screamed, "You shouldn't drink the filthy old stuff, anyway. And you know it. If you ever get another cup of tea, you'll make it yourself. I won't."

It wasn't long before I had a chance to get even. Every night Pa would have Ma read aloud to us, stories from the Church magazines or chapters from books. Pa was a poor reader himself, never having any school above the third grade. What was work for him was pleasure for Ma, who read easily and fluently. So it was that reading aloud was a regular part of our evening, even after we were quite old.

On this night we were all listening to the story but Pa, who had driven across the mesa that day. He leaned his head against the high back of the chair and closed his eyes. Every once in a while Ma would stop reading to see if he was still awake.

"Go on," he'd say. "I'm listening."

So she went on, for she had an interested audience without him. Soon he was sound asleep, his mouth wide open and his breath coming in deep, settled snores. Exciting as the story was, he was just too tired to stay awake for it.

When it was done, we all sat looking at him, and Ma took a piece of newspaper, rolled it into a long roll like a gigantic cigarette, and stuck it into his mouth. He didn't stir, but went right on with his heavy breathing. The sight of Pa with a giant cigarette in his mouth was to us the height of the ridiculous. We were all convulsed with laughter; it was really funny.

Since he still did not waken, Ma struck a match to the end of the newspaper. It blazed up and burned a little way. Pa got one big mouthful of smoke, and then things began to happen!

He leaped to his feet with a great yell and began threshing the air with his arms and stampeding around the room. Ma kicked the burning papers into the fireplace, laughing until the tears ran down her face. We all had joined full force.

Pa was mad clear through. He sat down sheepishly and regarded us with utter disgust.

"Laugh!" he yelled at last. "Laugh like you are crazy! If you don't shut up, I'll beat you all!"

But we were not afraid of him, and we couldn't shut up. We wore ourselves out in time, though little chuckles broke out from one to another, which set us all off again. An incident to remember with pleasure.

Old Tubucks

THIS MORNING DID NOT SEEM DIFFERENT FROM ANY OTHER. I had done the chores, had my breakfast, and started the cows out toward the pasture. The water was in the ditch after the most recent August washout, so I really didn't need to take them around the river road. They had made it a habit while the water was out, so I just let them go.

I trailed along, scuffing my bare feet through the dust and remembering that I had forgotten my bonnet again. It was not that I didn't want to wear it; I just didn't think of it. It didn't seem the same to be alone on this road after all the herds that had traveled it twice a day for the last three weeks. The cows went down the dugway to the stream from habit; I splashed through it without even holding up my dress — it was that shallow on this side.

I was looking at some houses we had started building on the sand bar when just a whiff of a breeze from the other side carried a faint, different sound. I stopped dead still to listen. It was not an owl — this wasn't the season or the time of day for owls. It was not a bullfrog, either — for the same reason. Just a low, guttural, half-moaning sound, and then a long silence. As I turned to go on and forget it, there it was again. Just once. Silence again. The sound repeated. Well, it was something alive; it must be. It had to be. I turned sharply and walked toward it, every sense alert.

[117]

Just around a bend on the other side of the island, near where the largest part of the water ran, I saw her — a cow buried almost to the ridge of her hips, and her head, with high, proud horns, stretched out upon the sand, which had hardened around her like cement.

"Oh, you poor thing!" I cried, running to her. "How could you be here so close and so long, and nobody find you?"

Again the moaning sound from her throat. Had she been trying to call someone for three long weeks? I myself had come this way twice every day since the high water, but sometimes there were others to talk to and sometimes, riding, I had not heard or paid attention. Had I been guided here today?

I wanted to cry for her — she looked so pitiful, so skinny and dry and hopeless, and the water only a few yards away. What could I do? Why had I left my sunbonnet home? I tried to carry a little water in my two cupped hands, but it leaked out. Then I had an idea. Taking my skirt by the hem, I scooped up a lapful of water and ran to her. Though some leaked through, she got three good, big swallows. Back I went for more, but alas! I filled it too full. When I stood up, my dress ripped from the belt to the hem and the water fell around my feet in one big plop. The pity of it!

Then it occurred to me that maybe this was the hand of the Lord, too, just like my finding her. I remembered how Grandpa had told of crossing the desert from Las Vegas during June, long ago before there was a road, and how he was nearly dead of thirst and starvation when some friendly Indians found him. They wrapped his belly round and round with a buckskin strap so he would not feel hunger so much, and two of them supported him to their camp not far away. Here the squaws measured out only a half a gourd of water and a few kernels of parched corn which he had to chew for a long time. Then they loosened the strap and gave him a few sips of water again, repeating this every hour or so until he could take a full meal. Too much food too soon would kill him ("Heap yakeway, purty dam quick," they said).

So maybe I should give her just a little food at first. I ran back across the river and climbed into the nearest field, where I found a clump of alfalfa that the mower had missed, tall stalks with flowers and leaves, as much as I could put my two hands around. As I

[118]

approached with it, I decided that I would name her Star, because she had a white spot right in the middle of her forehead, and Star seemed a romantic name. I knew that she did not belong to us, but I thought she was mine if I saved her life.

As I hurried on to turn the cows into the field, I made plans. This was Friday morning; Pa left with the mail long before daylight and would not be home until about five o'clock tomorrow afternoon. If he couldn't get her out then, I'd use the Scripture about the ox in the mire on Sunday, and in the meantime I would bring down the little brass bucket to carry water in and the sickle to cut the lucerne with. I'd not tell a soul until I talked with Pa. I'd have to disobey him, too, for he told me to leave the horses in the pasture. With all the trips I'd have to make, I'd simply have to ride.

I cut across the pasture and the hayfield to where the mail ponies were. At the fence I whistled. The roan came trotting up, her flaxen mane and tail still shiny from her recent grooming. A piece of rope for the ring in her halter, my toe against her knee, and I was off for home, eager to carry out my plans.

As soon as Pa had delivered the mail the next day I was there to meet him. I couldn't wait to tell him about Star.

"Pa, I found a cow in the sand on the riverbottom. She's in awful shape, in almost over her back."

"Take care of the team," he answered shortly, as though he hadn't heard a word. The team was always his first consideration after that long, strenuous run.

I waited until the ponies had rolled in the sand, shaken themselves, and had a drink at the trough, and then I measured out their grain and put on the nosesacks. While the horses ate, I would go in and tell Pa.

He was all washed and fresh and on his second cup of tea when I came in.

"Now what about the cow you found in the mud?" he asked.

I almost fell over myself trying to explain how I happened to hear her, and how far gone she was, and how solid the sand was around her. I even told why I didn't give her much at first, but she had really perked up even in two days.

"Any idea who she belongs to?"

[119]

"No."

"Don't you know any marks and brands?"

"Well, I know our own — a peak on the left ear and a swallow-fork in the right. She's got the tip cut off square on one and a slit in the bottom of the other."

"A crop on the left and an undercut on the right — the Adams marks. You go down to where she is, and I'll see if I can locate Thomas or one of the boys."

When I saw Pa and Thomas ride down into the river, I stood up on the sandbank and waved and called. Pa was riding Flax; he always looked heroic on Flax — a fine man on a fine mount. Thomas rode at an easy canter while Flax did a nervous little stepdance on the side — Pa was reining him in and touching him lightly with his spur. They rode up and looked at Star awhile and then got off and walked around her. She might be doing an act herself, for she just stretched out quietly as if she thought her time had come.

"The little gal there got the wind of her Friday morning, she says. Heard her a-moanin' or tryin' to beller. She been carryin' water 'n' hay fer a coupla days now."

Thomas looked at me as if he had seen me for the first time.

"Might be better to put her outta her misery," Pa suggested.

"You can't do that!" I cried out. "You just can't! Look how long she's been there, and how hard she has tried to get out. And then I heard her call, and I come, and I've brought her back to life when she was just a-breathing her last."

The men didn't have either gun or ax to kill her with, but I knew about Pa's pocketknife with the long, wicked blade that could cut her jugular in one quick stroke and let her blood out onto the ground.

Thomas looked at me again.

"Well," he said with some hesitation, "the hide is worth a coupla bucks."

Pa was not one to cut a man down on his price. "You name it; I take it or leave it," was his motto. Without another word he pulled two silver dollars out of his pocket and handed them over. Two dollars was the standard price for a hide after it was skinned and dried.

"You go on down and get the cows and leave the roan where you got her from. One more night won't make much difference to this

[120]

one here. Better come back this way." Pa was back on Flax and headed for town, riding along and visiting with Thomas.

By the time I got back, Pa was already there again, digging the sand away from one side of the cow, talking to her as he worked.

"Quite a time you've had here, Old Two-Bucks. We'll have to get at you to see if you're worth the price." Old Two-Bucks! The name Star just faded out of my mind.

I had already wondered how it was that Pa had two silver dollars so handy, loose in his pockets, without untying a pouch or counting out coins. Money was scarce in Bunkerville; paper money was not known. Most of our dealings were carried on with "Bishop's Chips," octagonal lead coins stamped denominations of 5¢, 10¢, 25¢, 50¢ and $1.00, and were good only in trade at the store which the Bishop ran. He took our butter and eggs, and our gleanings of wheat or barley and gave us these coins in return. Then his teams would haul the accumulated produce to the mining camps at Pioche or Bullfrog and sell it for money. We counted our silver as two bits, four bits, six bits, and a buck. *Two-Bucks* gave meaning to her name; besides, it was individual and different.

Before Pa had finished his digging, I heard a wagon, and here came the two Hancock boys driving our outfit, with our own little boys along. The Hancocks were new in town and were not to stay long, but for now they were anxious to get work of any kind and were big, strong, and willing. They brought another shovel and the way they made the sand fly would do your heart good.

In no time they had the hole finished, and one at the horns and the other at the tail had loosened Two-Bucks and laid her over on her side, leaving the imprint of her body opposite. Now to get her out and on the level. I thought they'd pull off both head and tail before they put a strap around her middle and all three pulled and lifted. Pa directed the handling of the wagon, backing it up to within a few feet of her head. Now some more shoveling to lower the hind wheels to the axle in the sand. Next a wide plank from the wagonbed to her shoulders and a rope around her horns to help with the pulling. Heaving and grunting and resting, pulling at her head with the rope snubbed around the upright in front, they finally got her in — just so much dead weight.

I rode with her and the little boys in the back, and sat near her head, talking to her and trying to reassure her, while the boys rubbed at her front legs to see if they would bend.

"Tubucks, Tubucks," they kept saying, slurring over the last syllable as though the word were a twin to the Indian *Tobuck*, which meant "very, very angry." She would give her own meaning to the name.

It was dark by the time we got home. Pa had the boys drive right into the stackyard, where they unloaded Old Tubucks, sliding her down the plank easily and then driving the wagon away.

"Don't bother with her any more tonight," Pa said. "She's had all the company she needs for now. We'll see how she is in the morning."

I was there bright and early to put a flake of hay within her reach and to try to bring life back into her legs. I brought a big pan of hot water with epsom salts and tore a towel in half to use for hot packs on her knee joints and scrubbed them all down with the curry-comb to help the blood to circulate.

When I got home from Sunday School, Pa had her suspended in the tarpaulin, with a rope through the endholes and fastened to the hayfork crane. Her feet touched the ground, but she didn't have to hold her own weight up, and her knees did bend a little now. She soon got tired, though, so tired that her head just drooped like a wilted flower, and I had to run for Pa to come and let her down.

School started the next day, and I was so excited with all the new books that I almost forgot Tubucks, but Pa seemed to think she was too important to trust to me, anyway. He hired Herb to ride the mail buckboard this trip.

The stronger she became, the more Old Tubucks seemed to resent us all. Even when she was still straddle-legged with weakness she would face us with a head-on threat of her horns. Griz she hated especially, though none of the other cows took him seriously yet; he was too young. At first Pa wouldn't put her in with the other cows for fear they would hook her, and then his concern was that she might gore one of them. So all winter she had full run of the stackyard, eating directly from the haystacks and drinking from the end of the trough on that side of the fence. By spring, when she shed her old hair, she was a beautiful young animal — a cow that had borne not more than two calves, maybe only one. Large and light-colored — if she had been a horse, we'd have labeled her a buckskin — wild and proud, she was the typical range animal.

Pa must have guessed when he paid for her that she would be with calf. Range animals have a way of caring for those details themselves. As soon as she began making bag, she got restless, always walking the fence, looking for a place to go over or break out, so Pa, sensing her need for privacy during her ordeal, drove her down to the salt grass pasture where there were a few other animals — cows and yearlings, and space and mesquite tree shelter. All the way down she darted this way and that, her head with the regal horns held high and her long legs now very active, her whole bearing that of a frightened wild thing running away.

I didn't see her often now, but at last I knew that she had had her calf. When I reported to Pa, he just said, "Leave her alone. Don't try to find her calf; it will be out in time. You keep your distance, even on a horse. Give her plenty of latitude!"

Within a week the calf, a fine little heifer, was following her around. She did not relax her vigilance and faced every intruder with a head-on threat. I was willing to give her all the latitude she wanted. So I named the calf *Latitude*; I thought it was a good name. It seemed somehow to just fit.

"We'll keep her in the pasture until fall and then beef her," Pa said. "A cow like that is no good to us. Some animals just don't tame, and Old Tubucks is one."

A banging on the screen door in the darkness and an urgent voice calling out, "Telephone from Littlefield! A flood a-comin'! The biggest in history! If you've got any cattle on the river bottoms, better get 'em off P D Q !" Running steps out and along the sidewalk to warn the neighbors below. The scratch of a match and Ma in her shimmy, her bob all awry on top of her head, was replacing the lamp chimney. Charity and I were already on our feet and pulling our dresses over our heads. Pa was in Moapa with the mail.

"Hurry now. Be careful!" Ma said, as we darted out.

Down the middle of the street, our bare feet silent in the dust but keeping perfect time, we ran. A light at the Adams'. Their stock would be by the upper fields, but they had big boys and horses to get to them. Across the log bridge that spanned the Field Ditch, we plunged into the dark tunnel of the lane, trotting a while and walking a stint to get our breath. We could not talk; we could only wonder how come a flood? We had seen no rain in months. Somewhere far away and high in the mountains there had been a cloudburst or a warm rain on last winter's snow, and we on the lower reaches of the stream got the disastrous results.

The darkness had dissolved into the gray of coming daylight as we emerged from between the trees to the pasture and hurried down the bank to the barbed wire gate. It took us both to open it and drag the wires their length against the fence so that they would not be in the way as the cattle went through. Nothing was changed. The cattle were still lying down, the blackbirds in the slough just beginning to stir and chirp. But there was the smell of the flood, and the river was running its full width, covering our island completely.

Each with a long stick, we started in different directions to rouse the cattle by yelling and striking at them. Fifteen head. All here and accounted for, and not too far away.

We had them all moving toward the opening in the fence when a sudden wave covered all the pasture and we splashed through water up to our ankles. Perhaps they sensed our panic; perhaps we crowded them too fast. All but five went through and up the rolling bank to higher ground and safety. These five were our dry cows and feeders for the sale next fall; they meant much in our family economy, so much that we must get them in.

Charity ran to turn them back and I stationed myself to head them in. "Easy now; take it easy now," I was yelling in the manner of the cowboys, while she was singing out for them to "Get along there, you 'onery old basties."

Success. Old Brin turned in and the others followed, even the calves, including Latitude. They all followed but Old Tubucks. Right at the post she panicked and tore off in the opposite direction, head and tail both high. And at the same instant another wave brought the water to our knees.

What to do now? I felt that I must go get her, but with the water at this depth I dare not go out toward the stream for fear of stepping off the bank. Maybe I could go to the high land and run down to where she stood at the end of the fence and the beginning of the jump-off place. If I could succeed, it would be worth it.

"Let'r go. It's her own fault." Charity was saying aloud what I thought. "It just serves her right. She's got it comin' to her.

"It's dangerous. Pa wouldn't want us to take the risk just for one crazy old cow," she went on. "Besides, it looks like everyone in town is there at the Place waiting to see the flood."

For a minute I hesitated, and then I turned resolutely and followed Charity across the bottom of Con Neagle's field to the high point where all the wagons were in line, parents high on the spring seats keeping the younger ones together, teen-agers out running around.

"It's a-comin'!" someone called, and everyone looked. A bank of black debris advanced like a rolling wall some three feet high, behind it trees, cottonwood and cedar, the ridge of a barn bobbing along, a churn, a limp little calf, some squash swinging near the bank.

People higher on the stream had lost everything — homes, corrals, crops. Our dam would be gone, but not much at the Ditch damaged (it was the local cloudbursts that wrecked the ditches). The breakers built out into the stream at such great labor and with such high hopes, the wooden ricks filled with rocks, the piles driven into the sand, the barbed wire entangled to catch and hold trees and limbs — all these were scooped out and tossed about as a man would destroy the play cities we children made on the island. Fields before the cutting edge, where the flood whipped into the bank on our side, would melt away in chunks as big as houses, and where it swung away to cut into the opposite bank there would be a large extension of new sand deposited which could be farmed for years, or until the river changed its course again.

So we would accept this. We would put the dam in again, and adjust as best we could. And Pa would praise us for our promptness in getting out the fourteen head, and say that we did exactly right not to risk our lives for Old Tubucks.

For me, this fell on deaf ears. I could still see her, proud and defiant, facing the sunrise and her certain death. I loved her for the service I had done her earlier; I admired even her suspicion and hostility. The thought that I could have saved her — but she would not — always gave me a pang, both for her misunderstanding and for my own inadequacy and lack of courage. I really should have saved her in spite of herself. That I still had Latitude left was some little comfort.

Fifth Grade or Sixth Grade

BECAUSE I HAD STARTED SCHOOL EARLY, I was in the fifth grade a
year ahead of other children my age. By this time the big rock schoolhouse was finished, and a very wonderful building it seemed to us all.

It was built in the shape of a cross, with a room in each direction,
with a large center place which the three school rooms could all use
together by opening the big sliding doors to the east and west. The
south room was set off by itself to be a library and a supply room,
and the place for the stairway, for the plan called for a large second-
story room lighted from the windows in the four gables. During my
stay in the school, this was never finished.

The beginners, first, and second grades met in the west room; the
third, fourth, and fifth grades met opposite them in the east room;
and the sixth, seventh, and eighth grades met in the north room,
which was wider and longer than the other two.

This year there had been an extra effort made to bring back into
school older students who had quit before they graduated from the
eighth grade. If we could get a large enrollment, the state would
increase our grant, and maybe we would have money for a band, and
more library books, and better equipment all around. If we could
graduate a class of six from the eighth grade, there would be provi-
sion for a first year of High School! This would mean a generous
grant indeed.

I hadn't even thought about school that summer, for I didn't seem to thrive at all, and I could see that Ma worried about me. Where at Moapa we had both weighed in the same notch at fifty pounds, Charity had gained in both height and weight until I looked small beside her. My music teacher, Lillian Bunker, had remarked that I had a "Swill-pail complexion," and that worried me a little. My rude awakening came when Sister Annie Cox came in as I was practicing on the organ. I had to sit on the end of my spine to reach the pedals.

"Straighten up!" she said, coming up behind me and hitting me between the shoulders. "Straighten up! Sit up and keep your mouth shut! You look like an idiot sitting that way!"

This was exactly what I needed, I suppose, but I was helpless to do much about it. Ma had already been so worried about my hunched back and flat chest that she sent for a shoulder brace to correct it. An instrument of torture, that's what it was. She would put it on and pull it tight, but I just couldn't stand it; it made me sick; it would kill me, I knew, if I had to wear it. So she put it away.

Another problem was that I could not breathe through my nose. They called it "catarrh" and tried salves and steam, and physic, none of which did a bit of good.

On the other hand, I didn't really feel sick. I wasn't as strong as Charity and never would be, but I could do my chores without any serious problems. I couldn't understand why they should continually fuss about me. I ate all I wanted at every meal, and if it wasn't as much as the others ate, it was still all I wanted.

As the time came near for school to start, I became excited. I would be in the sixth grade with all the other students, and Mr. John Gubler of Santa Clara, the teacher, was big and handsome and pleasant. I had never had a man teacher before. His wife, Mina Gray, a beautiful lady, had her two little sons in such clever two-piece suits. Not only was her dress of a fashionable cut, but she had such a load of flowers on her hat! I wondered how anyone could be a good Mormon and wear a hat like that. Not many women in Bunkerville had Sunday hats; they went bare-headed or wore their sunbonnets.

Since Ma had grown up in Santa Clara, she knew the Gubler family and Sister Gray, Mina's mother. For Ma, the best people in all the world lived in Santa Clara. So when Mina bore a beautiful testimony that Fast Day, we all decided that this couple would really be an asset to our town. They could be fashionable in their dress and humble in their hearts.

The next morning the schoolhouse doors were locked until nine o'clock, when each teacher opened her own room and rang her own bell. Mr. Gubler stood on the landing and said, "Sixth grade in the two east rows; seven grade in the two middle rows; eighth grade in the two west rows. Choose a seat and sit down."

There was a little confusion and some change of seating, until Mr. Gubler came to the front and called for attention.

"Good morning, students," he said. "I have chosen this way to seat you, but let's just look around and see if there are some misfits. In general, the smaller seats are near the front and the larger ones at the back. Look around you again and indicate what you want if you are not satisfied where you are." I knew that my seat was much too big, but those for the sixth grade all seemed the same size, so I said nothing. Neither did anyone else.

"Fine!" he said. "Just fine. Now let us all sing 'America' to begin our year. I like to begin the day with a song, and I know no song more appropriate." He gave us the pitch and then led out in a clear, strong voice, beating out the time with his hands and encouraging us to sing out.

At the close of the song, he stood in silence a minute and then said, "Let us unite in prayer."

We all bowed our heads while he said an appropriate prayer, and then made a short speech saying that we should have this brief period each morning, but should learn other songs to sing. The students would be expected to take their turn saying the morning devotion, and each would be notified the evening before in order that he might be prepared.

"On your desk you each have a plain card and three of the textbooks you will use this year. First, write your name on the card with the name of your parents under it. Hold it until all have finished. Now pass the cards from back to front putting your card on top of the one from behind you."

He insisted that we do just as he said, the student on the front row holding all the cards in order until he should take them. Slipping an elastic band around each pile, he then proceeded to call out the names, beginning with the front seat of the sixth grade and going down every row to the end of the eighth grade, taking time to look at each student to get the name right. All this took some time, but he made it seem important to do.

"In the roll book these will all be arranged alphabetically, but I want these now to help me get acquainted with you. Teaching is communicating, understanding each other; learning is the same."

At noon I went home elated, certain that this would be the very best school year of my life. Mr. Gubler had given us the last half hour or so to write him a private letter about ourselves: what we liked best to do, what we had trouble with, what we wanted eventually to become if we had yet any ideas about a career. These he would file and keep, but they would be just between us two. He would hold them in confidence. I thought that was a wonderful thing to do, and said that I should like to become a teacher.

At the end of the day I was even more delighted. We had all read and studied part of the time on assignments to be finished tomorrow. And then, just before dismissal time, we sang again, a jolly song about "I love to go a-wandering" where some of the group did one phrase and the others answered them. Everyone left in high spirits. I knew that it might not always go this well, for I remembered some of the pranks that some of the fellows had played on other teachers, and I was sure this would not be an exception. But for now, I had never had a happier first day of school, though I did feel quite alone, without a single one of my real friends.

The next morning I knew that something was wrong. Ma had been crying, and it was not like Ma to cry. We did our chores early to have plenty of time, and the younger ones were all off to school before Ma told me. Mr. Gubler had recommended that they take me out of school this winter, get a little horse for me to ride, and encourage me to be out-of-doors in the sunshine and fresh air. I needed my health more than I needed books; it was easy to see that I read well and wrote well for my age. But it was just as evident that I was not a healthy child, and in my best interest they should take me out of school.

Just then Pa came up leading a beautiful dapple-blue pony with a flaxen mane and tail. He slipped off his own horse and called, "Come and see what I've got for you! Her name is Selah, and she's yours to keep. Come on! Climb on her."

Pa was right. She was beautiful, not too little, either, but a nice-sized animal that even a man could ride. I really liked her strange-sounding name. I'd take time to look it up in the Bible, for I knew that I had seen the word somewhere in the Old Testament. I had never dreamed of having a horse for my very own before.

I rode her to the field to take the cows in the morning and again to go after them at night. But there wasn't very much reason to ride over the bare hills during midday. No animals were out; they feed only in the evening, some during the night, and again from just before daylight to sunrise. You can ride hour upon hour during the middle of the day and not see a thing bigger than a grasshopper. If I were to ride her, I must have some reason to go somewhere.

So on Thursday morning after I had taken the cows to the lower field, I decided to go on through town to the upper field, where Pa had a few head of dry cattle. I hadn't come in this direction very often, so I was interested in the big full barns at Steve Bunker's place, then Uncle Herb's and then Wittwers'. Next was the cemetery, with all the folklore of death and the possible return of spirits, then the beautiful rock house which Aunt Susan Hunt's three sons had built for her. Here was a house that was beautiful just because it was: the general lines, the dark stone trim. Past Uncle Nephi Hunt's and I was out of town among many big mesquite bushes and arrowweeds.

At the Gin Ditch I came to the gate of our upper field. The main ditch ran across the lower corner, so that the cattle always had water.

I went inside and rode among the little herd. They were all there but Latitude, the heifer calf of Old Tubucks. She was not in the field, that was sure. Along the riverbed farther up I could see a small group of cattle, so I went around by the road to the Mesquite crossing. She was not there, but away on up another mile or two some more cattle were standing in the sand bar.

I didn't go down onto the riverbed, but kept to a narrow trail through thick arrowweeds higher than my head. I turned a sharp corner to come head-on to another horse — a big horse, with a big man riding it, a strange man with a new Stetson hat and a fine getup: horse, saddle, bridle — the works, like you see in pictures.

He was more startled than I was. He looked like he had met a ghost or an Avenging Angel or something.

"Who in the world are you? Are you lost? Do you know where you are? Whatever brings you to this place?"

I hardly knew where to begin to answer him, but I started by saying, "No, I'm not lost. I'm a mile or so above the mesquite crossing, and I'm going down to look through those cattle there on that island."

"Do your parents know where you are? Who are your parents, anyway, and what are they thinking of to send you up here? Don't you know that with the least accident you could be killed, and your body never found for years? A child like you should be in school, and not wandering around miles and miles from any civilization — from any traveled road, even."

This last really got through to me. I had to bite my lip to keep from crying.

"I want to be in school! I love school! But my teacher said that I should be out-of-doors on a horse and in the sunshine and fresh air! I'd gladly go to school if they'd let me." And I did cry just a bit.

"Well, I'll be damned," he said, and turning his horse, galloped away.

I don't know how he worked — through the Bishop and Mr. Gubler and my parents, but evidently he convinced them that I should be in school — in the fifth grade if I seemed too out-of-place in the sixth, but where I would have the association of other children my age, and not be banished to ride the hills alone all winter.

Aunt Martha Cox was teaching the fifth grade this year. She was almost as old as my own grandmother, but she had taught school for many years and was an excellent teacher. She had a roomful, but gave me a seat at the front row of the fifth grade. She paid no particular attention to me — gathered up my papers with the rest, let me read whatever I found that was interesting, and encouraged me to memorize the poems in the reading book. She told the class often that words of wisdom and poems were better than money in the bank. No one can steal them from you, and you can draw them out on command. And you can train your brain to remember, like athletes train their leg and arm muscles.

Once a week we would have a short program in the later afternoon. Students could volunteer to sing or recite or read a short story. Once I volunteered, because I had found a high-sounding poem in a magazine, and I loved the long tongue-rolling words.

> The spacious Firmament on high
> With all the blue etheral sky
> And spangled Heavens, a shining frame
> HIS Great Omnipotence proclaim.

I said the verse slowly, pronouncing the long words syllable by syllable.

"That's very nice, indeed, Waneta," Aunt Martha said, "but the Psalmist said it much more beautifully. He begins, 'The Heavens declare the Glory of God, and the Firmament showeth His Handiwork . . . .' I'll not tell you where it is; you look for it and find it and let's see how much of that you can commit to memory." I've been grateful to her ever since for that assignment.

I had a happy winter. At recess I played jacks or hopscotch with the girls, and I felt very much a part of this little crowd. On the last day of school, when Aunt Martha handed out diplomas to every fifth-grader but me, I was quite taken back and hurt until she said, "I'm not giving Waneta a diploma because she got hers last year. She has been only a visitor in our class this winter."

I should add that many years later — about 1930 — I was taking my debate teams to Salt Lake City to meet several teams, among them the one from the LDS College. As I walked down the hall of one of the buildings, I saw Mr. John Gubler sitting at a desk at work. I went in and greeted him by name and asked, "Do you remember me? I'm Juanita Leavitt Pulsipher."

"Are you still alive!" he exclaimed. "I didn't expect you to last the winter. I couldn't stand the sight of you, so scrawny and pale among all those big, overgrown huskies!"

Bishop's Court

"Little pitchers have big ears."

I HEARD THIS EXPRESSION FIRST just the morning after school closed. Ma and a neighbor were visiting over their sewing — Ma mending and Ailene sewing at her own carpet rags.

"There's nothing more boring than sitting alone and sewing carpet rags. I figured you'd probably be working at a quilt in one stage or another, so I'd come over and we could both talk as we work," she said. "Sister Slade was quite upset this morning when she came for the milk. Slim saddled up and left early; said he had word there was a job at Modena, and he'd go ahead and get set up, and they could bring Nancy and the baby out as soon as he can get a pay day. Ain't no money jobs around this place. But Nancy thinks he's leaving to follow the little schoolteacher. The teacher's got away real early in a white-topped buggy, to catch the train at Moapa. Slim said he was going to Modena, but she don't believe him. He just took a change of clothes behind him on the saddle, besides his lariat."

She stopped to thread her needle, and then went on: "Seems that he danced with that little schoolteacher twice again last night, and when he come to dance the last dance with Nancy, she flounced out ahead of him and wouldn't go even one round. She thinks he's got a case on the schoolteacher, and judging by the way he dances with her, he just well might have. But Nancy don't do nothing to take off

[134]

any of her fat. Even leaves the care of the baby to her Ma mostly."

Ma had been to the dance last night. I was there, too, and watched the little fracas at the last dance: Slim did dance the waltz just before the "Home, Sweet Home" with the little schoolteacher, and it was easy to see that they were both enjoying it. And when he came to Nancy for the last one, she got up and stood a second, just until he got into the dancing position, and then turned and headed for the door.

Now I was sitting on the floor with my back to Ailene. Just after New Years there had been a Bishop's Court held in our front room. It didn't begin until quite late; all three of us girls slept upstairs, but I was the only one awake. With the doors all shut, I couldn't really hear what went on, only I did know that Slim was brought in by Uncle Jess, the constable, and that Nancy and her parents were there. The meeting lasted quite a while, and Nancy and her parents left first.

Slim was kept until after they were gone, and there was some talk between him and the Bishop. It ended by a quiet wedding in which Slim and Nancy were married, but no reception was held. They weren't related to anyone else in town, and didn't have any place to hold a reception. Slim moved in with Nancy's parents, helped with getting wood, worked some on the water ditch, and even hauled manure for the Adamses for which he got a half a beef. He was pleasant, cooperated in every way, and they seemed to be doing just fine.

Their baby came early, a beautiful little girl whose head of yellow hair was clear evidence of whose child she was. In the meantime, everything changed; Slim was baptized and started coming to church. He loved to sing in the choir, for he had a remarkable tenor voice, so that in the annual concert, he had a solo part in one of the songs, and sang a duet in another with the new lady teacher who taught the first three grades.

The belle of the town, who had been so infatuated with Slim during the last holidays, left to go to school at St. George, and before long it was generally known that she had a boyfriend from one of the best families there. The wedding was in early spring. Her parents went up to go through the temple with her, and the groom's family entertained in their fine home. But she had no desire to come back to Bunkerville, even for a visit.

For a while it really seemed that here was a case where they all lived happily ever after. But now Nancy was jealous of the little schoolteacher.

Last night Slim had danced first with his wife, and in spite of her weight, they danced well together. They even talked to each other during the rest intermission, and she held up to the end, which very often she couldn't do.

But how he could dance! He went the rounds, giving the girls a thrill whether on a polka, Schottische, quadrille, or hostler's four, seeming to enjoy them all equally. But the wife was jealous only of the little schoolteacher who got the other waltz. Only a few hours earlier, I had learned that she was justified.

Twice before during the past two weeks I had met this girl going down the lane alone as I came up with the cows. I thought nothing of it, for I knew that it might be pleasant to walk out anywhere after a long day of school, and where was a better place than this shady lane? Each time we greeted each other with a "Hi!" but did not make any conversation. I did not think it at all strange that she should be there.

Then just the night before, after I rounded up the cows and started them up the lane, I decided to go back and get Selah and ride her home. Her bridle was hanging on a nail in the lone cottonwood tree. As I came to it I saw them. Such a romantic picture!

The last flood had washed so much of the land on our side down into the river — almost our whole field. But in one place a big piece had slid down about five feet from the top and stayed there, making a good, grassy seat wider and longer than a sofa. They were sitting together watching the glow of the sunset, his arm around her waist and her head on his shoulder. His horse stood just across a trickle of water, the reins over his head, on the ground, and the water all so brilliant it almost hurt, it was that beautiful.

I sensed that I had seen what I should not have seen, so I took the bridle and went across the field to where Selah was feeding, called her, got on, and went out the other direction the long way home, galloping along the hill road.

I had the milking all done and was crossing the street with the bucket of milk, when Slim passed on his horse, heading toward his home. Instantly I knew that he had brought the little schoolteacher behind him on the horse up the river road, and had let her off down near the high school building, so that she could walk the two blocks from there to her boarding place, while he doubled around in the other direction to where he lived.

Often I have wondered about Slim and the little schoolteacher. Did she go to her home, and then elope from there with Slim to Alaska, or some other distant place, where they could make a life together? Or did he really get a job in Delamar, and send for Nancy, as her parents said he had done when they left Bunkerville. They were very close-mouthed about it all, saying no farewells but just pulling out in the very early morning. I never knew.

The things that went on in a Bishop's Court were supposed to be kept secret; at least all concerned were counseled to accept whatever decision was arrived at as final, and not to discuss the matters of the Court in their families or with their friends. That was so hard to do that it was never done. Too many people were bound to know about it, about the differences that grew to such serious proportions that they must be submitted to the Bishop's Court for settlement, about the written summons to appear, about the arguments and the final settlement. Questions should be settled by the right and wrong of the matter, not by legal technicalities, and in the end, both parties should be satisfied.

I knew all about the case between Thomas Henry and Jim Albertson, having pieced together most of it from the conversations at home and around the Post Office even before the Fast Day when both men bore their testimonies and asked forgiveness of each other and the ward for their hot-tempered quarrel. It all grew out of trouble over the water. Each man thought it was his water turn, and the crops of both were burning up. Thomas Henry had it running on his field, and Jim pulled out the headgate and turned it on his. As soon as he saw that the stream was failing, Thomas went back to the ditch and changed it again. The third time, he sat down with his shovel across his knees to guard the dam.

When Jim came back, there was an argument which grew into a scuffle and then a fight in which there would certainly have been serious injury or even death if some neighbors coming along the road in a wagon had not separated the two.

At this trial there were no witnesses called — only the three members of the Bishopric, the ward clerk, the two men involved, and the Watermaster. Instead of proceeding with a review of the case and a statement of the evidence, Bishop Jones asked the group to join in singing a hymn, "Truth Reflects upon Our Senses." Handing each man a song book, he told them the page, and when all were ready, he led out in a clear, strong voice. It was almost a solo, for Pa couldn't carry a tune, the other counsellor, Brother Iverson, was hoarse, and neither Thomas nor Jim felt like joining in. But the Bishop went right on through all four verses, supported weakly by the ward clerk and the Watermaster, while the others read the words from their open books.

The song was all about keeping peace with your brethren, and about removing the beam from your own eye before you try to pluck the mote from your brother's. That finished, he asked them all to turn to another page, and they would sing, "School Thy Feelings, O My Brother," and again the Bishop sang, with a little assistance,

> School thy feelings, O my brother
> Train thy warm, impulsive soul
> Do not its emotions smother
> But let wisdom's voice control.
>
> School thy feelings, there is power
> In the cool, collected mind
> Passion shatters reason's tower
> Leaves the clearest vision blind.

and so on to the end.

After that, Pa offered prayer, and asked God that the spirit of brotherhood and love and forgiveness should be with them in their deliberations, that they might all have wisdom in the settlement of whatever troubles lay between these, their neighbors and brethren.

Then the Bishop began to talk. He would not ask them to tell what had happened, he said; he could almost guess what had happened. It had been unusually hot, the water had been out of the ditch, both fields needed it, and needed it bad; each man sincerely thought it was his turn. It didn't really matter who struck the first blow. All that did matter was that someone interfered before something was done that one or the other would regret all his life long, and for that both should thank God.

Next he began to remind them of their long years of association, of working together to build the dam and the ditch, of serving together on the recreation committee. Turning to Jim, he asked, "Who was it that sat up night after night with your little George, and told him stories, and rubbed his little aching legs. Who was it that washed his cold body and prepared it for burial?"

Seeing that Jim was close to tears, he turned to Thomas. "Who was it that guarded your interests while you were on a mission? That left more than one sack of flour on your porch? That saw to it that your wife had wood cut for the cold months?"

Before he could go on with his appeal that they not let a few minutes of passion wipe out years of neighboring, Jim was on his feet.

"To hell with the water!" he cried. "Let the damn grain burn up for all I care," and he strode across the room to meet Thomas Henry's outstretched hand.

So everyone was happy, and the Watermaster arranged the turns so that each should have it his full time before it went on to the next in turn.

Not all cases that came before the Bishop's Court were so well-settled. Sometimes the Bishopric themselves could not agree upon a decision, so submitted the case to three arbiters for settlement — one man selected by each of the contesting parties and one to represent the Bishop. Once a decision was reached, especially if the Bishopric were unanimous in it, the contestants usually accepted it. Not to do so would be to forfeit their membership in the Church, which was the worst possible punishment, the thing that brought the most rebellious to terms.

There was one story which Pa liked to tell of a young outsider who had come into a Mormon town and become so free with the girls that before long three different fathers came to the Bishop, each claiming that the young man should marry his daughter to save her good name. When he was called in to the Bishop's Court, the young man was defiant. Was it his fault if the girls were fools? Could he help it if they threw themselves at him? Throughout the whole proceeding he was sneering and scornful.

"Well, young fellow," Erastus Snow said in his slow, deliberate way, "It looks like if someone else don't kill you, I'll have to."

That was enough. Before morning the young man had fled the state, and the court had accomplished its purpose.

Unless there were visitors, the preaching in our Sunday meetings was done by members of the congregation, selected by the Bishop. Each spoke according to his interest and background, often reading from the Scriptures and illustrating from experience on the farm or freight road or cattle roundup. Those who had filled missions for the Church always had an unlimited fund from which to draw, stories of strange lands and people and of God's watch-care over His servants. Always a few general themes ran through the meeting: God fits the back to bear the burden; you do your part and God will do His; accept in faith what comes to you whether you understand it fully or not.

The courting couples on the back benches found devious ways of enjoying the close and quiet intimacy of those two hours. One girl told me how her silent, bashful beau had with evident carelessness left his hymn book open to the title, "Shall We Meet?" Although he did not direct her attention to it by either nudge or sign, and she pretended not to notice, she soon left hers open to "On the Banks of the Beautiful River." She was not sure that this was a conversation until at the end of the service he took her arm and said, "Let's get out of here." Without a word he steered her toward the long, shady lane that led to the river.

The next Sunday she noticed that his book was open to "Abide with Me." She waited until the closing song was announced before hers answered, "Not Now, But in the Coming Years." Late that night with the encouragement of an empty living room and a peach-wood fire, he said suddenly, "The coming years seems too far away. Don't you think we could manage it by fall?"

When finally it came time to close the meeting, the Bishop always called someone from the audience to offer the benediction. A young man hearing his name called would usually start, and with a dazed, hit-on-the-head expression, make his way to the stand, mumble,

[140]

"Please arise," and proceed with a short, one-breath prayer. An experienced elder under the same conditions would come forward with dignity and pause a moment before he said clearly, "If the audience will please arise, we will be dismissed." After waiting for the women to finish pinning on hats and adjusting skirts and for complete silence, he would clear his throat, lift his arm to the square and proceed to ask God's approval of what had been done and His protection as we journeyed to our several places of abode. By the time he had finished, the youngsters at the back would have edged out into the aisle ready to bolt with the "Amen."

There was one time when a weary brother had slept through all the first talk, and in the lull before the second, was nudged by a youngster who whispered, "Bishop just called on you to dismiss!" With a snort he stood up, pulled down his vest to collect his wits, walked up the aisle, called upon the audience to arise, and closed the meeting in the middle. The Bishop, a broad grin on his face, made no move to interrupt, and surprised boys whooped as they jumped in flying leaps from the top step.

When I think of our life among the cactus, and with the constant threat of quicksand, when I remember how, with all the differences in our little community, we still could live together and work together, it makes me think of the strength of our society. I like to think of our Bishop's Courts, with all their faults and with all their mistakes. They were still essentially and fundamentally right, for their purpose was to see that justice was done, not according to legal technicalities alone, but according to plain human right. And their purpose was more — it was to see that good feelings were established, and that people shook hands and parted friends.

All on a Summer's Day

USUALLY I TOOK THE COWS TO THE PASTURE IN THE MORNING and came for them in the evening, but now, for a few days, I must stay all day and herd them. The big pasture was being flooded; the cows could not stand in the water or the pasture would be ruined. Pa had harvested the wheat in early June and plowed about half the stubble under for the fall crop of corn, melons, and squash. These were all growing well; a cow could very quickly ruin the young corn, so my business was just to stay where I could protect the crop. There was plenty of good feed in the lower part of the field, too, so my assignment was not at all hard.

Our land was separated from Con Neagle's by a "live fence," a row of cottonwood trees planted so close together that their trunks would almost touch up at the "topping head," while brambles grew between them so thick that nothing bigger than a snake or a field mouse could get through. The only point of entrance was the field ditch when it was empty — and today it was.

I was playing in this damp ditch when my cousin Charles came up from the sloughs along the river. His cows were in the field below ours, and he had been robbing blackbirds' nests. Both his hind pockets were full of eggs; one mudhen egg included. He was very proud of himself, for usually it took two to rob a mudhen's nest — one to decoy the mother away and the other to slip in behind and get the eggs. Since this nest had only one egg, he was sure it was fresh. He would puncture it with a mesquite thorn and have the shell for the center of blackbird eggshell beads.

"Look! Look! There comes Old Brock straight for the corn," Charles said, suddenly. "There'll be Hell-a-poppin' if she gets started!"

I ran as fast as I could, drove her well back in the other direction, and as I turned around, I could see Charles starting to climb up the willow tree on the ditch bank where I had been playing.

"You get down from there," I yelled. "That's *my* nest, my very own. You know that's my nest! I been watching that nest ever since the birds started building it! The eggs won't be any good to you! They're nearly ready to hatch! Don't you touch that nest!"

The little yellow-breasted warblers had been so busy building that dainty little nest. I had seen them pull the hair from Selah's mane and tail; once the father bird came carrying a long yarn string. I thought how wise the birds were to put the nest way out near the end of a limb, safe from cats and boys.

Charles had trouble getting up to the top of the trunk; it was slick and hard to climb. Now he perched among the limbs and branches, with an even greater challenge to get to the nest. I came running back as fast as I could.

"Don't you touch them eggs!" I called again. "You'll be sorry! You promised you wouldn't! You know you did! You'll be sorry!"

My concern seemed only to urge him on, and as he neared the nest, lying flat on his stomach and reaching with all his might, I grew more eloquent.

"You dirty, rotten, lying skunk," I called. "You stinkin' liar! You'll be sorry!"

But it was no use. He reached and stretched, seeming to enjoy the fact that I was almost in tears. To cry over a bird's nest!

At last he did get them — two tiny eggs — and for want of a better place, put them into his mouth. They would have been crushed in his shirt pocket, and his pants pockets were already full.

Boiling with wrath, I waited at the foot of the tree, and the minute he came within reach, I slapped him as hard as I could on one hind pocket and then on the other. He jumped to the ground and started

[143]

to yell at me, breaking the eggs in his mouth, which sent him gagging and spitting.

"Dam' your heart! Wait till I get hold of you," he yelled.

"Yes, wait till you do!" I bantered, running across a patch of sand-burrs. My feet were tougher than his, and I had a stout stick with which I could defend myself.

I had been so furiously angry that I had wanted to pull his hair and scratch his face, but the sight of all that yellow goo behind and the expression on his face as he spit out those baby birds took it all out of me. I was ready to bargain.

"If you'll not hit me, I'll come back and help clean your pockets out, and we'll go over to Con Neagle's patch and get a melon. They're getting ripe; he took some home last night."

"OK," Charles said. "That's a helluva mess," and he stretched and twisted to try to see. Indeed, he was right; it *was* a mess.

I got the can I had to carry water in for my muddish-making project. But the ditch was dry. Con had the water out on his lucerne, just beyond his melon patch.

"You check the cows while I get these burrs out of my feet and I'll soon have you clean as a pin," I promised.

Charles ran through the stubble to the big polegate. From there he could get a view of all the lower pasture and count to see that the cows were all accounted for, either feeding or lying down.

"Safe as a dollar in the Relief Society Bank," he announced as he came back. "Now what we waitin' fer?"

I led the way up the dry ditch, stooping easily under the barbed wire fence, and going on to the headgate behind which the water was backed up to run on Con's alfalfa field. I had to make a step in the high bank to reach the water, then back down to pour it into his pockets, stir it around with a stick, and scoop the eggshells and goo out with my hands.

After several canfuls in each pocket, Charles thought they were clean enough. I knew they'd be pretty stiff when they got dry, but if he was satisfied, I was.

We were already so far up on Con's property that we had only to climb out over the ditch bank to be in his melon patch. These were early watermelons, not as large as the fall ones would be, but sugar-sweet. He had his fall garden in his upper field: large, long water-melons, mushmelons, casabas, pumpkins, squash, and fall corn, for Con made a business of farming, and his fall crop, like our own, was just getting a good start.

We made our way through the willows and were down well among the vines, when Charles said in a stage whisper, "*Jee-hosiphat!* Here comes Con!" And as fast as he could, he disappeared into the willows, and on, I knew, down the dry ditch to our field.

I looked up. Sure enough, there was Con driving along the side of the ditch in his wagon. I knew instantly that he had come to change the water from the alfalfa to the melon patch. This he would do by pulling the headgate from its present position and putting it into place right on our fence line. Since I was sure that he had seen me, I decided to stand my ground and take my medicine. If I ran, he would tell Pa. Then I'd have to march over to his place and ask forgiveness and pay whatever damages he asked for. It was better to face it now. So I went on, stepping carefully between the vines, stooping once to thump a melon, and all the while watching the progress of the wagon.

"Whoa!" Con said loudly, pulling his team to a halt.

I just stood in my tracks while he wrapped the lines around the brake and climbed out of the wagon. His place in town was just across the street and "kittern" from ours — that is, we were on the northeast corner of our block and he was on the southwest corner of his, but his fence line was covered with pomegranate bushes so thick and tall that no one could possibly see inside the yard. All our activities were in the other direction — to the school, the church, the Post Office, and the store. So for the first time in my life I saw him at close range.

With all my fear, I couldn't help wondering what made him so bowlegged, and how could his levis stay so low around his hips without falling down? The round tag with the BULL DURHAM sign for the sack of tobacco in his shirt pocket advertised the fact that he smoked, and his heavy, light-brown mustache was stained, as if to prove it if further evidence was needed.

"Can't you find a ripe one?" Con asked, and I was surprised at the cordiality of his tone.

[145]

"Not yet," I answered, much relieved.

He came toward me, all the while looking for a ripe melon.

"Do you know how to tell when a watermelon is ripe?" he asked.

"I think I do," I told him. "I can't always be sure by the sound when I thump it, but I look to see if the quirl and spoon are dry."

"That's a pretty good sign," Con agreed. "Then if you take your thumbnail and scratch the skin just a little, and if it peels off easy, that's another good sign. Of course, thumping is best. Come here and listen to these two."

One had a dull, heavy sound; the other a clear, higher note. I looked for the curling, spoon-like leaf and the tightly-coiled tendril on either side of the place where the melon stem fastened onto the mother plant. Yes, the quirl and spoon were dry.

Con pulled the melon off, and opening his pocketknife, ran the blade all the way around it, then tapped it lightly on the ground. It popped open, all its luscious, red heart on one side. He cut off a big hunk of this core and held it out toward me on the end of the knifeblade.

My hands weren't exactly clean, but I took it in my fingers and leaned way over to eat it so that the juice wouldn't drizzle down the front of my dress. Such a wonderful, sweet melon! Never had I tasted one better! Con gave me a second piece of the heart, before he ran the blade all around the edge of the rind, as if he felt that all that was edible should be eaten. I thought of Charles hiding in the brush and watching with hungry eyes, but decided not to mention him unless Con did. Con evidently had other things on his mind, for he wiped the knife blade on his levis in two swift strokes, snapped it shut and put it into his pocket. In the same movement he produced a thin little package of tobacco paper. How skillful he was with it! One sheet separated, made into a little trough; the tobacco sack opened just enough; exactly the right amount sifted into the paper; a quick foldover, licking the edge with his tongue, and Con was ready to light up. The match flickered a second, caught on, and was flipped down and stepped upon in less time than it takes to tell it. Now Con could squat on his heels, relax, and carry on a conversation.

"I don't blame you kids for coming over here after a melon," he said. "The weather's so hot and the water so dam' bad. So I don't blame you. I don't mind if you get a melon once a day, if you're careful not to tromp on the vines, or plug the melons. One thing I can't stand is for kids to go through a patch plugging the melons to see if they're ripe, and then turning them over to rot. Just as well pick it in the first place — 'taint no good after it's been plugged."

"Pa gets awful mad at kids that plug melons, too. But me—I don't have a knife, and I'd not plug melons with it if I did," I promised.

"That's all right," Con went on. "You're older and got more sense than most of the kids. You just be careful of the vines and don't take more'n you can eat. But mostly, stay off for a day or two after the water's been on. Or stay along the edges where you don't get into mud up to your knees."

Then as if he had a new idea, Con stood up, picked up the rinds of our melon and threw them one-at-a-time spinning into the brush where Charles had hidden. I imagined that he smiled a little.

"Better get goin,'" Con said, and started out. Then he stooped to thump a small melon. He picked it and held it out to me.

"Here, take this with you. I'm turning the water in here to run all night, or a good part of it. I may have to camp here. But this is a ripe melon, and it will be better to have it now than try to get it tomorrow."

Charles waited until Con had turned the water onto the melons and started off in the wagon before he came out. He would eat the melon I had brought; Con understood that he would eat it; this was just Con's way of sending him a gift.

"Con was just smart," Charles observed, as he finished the melon. "He knowed good and well that we'd steal some of his melons, and we wouldn't take as many if he was decent about it. He must-a heard about Uncle Jim and his apricots."

Charles was right. Everybody in town had heard about Uncle Jim's apricots, and how he had told some of the boys that, "Every year you've got my apricots. This year I plan to enjoy them myself. I warn you! You'd better stay clear."

Uncle Jim got a shotgun and moved his cot out under the apricot tree. The boys waited for his snores to be deep and regular. Then they climbed the tree, ate some apricots, saved the pits, and put them into his shoes. When still he didn't rouse, the four of them each took a corner of the cot and carried it out to the sidewalk, where he found himself the next morning, his shoes, full of apricot pits, set carefully beside it.

Of course they shouldn't have done it; they were stealing what did not belong to them. On the other hand, Uncle Jim should not have dared them.

As for me, Con had treated me fine; he had trusted me and talked to me like an equal. Now I would look out for his interest in every way that I could.

His melon eaten, Charles had nothing else to do. He had brought only dry stock to the pasture this morning, leaving the two milk cows to be fed at home. When he decided to cut across Uncle Tom's field to where two of the boys were gathering up the last small load of hay and ride to town with them, I agreed that he'd be smart to do it.

I was glad to see him go, because he was always doing such things as catching grasshoppers and experimenting with them, trying to see which could jump the farthest; pulling out a leg to see how much difference it would make, tying several of them together with a yarn string for a team. None of which I liked at all. The only animal that he left alone was a toad; he had a strong superstition about toads, more than just the fear that they would make warts on his hands. Witches and haunts were in some way connected in his mind with toads, and Charles was full of fears about the supernatural — spirits both good and evil.

That night as I stretched out in bed, I thought of the doings of the long, long day. Would the little warblers get busy and make another nest and lay their eggs in a better place, and still have some baby birds this season, or would they just die and leave no little singers to follow them? I could never forgive Charles for robbing that nest — never as long as I live, I told myself. How different he was from Fred Hoskins!

Only last Sunday School Fred was sitting on the end of the bench in front of me. Just as the Sacrament was being passed and he took his piece of bread, he jumped up and bolted for the door, dodging the brother who stood there and running past him down the steps.

He didn't come back until just a few minutes before our class was over, when he slipped quietly into his place.

"Welcome back, Fred," the teacher said, "We thought we had lost you. Would you care to tell us what it was that called you away in such a hurry?"

"Well, you see, it was like this. Last Monday we were hauling our hay out of the field just across the Big Ditch, and Dan sent me over to the apricot tree to bring a pitchfork that he had left there. Just as I came up, a baby robin fell down right in front of me. It hadn't any feathers to speak of; it just got out by accident, and it was too stunned to hardly try to get away. I caught it and thought I'd climb up and put it back in the nest, but Dan yelled for me to get a move on. I knew I couldn't take the bird with me, so I took out my top-string and put the slipknot over one leg and set it on the ground and tied the other end around one of the suckers at the bottom of the tree. I thought I'd come back later, but I didn't. When we got home, we had company from Mesquite and I completely forgot until this morning. Just as I reached for the Sacrament bread, I remembered that baby robin, and I couldn't sit in that seat a minute longer. I ran all the way down. I expected that maybe I'd find the bird dead and eaten, but I could get my top-string. Well, I was wrong. The bird was still tied, and still struggling to get free, but it was now full-grown, all feathered out. And its mother in the weeds was making an awful fuss. She had been there all week guarding that little bird and feeding it. All the others had left the nest. And was I ever happy to turn this one loose! It flew to the top of the tree, with the mother bird, and they seemed to be having a celebration of some sort when I left."

The teacher was right touched by the story.

"It seems that mother-love is not confined to people," she said. "The mother robin certainly had it, too."

But that was not all. I decided that I was glad that Con had caught me in his melon patch. Now I admired the man. His farm was the best-kept of any in the valley. His team was sleek and well cared-for, and his outfit in good shape. He himself was a smaller man than I had thought he was, but his blue eyes looked straight at you — a man you could trust, and one that would give you a break. I didn't even mind the tobacco; there in the open it smelled rather good. Pa drank tea and so did Grandma Thirza, and that was against the Word of Wisdom, too. From now on, I'd always speak well of Con, and I'd look out for his interests. I could make quite a difference in what happened to his melon patch, and I would see to it that we never took more than one melon a day.

The Lord's Vineyard

I WAS ALWAYS GLAD WHEN IT WAS MY TURN TO TAKE THE MILK
IN TO GRANDPA'S HOUSE. I liked to linger a while, just to learn
more about Pa's folks. Tall and slender Aunt 'Ress had devoted
herself to the care of her parents, and on that lonely ranch she had
little chance for social life. But she always seemed cheerful and happy
in keeping things clean and neat, and her father well-groomed.
She often had some little goodie for me, too.

Grandma Thirza was little and spry, and very definite in her
speech. If her first concern was for Grandpa, her second was that
she be well-dressed. We called her "Toggy." For us the expression
"all togged up" meant not only wearing your best clothes, but wearing a little too much in the way of decoration. Grandma Thirza
would put on a brooch and beads, a fancy back comb in her hair,
an embroidered cape, and a ring or two, and carried herself like a
real aristocrat. She always took two handkerchiefs, "a show and a
blow," the first lace-trimmed and the second heavy-duty and hidden
in an inside pocket of the cape. She always had a bit of perfume,
bergamint or rose leaves, and she never entered the church door without stooping to dust off the toes of her shoes.

She also had a train of superstitions and taboos: no one should
ever pay back salt — if a neighbor borrowed sugar or flour or a loaf
of bread, Grandma expected it returned, but not salt; to break a

mirror, to open an umbrella in the house, or to bring a shovel or ax inside were all fateful omens, bound to bring bad luck.

Grandpa Dudley had been a tradition long before Pa moved him and Grandma Thirza from the Leavittville ranch to the two-roomed rock house near our place. From Pa we had heard many of the stories of Grandpa's work as an Indian missionary, of his bravery and his endurance. Now he had grown too old to live off alone, even with two of his wives, Grandma Thirza and Grandma Maria (who had since gone to live with her youngest son) to help him.

Often I lingered to hear Grandpa talk or sing. Though he never talked directly to me, I think he was conscious of my interest and told many stories for my benefit. One evening as he sat on his low, straight chair, the firelight brightening the ruffle of beard under his chin and the shock of upstanding, snow-white hair, he began to sing. He often sang ballads or hymns, but this was an Indian song.

"Ki-yi-yi-yi, ki-yi-yi. Ki-yi, ki-yi, ki-yi-yi-yi," he sang, tapping out the uneven rhythms with his cane. The song changed from the ki-yi's to a series of guttural sounds, deep and full, like grunts almost, and then rose in a shrill, eerie cadence.

Strange how an old man before a fireplace could fill the room with an Indian song and a tapping cane tom-tom until I could almost see bare, brown bodies circling around a campfire. Finally the song ended in a succession of short, low notes, and a long wail in a minor key. For a long time Grandpa sat looking at the little blue flames that played around under the back log without seeming to touch it. Then he let his cane fall back against his body and stretched his hands out to the fire.

"I thank God that these old hands have never been stained by human blood," he said in a deep, earnest voice.

To me, that meant that he had never had to kill an Indian. Why else should he shed human blood? It was many, many years before I learned the real meaning of that statement and that it referred to the massacre in 1857 of the Fancher party by Mormons and Indians at the Mountain Meadows. Another story that developed a new meaning was one to the effect that

> My brother Lem and I were taking our wheat to the mill at Parowan;
> out on the Buckskin Flat three armed horsemen dashed up to my wagon

[152]

from the side and stopped the team. "What is your name?" the leader asked loudly.

"Dudley Leavitt," I answered.

"Somebody has been talking," he said. "Stories are leaking out."

"I don't know what you mean. What are you talking about?" I said.

"The affair at the Mountain Meadows."

"I know nothing about the Mountain Meadows; you yourself have made the first mention of it to me. Now, there's a man in the wagon behind me there who will not be afraid to tell his name, either. You may go back and tell him also that there was something happened at the Mountain Meadows. I'm sure he has never heard anything yet, so you may give him the news."

With an oath, he turned his horse and they all galloped back toward their hideout.

Could this have referred to the pact that was made among those who participated, that they would not discuss the massacre, and that any who did should receive the death penalty?

Another story had little meaning to me then, but now seems very significant.

I was with a group of elders that went out to visit the spot with President Brigham Young the first time he came south after it happened. The soldiers had put up a stone monument over the place where the bodies were buried and a wooden cross that said, "Vengeance is mine, saith the Lord. I will repay." Well, President Young read that to himself and studied it a while and then read it out loud to us, but he said, "Vengeance is mine, saith the Lord, I HAVE repaid!" He didn't say a word, but he lifted his right arm up to the square, and in five minutes there wasn't one stone left upon another. He didn't give any order. He didn't say a thing, but we all understood that he wanted it torn down.

Grandpa had come with the first Mormon missionaries to the southern Indians in 1854, living first on the Santa Clara Creek, and moving down onto the Virgin River to live the United Order. But he considered all his life a mission, so eager was he to further the work of the Lord. As a boy in Illinois he had known Joseph Smith, the Mormon prophet, and had become wholly converted to his teachings; he had known Brigham Young, and had the same implicit faith in him as the mouthpiece of God. Now, looking back over his life, he often talked of the Prophet Joseph and of the grief of the people when he was martyred by the mob at Carthage jail; he told of the hard days at Nauvoo when his family were driven from their farm across a frozen river; he told of experiences crossing the plains to Utah, his Zion. But mostly he talked of his work among the Indians, his labors "in this part of the Lord's Vineyard."

These Indian stories kept me wide-eyed and open-mouthed, and colored my dreams at night. No matter how difficult the situation, Grandpa always came out victorious in the end, something like the good heroes of our modern comics. He always said that the hand of the Lord was over him, but there were times when I felt that the Lord was pretty slow to stretch forth His hand to Grandpa's aid. At other times He was very prompt.

"I was traveling down the Mogutsa," Grandpa said one evening. "The night was dark and stormy. I heard a crackle in the brush and the Spirit made known to me that I was in great danger. I stopped short and stood still. Just then a flash of lightning showed me at least twenty Indians, all with their bows drawn to the last notch. I yelled out, 'Wamptun! Wamptun! Tickaboo!' I thought if I told my name and said that I was a friend, they would not harm me, but they were mad. One of their men had been killed by a white man, and they were out to get revenge.

"They took me down into a deep wash, where they had a fire built against the bank. They put me against this steep wall behind the fire and they all sat in a half-circle on the other side, trying to make up their minds how to kill me.

"The Spirit prompted me again. All at once I knew just exactly what to do. I reached into my pocket and pulled out a small notebook, and with a stub of a pencil, I started to make big marks on the paper. One Indian close-by saw what I was doing, and in a little while they were all watching me. I never said a word, but kept writing in big marks and circles. Then I tore off the sheet, stuck one end into the flame, and when it started to burn, I stood up and held it up as high as I could reach, and started to pray, part in Indian and part in English.

" 'Hai, Shanob, Shanob. Hear my prayer and deliver me. Wamptun, tickaboo Indians. Let them not kill me. Wamptun no yakeway. Let Wamptun go pronto, purtydamnquick.'

"I held the burning paper up and talked to God all the while it burned. Well, you should have seen those Indians. They looked at each other and began to jabber. All of a sudden they decided that they had better get me out of there before my letter had time to get up to Shanob. They guided me back to the road and set me on my way, as glad to get rid of me as I was to be rid of them. I sang as loud as I could all the way back, "God Moves in a Mysterious Way, His Wonders to Perform."

Grandpa's religion was really a living thing. When he prayed, he talked man-to-man with God; when he sang the hymns, they took on a special meaning; and when he quoted Scripture, rolling the sentences and speaking in a voice that was groomed to fill all outdoors, I was filled with awe: "Hear, O ye Heavens, and give ear O earth, and rejoice ye inhabitants thereof! For the Lord is God, and beside Him there is no other. Great is His wisdom, marvelous are His ways, and the extent of His doings no man can find out. . . . ." It has never sounded quite the same since.

Grandpa considered himself important in the general scheme of things. As he figured it, God had work that He wanted done in this part of His Vineyard, and it took men like Grandpa to do it. If the Kingdom were ever to be established on the earth, he must help to establish it. He needed God—but, quite as importantly, God needed him.

A visiting brother once looked over a field of wheat on newly-cleared land.

"That is a good crop that you have been able to raise, Brother Leavitt," he said. "You have had the help of the Lord. Between you and the Lord, you have done all right."

"Brother," Grandpa said gently, "you should have seen that piece of land when the Lord was trying to run it without me."

One of his pet notions was the importance of being well-born. To him, that meant having a good father, just as in breeding animals it is important to select a good sire. "Blood will tell," he always said. "Blood is thicker than water." In evaluating a man, he always judged him by his father. In his own case, he considered himself the important factor in the heritage of his children, though he had the highest respect for all his wives. "If I plant carrots in this field and this and this, they will still all be carrots," he said.

One evening when I went in to take the milk, I found him talking to another old man. He looked to be about Grandpa's age, except that he was smaller and wiry and wore a full beard. They sat on opposite sides of a little table talking about a horse, and I squatted against the side of the fireplace to listen while Grandma measured out her milk. Since she forgot to remind me that my mother would be waiting, I forgot to leave.

"I heard that you had bought Old Maje from Davis," the visitor said, "so I come on down here to see if you still had him or if he is dead. It's a long ways to come just to see a horse, but I'd go farther than that to see Old Maje."

"Well," Grandpa hesitated — "he died about a year ago. He was a good animal. I hated to lose him."

"A good animal! I'll say he was a good animal! I raised that horse from a colt, and I ought to know. I've had a lot of horses in my day, but never another like him. I'd never have left him when I went into Old Mexico, but I was traveling with others, and I thought I would be back in less than two years. My brother wanted to keep Maje; he needed a horse, and I knew he would be good to him. But my brother died suddenly and his wife went back to live with her folks, so she let Maje go. I followed him through three different hands before I got to you. Let me tell you about . . ."

I listened while he told of the horse, how intelligent he was, and how understanding. I understood the feeling that the old man had for his horse, for in this hard land where a horse often shared hunger and thirst and exposure with his master, there grew up a real bond between them. I understood even better now, since Pa had given me Selah.

"What I really came for," the visitor said at last, was to see if you would sell your interest in Old Maje for the eternity. I'm getting to be an old man. I won't be here much longer, and heaven just won't be heaven for me without that horse."

Whereupon the visitor produced a paper and read aloud the agreement deeding to Dan Jones all rights of ownership to Old Maje for

1. Littlefield, Arizona, looking east across the Virgin River toward the Virgin Mountains, ca. 1900. *Lynne Clark Collection.*

2. Bunkerville, Nevada, looking north across the Virgin River toward Flat Top Mesa, ca. 1900. *Lynne Clark Collection.*

3. Henry and Mary Hafen Leavitt. *Utah Historical Society*.

4. Grandmother Mary Ann Stucki Hafen (with Annie Woodbury Hafen) and her home in Bunkerville. *Lynne Clark Collection.*

5. Pioche, Nevada, ca. 1900. *Lynne Clark Collection.*

6. Dudley Leavitt, wives Mary and Mariah, children Daniel
and Ira. *Utah Historical Society.*

7. The Arrowhead Trail car, 1918. *Lynne Clark Collection.*

8. St. George, Utah, looking southeast, with the Hurricane Cliffs forming the horizon, temple at left and tabernacle in center, early 1900s. *Lynne Clark Collection.*

9. The author's first school at Bunkerville, 1917. She is standing at left. *Juanita Brooks Collection.*

10. Thomas D. Leavitt home, Bunkerville, 1918. *Juanita Brooks Collection.*

11. St. George, looking northeast toward Zion Park, early 1900s. *Lynne Clark Collection.*

12. School house at Mesquite, ca. 1920. *Lynne Clark Collection.*

13. Sunday School at Mesquite, ca. 1920. *Lynne Clark Collection.*

14. The author, ca. 1920. *Juanita Brooks Collection.*

15. Fourth of July at Enterprise, Utah, ca. 1915. *Lynne Clark Collection.*

16. Dixie Academy Building, St. George, ca. 1925. *Lynne Clark Collection.*

17. Daisy, Juanita, and Eva, ca. 1925. *Juanita Brooks Collection.*

18. Corner of Tabernacle and Main Streets, St. George, looking west, ca. 1930. *Lynne Clark Collection.*

19. Picking strawberries near Provo, Utah, 1927. Juanita at left. *Utah Historical Society.*

20. In Yellowstone Park, 1927. Juanita at rear. *Utah Historical Society.*

21. Juanita and Ernie, ca. 1928. *Juanita Brooks Collection.*

22. Main Street, St. George, looking south toward the tabernacle, ca. 1930. *Lynne Clark Collection.*

23. Dedication of the Mountain Meadows Massacre monument, September 10, 1932. *Utah Historical Society.*

24. The wedding dinner at the Brooks home, May 1933. Will and Juanita in front; Mary and Henry Leavitt, Grandma Hafen at Juanita's left. *Juanita Brooks Collection.*

25. The family of Henry Leavitt (who died in 1944) in the mid-1940s. *Standing (left to right)*: Francis, Charity, Melvin, Mary, Laurel, Daisy, and Dudley. *Sitting (left to right)*: Eva, Aura, Mary Hafen Leavitt, Juanita. *Juanita Brooks Collection.*

the hereafter, and both men solemnly signed it, though Grandpa had to blow his nose hard and Brother Jones had to wipe his spectacles to see where to put his name.

Grandpa thought of all his life as a mission. Whether he was preaching to Indians or chasing them, whether stampeding cattle or building a dam, he thought he was laboring in the Lord's Vineyard. Sometimes it looked like he was trying to establish a vineyard where the Lord never intended one to be. He broke the ground, cleared off the brush and rocks, struggled with the river, killed the rattlesnakes, and left his part of the Lord's Vineyard better than he found it.

He knew that try as they would, his children could never become wealthy here; they could hardly become situated comfortably. For him, wealth had no value except as it might aid in promoting God's work, the establishment of the Kingdom. If his children could raise families who were honest, who walked uprightly, who paid their debts and helped their neighbors, who kept the Word of Wisdom and were prayerful, they would have succeeded. And only in this way could Grandpa succeed in his labors in the vineyard of the Lord.

Now here this man was who had been so lithe and strong, spending his days on this low, rawhide-bottomed chair, taking it along with him, sitting and reaching with his powerful arms.

"These old, useless, crippled legs," Grandpa told one of his sons. "How glad I will be to get rid of them. There is so much that I could do if I were not chained to this worn-out body."

A neighbor asked him how he was.

"My mind is active, but my feet drag," he answered. If my feet would follow the dictates of my head, I could get over the ground like a mountain sheep."

During the summer he lagged a little. He spent more time indoors, musing over the past or sitting in that quiet, semi-blank state which he called "studying." He admonished his children all the more to walk uprightly before the Lord and to keep themselves unspotted from the sins of the world.

One evening as I sat on the floor before the fireplace, he began to sing. Not that that was unusual. He often sang. But in some intangible way, this was different. He began the hymn, "Come, Let Us

Anew." When he came to the last verse

> I have *fought* my way through
> I have finished the work
> Thou didst give me to do

I felt as if I were listening to the death chant of some warrior. It was his announcement of the end. I found myself trembling. The next lines

> And that each from his Lord
> Should receive the glad word
> "Well and faithfully done,
> Enter in to My joy and sit down on My throne."

expressed his faith that he would be greeted by a kind friend who would approve his life's work.

The next day as I took the cows to the field, I saw the empty shell of a locust on a twig of a catclaw bush. I had some trouble to break off the branch because of the thorns, but I thought it was well worth it, it was so perfect and delicate and beautiful. I took it proudly to show Grandpa, and thought maybe Grandma or Aunt 'Ress might want to hang it somewhere for a decoration. Grandpa studied it a long time and then handed it back.

"That is how it will be with me soon," he said. "One of these days I shall step out of this old shell and be free. It will be a welcome release — a Promotion, that's what it will be."

Neither Grandma nor Aunt 'Ress seemed interested in the locust shell, so I took it home to arrange on the organ, up by the mirror where the little ones couldn't get at it.

As I left, Pa rode up on Flax, and Aunt 'Ress met him out by the wall. After they had talked awhile, Pa rode away without going in. Instead, he went to the homes of his brothers who lived in the lower end of town and left word that Grandpa was failing; it would be nice if the older grandchildren would come in groups of four or five and call on him, not to stay long, but to let him know that they were concerned for his welfare and loved him.

The next morning Grandpa did not get up. During the day, word went out that he was down, so many of his family called on him. He knew he was near the threshold, but he was calm. He had faced death many times, from heat, starvation, Indians. Now it held no fear.

The Lord's Vineyard

In her eightieth year, Mabel Leavitt Rushton, daughter of Dudley Jr., told her remembrance of Grandpa's counsel to the grandchildren who came to call on him during the last few days of his life.

> Six of us went together that afternoon to see Grandpa. There were Minerva and Orson and me from our family, Ralph and Roxie from Uncle Lon's, and Ernest from Uncle Frank's. We were all between fifteen and seventeen years old. Grandpa seemed so glad to see us. Aunt 'Ress propped him up on pillows, and he talked to us right frankly. He told us he was very glad we had come, because he would like it if we young people would take care of his body the night before the funeral.
>
> "I hope you won't be afraid. I wouldn't harm you living, and I won't harm you dead. Two of you can come in at a time if you want to, or even three. But the cloths must be changed about every half-hour. I'd be sorry if my face was black.
>
> "If you get sleepy, go out and run around the house a time or two, or up and down the sidewalk, but don't all leave at once."

On the second day he still had visitors. He was too tired to talk, but his eyes knew everything until he fell asleep. It soon became evident that he would not wake up. His family had all been summoned; they should stand by at the end.

There was something dignified about his passing. No hysterical weeping, no shaking him and calling him back, no nurses punching needles into him or poking oxygen tubes up his nose. His family accepted the inevitable as he would have wished. Some walked in the yard, or wept quietly in the other room, but where he lay, all was peace. The son who sat beside him touched his lips with water or shifted him slightly, holding his pulse and watching his breath grow shorter. Death crept up so softly it was hard to tell when the end came.

As Mabel Rushton later related,

> We followed his directions, and found that we were not afraid at all; instead, each one was glad to take his turn.
>
> Best of all, Grandpa had seen to it that there were cookies, candy, and nuts for us to munch on during the night, so that it was almost like a party. When Aunt 'Ress came at daylight, we were all still wide awake. We felt proud that we could do this last little service for Grandpa.

[159]

The funeral was held in the little rock church. The bell was tolled once for every year of his life, a long announcement. Within the building, everything about his place was white, the coffin covered with white flannel (the handwork of his friends), the chairs on which it rested draped in sheets. Sheets also disguised the pulpit, the word FATHER outlined across the front in quickly-wilting pink oleander blooms. Oleanders and zinnias in fruit jar vases stood in an uncertain row across the stand, and a spray of homemade paper flowers, in pink and green, graced the top of the casket.

During the services, while the different speakers told of his accomplishments and extolled his virtues and assured his wives and children that he would come forth in the morning of the First Resurrection crowned with glory, immortality, and eternal life, it seemed to me that his passing marked the end of an epoch. It was as if the curtain had fallen on the first act in the drama of the Southwest.

At the close of the funeral, when the lid was removed from the coffin and all the audience marched around single file to view the remains, the weeping was unrestrained. As I passed by, I could see only peace on his face, and dignity, as though he knew he were being looked at and held a pose for it. Why should they cry so? Why should a daughter swoon and have to be carried out? I could think only of his own eagerness for the end, and the one word he used to describe it: "Promoted."

The Outsider

He came in on the mail rig from Moapa. Pa stopped at the house just long enough to set his suitcase on the porch and tell Ma that he might be here for two nights, depending on whether he got done the things he had come to do. He was an Outsider, Pa said, but he seemed very nice and she needn't worry; he'd make some contacts up town and likely be back in an hour or so.

An Outsider! I had never visited with one before in all my life. Most of our visitors were relatives who came in wagons from Mesquite. Those who came representing the Church leaders in St. George always stayed at the Bishop's home and spoke to the people in meeting, reminding us of our part in the great plan of establishing the Kingdom of God upon the earth and making the desert blossom. They always praised our efforts. Even the drummers who came to sell things at the store were from ZCMI in Salt Lake City, and Church men also. And the trustees wouldn't think of hiring a teacher who wasn't a member of the Church or who didn't keep the Word of Wisdom.

What would an Outsider want in our town? What was he here for, anyway? At our family prayers each morning both Pa and Ma (when it was their turn — the older children shared in this, too) always asked God to remember the missionaries who were abroad preaching the Gospel to those who sat in darkness. While this might

[161]

be only figurative, I had somehow the idea that all Outsiders would be underprivileged.

Ma was a little troubled at having to entertain him. We weren't set up to run a hotel; we had enough children to fill our house. But she marshaled all hands to help, one to clean the washdish outside the kitchen door on the back porch, wipe off the splashings from the oilcloth behind it, and put a fresh towel in the roller; another to carry fresh ashes and a new catalog to the outhouse and clean it out. She would change the sheets on our bed upstairs, pick up our things, and arrange them. I swept the front porch and dusted the living room.

I had hardly finished when the Outsider came. Instantly I sensed that there was something different about him, even more than that he was wearing a suit and tie on a weekday. Sitting in darkness, indeed! He seemed so vibrant and alive that just standing there, he made things seem different. Could he have a drink of water, please? I ran to get it.

As I handed the cup to him, I noticed how soft and white his hands were, with the half-moon showing clearly on his fingernails and no dirt under the nails. He sipped at the glass gingerly. This was clearly not his first taste of the Virgin River water. Noticing my interest, he asked, "Is it all like this?"

"Yes," I said. "Only that out of barrels is worse. We don't mind it, but strangers always say that it tastes like a dose of epsom salts."

"A good comparison," he admitted, then added generously, "but this really *is* better." And he drank it quickly as an ordeal to get through.

It was still not sundown. If I would direct him to the home of some of my grandfather's descendants by his Indian wife, he would appreciate it very much. He was representing an eastern university where people of Indian extraction could get a free education, he explained. So I pointed out the house where Aunt Annie lived, just one block south, and Aunt Janet in the other direction about three blocks away.

So that was why he was here! I told Ma, and together we wondered how much he had learned from Pa on the trip over, but he evidently did know about Grandpa's five wives, and that one of them was an Indian girl. Pa likely wouldn't go into any detail of how Grandpa

[162]

had come to marry this girl, or what it had meant to the rest of the family to have Grandpa referred to by some of the uppity-ups as a "Squaw man." We had all been trained to call all of the wives Grandma.

Now here was this Outsider come to offer these children a very special opportunity not open to any of the rest of us. Some of the older grandchildren were already married, but others just might be interested. In any event, the fact that we knew what the Outsider was in town for cleared the air for us all.

Before long he was back. Ma showed him where he would sleep, and the toilet facilities, and told him to make himself at home. He seemed to sense that we would be more comfortable if he spent his time in the front room, so that is what he did, moving about it easily and casually as if he appreciated our efforts to have it attractive. He looked at the organ with its latticework and its display of nick-nacks, with my one boughten valentine in the center, and then sat down to it briefly and sounded out a few chords and ran a bit of melody with his right hand — not much, to be sure, but enough to show that he could play if he wanted to. I was so proud of that organ. There was only one other in the whole town, so when the Outsider said that it had a fine tone, I felt that he had paid a very special compliment. With him in it, the room did not look so grand as when our Mesquite relatives visited, though the organ did help to redeem it.

At supper he met all the children, repeated our names, and remembered them. He ate our homemade bread and new milk, with the extras of molasses and preserves and butter and cheese, as though he enjoyed it, except that he paused a little on the milk at first. Ma always apologized if she had to serve morning's milk, even though the cellar kept it quite cool. She thought that fresh milk was much more healthful and palatable; it was the way everyone else did, besides.

The Outsider made talk for us all, asking what grades we were in at school, and what we liked to do. He mentioned that on the way over the Mesa today he had seen his first mirage, and told how real the lake and trees and buildings looked, which led to our story of the Davidsons who had died of thirst about there, and of the dangers of mirages in general. He mentioned that he had traveled in Mexico

[163]

and South America, but had never before ridden over a desert stretch such as this. This gave the little boys a chance to tell him about Old Griz and how Pa had found him out there, just about dead, and everyone got into the conversation until it seemed almost like a party.

When Ma thought the younger ones should go to bed, he suggested that maybe we could have a little picture show first. So with just a bit of adjusting of the lamp and some clever use of his hands, he made shadow pictures on the whitewashed wall. With a running commentary, he gave such an interesting program that no one wanted him to stop, not even Pa.

After the younger ones had gone to bed and things were cleared away a bit, Ma said she thought she would go to the dance. The Outsider said he would like to look in on it too, if there were no objection.

While we got ready, the Outsider sat in the front room reading. Ma had hopefully set the Bible and the Book of Mormon out on the stand and two or three tracts explaining our faith. Whether he looked at them was not so important to her as whether she did her duty by making them available. In the meantime, Pa had gone out to the corral to check on the animals and to see that things were generally in order before he went to bed.

On this night I took special pains with my shoes, blacking even the heels, and using two stovelids of soot in the process — the back lids near the stove pipe, which were always best. I touched up my hair with a bit of butter and rubbed some talcum on my face with a flannel cloth. I would pinch my cheeks a little just before we got there to make them red.

The crowd was all gathered and the dance ready to begin when we got there. The benches had been pushed back around the walls, with the surplus ones stacked on the back of the stage. The lamps were all cleaned and filled, the tin reflectors behind them polished. The girls sat demurely on one side of the room and the boys on the other, while a few couples who were going steady stood together near the door. The Outsider did not know the rules of our dances, for he came along with us and sat on the women's side of the hall — our men would have dropped dead before one of them would have done that! But the doorkeeper had accepted his fifty cents without giving him a ticket, so that he could sit where he pleased.

Ma certainly did enjoy the dances. Besides the music and the activity, there was the chance to visit with other women, to note the new dresses and decide whether they were homemade or had come from Montgomery Ward or Bellas Hess. She had noticed who danced with whom, and how, and sometimes discovered a budding romance before the people were conscious of it themselves. She often held a baby while its younger mother shook off her cares in the wide whirlings of a quadrille, or she exchanged experiences with one in a shapeless "mother hubbard" who couldn't dance herself, but came along while her husband did. There was an unwritten rule that so long as he sat out the first and last dance beside his pregnant wife, a young man might dance as much as he cared to.

So on this night I sat between Ma and the Outsider, who was on the end of the bench near the stage. The musician, his hat pulled low over his eyes to protect them from the glare, was absent-mindedly pulling his accordion in and out in long, windy chords, as though he were tuning it up.

The floor manager stepped to the center front.

"Give us your attention, please, and we will begin this dance. Brother Bunker, will you offer the opening prayer?"

"Friends, Romans, countrymen, lend me your ears!" the Outsider said *sotto voce* to me. As Brother Bunker came forward, he offered the stock petition for such occasions, asking God to help us all to enjoy ourselves in wholesome recreation, and praying that no accident or evil might mar the activities.

"Fill up the floor for a waltz," the floor manager next called out.

The boys all hurried across the hall for their partners, and all promenaded arm in arm in a grand march until the floor manager gave the signal. This first waltz was precious and prolonged. Watching the musician, the Outsider imitated the jerky movement of the accordion and said, "Link-ed sweetness l-o-n-g drawn out."

It was as if he had shared with me a delicious tidbit. I knew that he did not make these up; he had found them in books.

As the dance went on, the men had to dance in turns and by numbers, either odds and evens or numbers 1 to 24 and 24 to 48. Each dance was repeated so that no one was cheated. Ambitious young men who wished to dance every time must either buy two tickets, or perhaps borrow one from an older man who would sit his out.

The calling of the dance was important in the selection of a partner, for one who could waltz well might become confused in a quadrille, and another who could do the one-two-three-kick of the schottische would be like a cow-in-tow on the polka. At the end of each dance the young man accompanied his lady to her seat and then returned to his own side of the hall.

Through it all the floor manager moved among the crowd, not dancing himself but seeing that none of the boys should "wring on" or get too rowdy, and keeping his eye on the conditions in general. Meanwhile the Outsider seemed mildly amused at the gusto with which the young men stamped and whirled and swung their partners.

During the intermission the floor was swept, two boys pushing the dirt ahead of them in a long windrow. A few couples walked out during this process, but most of the people remained in their places. The floor manager walked back and forth behind the sweepers, whittling off a candle and scattering the shavings. Someone called from the sidelines for a stepdance by Uncle Tom and Aunt Lene.

"Uncle Tom and Aunt Lene will do a double-shuffle," the manager called out without stopping his knife.

Uncle Tom was tall and angular; Aunt Lene was short and plump. Both had great-grandchildren, so should have given up dancing long ago, yet they came promptly to the center of the hall and faced each other. The accordian started, lively, staccato. They waited for the exact note, bowed deeply to each other, and began. Holding her skirt up slightly with one hand, Aunt Lene swayed gently as her feet did little shuttle steps in and out under the hem. Uncle Tom gyrated in a circle around her, one foot shuffling forward, the other kicking outward, one arm close at his side, the other flapping loosely in time with the kicking foot — the whole not unlike the preenings of an amorous turkey cock. There was a double figure eight, where they passed back to back in the middle of it; there were intricate cuttings in and out, until at the end, when they faced each other again and bowed.

The Outsider clapped and clapped, and even stamped his feet in approval too, as some of the others were doing. "Come and trip it as you go, on the light, fantastic toe," he said. "Truly a *fantastic* toe!" Then when the floor manager shouted for everyone to fill up the floor again, he said right out loud, "On with the dance! Let joy be unconfined!"

I was so thrilled to see how he entered into the spirit of the party. I knew that he was saying things out of books again, but such appropriate things! Such unusual things! Surely he was not one who had been sitting in darkness, and whatever light he had I wanted some of.

At last it was time for the Home Sweet Home waltz. Some of the married folks just waltzed as far as the door and went right on out so they'd not have to wait through the closing prayer. Others danced around once or twice before they escaped, so that by the time it was half done there was plenty of room on the floor.

The Outsider turned to me. "Would you like to try this one?"

Would I! I who had not danced at a grown-up dance in my life, would I like to dance with him, the best-dressed and handsomest man there! I stood up, but my heartbeat nearly deafened me. As we started, I looked down, because I didn't know where else to look.

"Don't watch your feet," he said softly. "Hold your head up. Listen to the music. Get the feel of it, and your feet will take care of themselves."

I did, and it worked. We went all the way around the hall twice without breaking step once, as though just by his skill he carried me along. I could not talk; I had nothing to say. He hummed the tune and kept his head up too, above mine.

As we started back to where Ma was still standing and visiting, I said, a little breathlessly, "Thank you. That was a new experience for me."

For a second he saw me. Then he quoted again: "All experience is an arch wherethro' Gleams that untravell'd world whose margin fades for ever and for ever when I move." He stopped as if at a loss to go on, then added, "You know. That *untravell'd* world."

We had stopped. His hand was on my arm just above the elbow, and I leaned against him just the least bit, hardly conscious that the door keeper had closed the door and was standing in front of it, that the floor manager had called on Brother Jones to say the closing prayer, and that Brother Jones had asked the crowd to "Please arise, and we will be dismissed." I stood with bowed head, not heeding the prayer but with "that untravell'd world whose margin fades for ever and for ever when I move" saying itself through my mind.

With the Amen, the door was opened and the general leave-taking made any further talk impossible. Outside I walked on one side of Ma, the Outsider on the other, down the road. He asked about the musician and about Uncle Tom and Aunt Lene, so that Ma had a good time explaining how things were in our town, even the using of the meeting house for the dance. Ma invited him to go to Sunday School, but he excused himself, saying that he had an early morning appointment that would prevent it.

Ma served breakfast to him and Pa by themselves the next morning while we were doing the chores. I guessed that he had met with no success in Aunt Annie's family, or any of the others. They did not want to be classed as Indians. They were not Indians; they were descendants of Dudley Leavitt, born under the Covenant and with special blessings already promised.

When I came in from Sunday School, he was gone. He had found a way back to Moapa with someone who was going, and he would get there in time to catch the night train, which would save a full day. My heart was like lead. I had thought that I would see him at dinner, at least, when we would have an ironed tablecloth on and Ma was serving chicken and noodles, her very best dish.

That afternoon I took the mail ponies down to the pasture and rode Selah back, coming by the hill road. It was just past sundown, so I rode to the top of my favorite knoll, where I could see far in every direction. At the west, the Mesa stretched endlessly, pink in the reflection of the evening light.

Out into the vivid sunset the Outsider had gone to Moapa. Where would he go from there? I realized that while he knew a great deal about me, I knew almost nothing about him, not even his name. I looked over my world here on the edge of the desert, its sun-blistered miles of rock and clay — a barren world, full of emptiness. I knew that there were places where grass and trees and flowers grew just for the fun of it, without having to be nursed along by irrigation. "That untravell'd world whose margin fades for ever and for ever when I move," I said to myself. Did that mean like chasing the end of the rainbow? Or like going off the road to find the greenery and water of a mirage? Or was it not the physical world at all to which the Outsider referred — but the world of thought, of knowledge?

So sitting astride my dappled pony, my bonnet on my shoulders, my braids undone, I studied this out and determined that I would see some of the world beyond the desert, that I would go to a college or a university or whatever it was that one went to in order to learn of books, and how to talk like books. I would not wait for life to come to me; I would go out to meet it.

As I watched the glory in the west bloom to such brilliance that it almost hurt to see it, and then begin to fade, it seemed almost like the bright spot which he had made in my life. Maybe when I was all grown up and out in the great world, just *maybe* I would meet the Outsider there, and I would be so changed that he would not know me. But I would tell him, and then he would remember. Just like a storybook.

Selah

"THERE'S A MAN HIDING IN THE BRUSH AROUND THE SALTGRASS PASTURE," I told Pa as he sipped his tea. "He puts his horse in every night after I take the cows home, and takes it out before I get back in the morning. He's been there two or three days now."

"What makes you think so?"

"Well, there are tracks around the gate, tracks of a big man and a big horse with no shoe on one front foot. I've noticed them fresh every morning, but forgot to tell you when you were in last time. This morning the water had run around the gate, and they were plainer than ever. He wears a big shoe, lots bigger than yours. The right one has a hole in the sole and the left one is cracked all across. The horse is big, too, bigger than Old Maje."

I could see that Pa was pleased with me. Part of it was that he had washed off the dust and grime of the mail run, and had downed one cup of tea. This always put him in a good humor. Then he was proud that I had been so observant. He himself had a reputation among his fellows for reading tracks. They would say that he could follow miles behind a herd and tell how many head were in it, what age and color they were, and whose brand they carried. Exaggeration, of course, but with some truth in it.

He studied a minute and then looked at me sharply.

"You ain't scairt of him, are you?" Pa had a scorn of fear.

"Well, no. Not exactly. But it makes me feel kinda funny, knowing that he is somewhere close around and likely watching me all the time. I hurry right on for fear I will see him. I think he knows that I know he is there."

"You don't have no call to be afraid. No grown man is going to harm a little girl like you. No man will molest a girl who don't invite it. If you know where you're going, and set out to go there, ain't no man going to stop you. It's the girl who dawdles along and giggles and accidentally drops her handkerchief that gets picked up. The girl that gets taken advantage of usually gives a come-on herself."

I knew Pa wasn't talking about me. He was thinking of another girl older than I who had come home to have a baby, and said that she was forced. Pa thought I looked too young. Though I was now thirteen going on fourteen, I was still skinny and flat-chested and wore my hair in braids, while many of the girls my age were young ladies.

Pa sipped his tea in silence for a minute and then decided.

"We've got plenty of good pasture," he said. "I don't think we'll miss what one horse eats during the night." Pa would be as glad to feed a hungry horse as a hungry man. Still he might have thought it important to know who was camping down in the brush at the bottom of the field and putting his horse into the pasture to feed every night.

It was such a good pasture that I left Selah there all the time, to husband the hay in the stack for winter. As the days got shorter and the weather colder, I'd ride her all the time. I'd usually call her and have some bit to give her, then race her around just for the fun of it. I'd stopped worrying about what her name meant, for no one else seemed to know its meaning, either.

It wasn't the horse eating our feed that troubled me, it was knowing that a man was hidden somewhere. At this time of year — early November — a man could live well in the lower fields. The days were still sunny and warm, the nights only cool. The last of the fall corn had not been all picked; there were roasting ears a-plenty. The casaba melons were not quite ready, but other melons were, and there were whole fields of squash and pumpkins ready for harvest. There were a few trees of late clingstone peaches along the fence line between Hardy's and Wittwer's land, and the brush was full of quail for anyone who knew how to trap them.

Saturday morning proved my intuition right. He was near and watching me every time I came down. I dragged the heavy pole gate just open enough to let the cows through, going ahead of them as usual to keep them going against another fence and into a second gate, this one a wire gate — into their pasture. It was an awkward setup, typical of Pa's slipshod farming. He had fenced off a part of the field for the cows, where there was some fodder left from the summer crops, with some clover and Johnson grass and other browse, but to get them there, I must herd them across the bottom of the lucerne, which was now heavy — just ready for its last cutting.

Usually I had no trouble, for the cows were slow, plodding things, and the distance only a few rods. This morning they must have sensed the stranger in the brush, for they came through on a trot and headed straight for the lucerne. Like one possessed, Old Brin ran past me right into it. The field was swampy with irrigation water, and to chase her I must tromp into the mud at every step. Then I hit a gopher hole and one leg went in to my knee. I fell, and came up with both arms mud to the elbow. I had been calling out and hollering at her; now I was crying with anger and frustration.

Suddenly he was there, standing just at the right place and waving his arms at the cows. He made no sound, but the animals now were docile and went obediently down through the opening into the pasture. Pretending not to see, I hunted for water enough to wash off my hands and arms and one muddy leg. I found enough for my hands only.

By this time the stranger had vanished — just disappeared entirely as though he had never been there. It took all the courage I could muster to go back and close the two gates — the wire one with the wooden arm around the upright, and the large, heavy outside pole gate — for the rule of the shut gate could not be broken for any reason whatsoever. Again I saw the tracks, familiar now, of the man who had come out to head the cows back.

I wondered a little about the Three Nephites who are said to be still upon the earth in their resurrected state, but this was a young man — a large young man with a heavy black beard and thick black hair.

I waited to talk this over with Pa, but he had sent the mail rig home from the Post Office, while he went to the town corral where the stock from the fall drive were held temporarily, and the men of town came to get their own. Saturday night I went to the dance with Ma, and got so interested in watching who danced with whom, and how, that I forgot all about the dark-complexioned man hiding in the brush.

Sunday morning I followed the cows to the field, happy and carefree. At the pole gate I stopped in amazement. There was the story as plain as if I had seen it enacted. Big man's tracks leading a big horse into the field and the same man's tracks leading Selah out! I was so stunned that I could hardly pull the gate open and follow the cows to lock them in. But these were my chores, and I did them automatically. In the middle of the field was a large, raw-boned horse with a saddle sore on his back. I sat on the ground against the gate, utterly bereft. For a while I was so full of self-blame that I couldn't even cry.

Why hadn't I told Pa that I *was* afraid of this stranger? Why didn't I go myself to Uncle Jess, the Sheriff, and tell him about this man hiding in the fields? Most of all, *why* hadn't I ridden Selah home last night as I had planned? She had come at my whistle, and I had ridden a couple of turns around the field, and then I had actually gotten out of the lane gate to ride her home by the hill road, but had come back and left her. At the sight of that raw-boned big horse in the pasture, I burst into tears, sobbing myself out on the ground.

What to do now? Get to Pa with this word as soon as I could; he would know what to do. So I started for home on the run, crying as I went, until a sharp pain struck me in the side and forced me to a slow walk.

In the back of my mind, I knew I was being foolish. The man had evidently left by dusk. If Selah survived the first twelve hours, her rider would have to seek a hiding place, with feed for her. He would stay with his pattern of traveling at night and hiding up in the daytime. But he was a big man and she was a little pony, and if he should whip her and force her beyond her strength until she should fall dead — the thought was torture.

I knew just what had happened last night. He had tried to catch Flax, the beautiful sorrel; next he would try the wily mail ponies, but they could easily evade him. Only Selah, gentle little Selah, who had known only kindness and affection, would allow the stranger to approach.

When Ma saw my swollen eyes and mottled face, she was frightened. "You silly girl," she said, "You'll kill yourself running so far. Crying and running won't get Selah back. You lie down there and compose yourself."

Ma tried to call Littlefield to tell them about the stolen pony and ask about a large, dark-complexioned young man. But the local operator said the line was out of order; it had evidently been cut during the night.

As soon as Pa came home, I started blaming myself. "I knew that I should bring Selah home last night. I got on her and started out the lane, but I remembered that you had said to leave her there, so I took her back. If I'd brought her home, he'd have managed to get one of the others."

Pa let me talk myself out, and then said kindly, "My girl, I think you should follow your hunches — that is, if you have a strong feeling you should pay attention to it, whether it goes against my counsel or anyone else's. But be careful. In general, it is better to do your assigned duty.

"You did the best you could. That is all any of us can do. But you must learn that life is full of sorrow and disappointments. When it comes, we must take it with patience. This may teach you to follow your own inner guide in the future."

So all the family went on to Sunday School, while I at home lived over the happy times I had spent with Selah on the hills in the spring evenings. By the time the family came home, I was partly reconciled.

The days wore into two weeks before we had any word of Selah. Uncle Herb, our mail driver from Bunkerville to Littlefield, came with the report that she had been left at the Amm Truman Ranch, away off the highway on the Mogotsu branch of the Santa Clara Creek. The rider had been a week going that distance, which meant short travel-stints and long rests. All this, I thought, was a direct answer to my prayers. The Trumans were pleased with the exchange, preferring Selah to the animal he had taken.

Alive and safe! What a joy! Now we could write some letters, and arrange for her return. The letter was mailed. Weeks passed, and no reply. Then Uncle Herb stopped in again to have breakfast with us before he started the up-the-river-run to Littlefield. We had just started to eat, when he said, "Amm Truman is in town. He had been drinking some last night and was saying that as sure as God lives, Hen Leavitt will never get that little mare back."

"Well, then, we'll never get her," Pa remarked quietly, "for God sure does live."

"Talk of the Devil and you'll smell the brimstone," Uncle Herb said, looking out the window. "Here comes Amm now."

Pa seldom waited for a friend to knock if he had seen him coming, so now he opened the door just as Amm reached the steps.

"How are you, Amm?" he said in his friendliest voice, holding out his hand. "Come on in. Will you join us at table?"

"I just et," Amm answered. "I'll wait out here. I'd like to talk to you alone."

Pa went right on out; I jumped up to the window to watch. I thought this was a conversation in which I might have something to say, but Ma insisted that I come back and finish my breakfast, or I'd be late for school. I waited to see the two men cross the street and settle themselves on the pole fence of the horse corral, side by side, their backs to the sun. They were both big men — over six feet tall — but Amm was broader through the shoulders than Pa. If there should be a fight, I'd bet on Pa, though, as being quicker and more agile. But this didn't seem to be an argument; it was more like a visit.

They were still there when I left for school, and Pa wasn't home at noon, so I had to wait until evening before I could learn about Selah. I saw him at the stackyard and hurried to talk to him.

"When are we going to get Selah back?" I asked eagerly.

"We are not going to get her back."

"But she is mine. You have no right to trade off my horse without even talking to me. You gave her to me, you know you did! And she is mine. You have no right — "

"You sit down and listen to me." Pa's voice was almost stern. "You're getting a big girl now. Don't act like a baby. Selah was yours as long as she was here, but she was stolen and taken away and that has changed everything. It wasn't my fault, nor yours, either, I guess. But it happened. That's how life is with everybody. We have something today and tomorrow it is gone, like the river taking the grain field, and Aunt Dora's baby dying so sudden. We have to face up to these things and take them the best we can.

"You fretted and grieved for fear the man would mistreat Selah. You always made that more important than getting her back. Well, it seems that your prayers were answered. The man took ten days to make it — evidently stopped at Johnson's fields one day and on to the Big Bend the next, then to Littlefield, then to the Beaver Dams, all of them only a few miles apart. The only long, hard ride was when he went over the mountains to the Santa Clara Creek. From there he took a day or two more before he got to the Truman ranch. He seemed to know the territory well.

"Amm said that Selah was in good shape, but the next ride to Modena and the railroad was a long, hard one, so he left Selah in Amm's corral and took a bigger horse, more like Old Bonyparts that he left here.

"Amm thought she was really a gift of the Lord. You see, his daughter died a month or so ago, and left two orphaned children, a girl and a boy — little children, one too young to go to school. You know how gentle Selah is with children — well, she was really a godsend.

"We could go to Las Vegas and take our replevin papers and hire a lawyer and take the matter to court, but it's just not worth it. We would get the pony back at too high cost — besides the money and the time, I would lose a lifelong friend, and two little children would cry more for her loss than you did.

"You are getting a big girl now. It's time you put away childish things. In a few months you'll be fourteen, and start in high school next fall. We'll have to start Melvin to look after the horses. When you want to ride, you can ride Flax, and maybe with some of the money we get from Selah, Ma can buy you a real riding skirt."

Pa didn't have to tell me anything about riding Flax; I knew from experience. But a split riding skirt! That would really be something — it would mean a saddle, too, like a real grown-up lady.

And I really was getting to be a big girl now. I knew that in more ways than Pa did. Only last Sunday afternoon as I was following the cows up the lane, I met two couples who had started down for a walk into the fields after meeting. They were taking shelter under the thick cottonwoods from a little skift of rain. It was hardly more than a sprinkle; I hadn't even noticed it.

"Here you! Come here a minute!" one of the girls called, as I came up alongside.

"Just look at this," she exclaimed, taking hold of my shoulder and pulling me around to face her. "Look! See what the rain has done to this kid's hair! Curled it all up around the edges and under the braids at the back. Here I spent an hour this morning with the curling irons and lamp trying to put some curl into mine, and the least bit of rain straightens it out like carpetrag strings. And she don't even know that she has curly hair." She began to loosen up my hair and push a wave in at the front.

"There!" She said at last. Now don't you ever pull your hair into tight braids again. Try to do something else with it. You just don't know how lucky you are!"

The rest of the way home, I had walked on air. I, with my skinny legs, and narrow face, and sallow complexion and big teeth suddenly had curly hair to compensate a little. All the world was rosy.

At night I studied it out about Selah. She would always be a warm glow in my heart and the central figure of many pleasant memories. But life was ahead. Life was exciting and wonderful. Several cars had come into town; one had signposts marking the new Arrowhead Trail from Salt Lake City to Los Angeles. One post was set right at the corner above our corral: SALT LAKE CITY 385 mi. with the arrow pointing east, and LOS ANGELES, CALIF. 385 mi. with the arrow pointing west. Here I stood just exactly halfway between those two great cities! Maybe I would get to visit them sometime, at least one of them!

Pa was right again. I must put away childish things.

PART TWO

That Untravell'd World

Bunkerville High

WITH TWO FULL YEARS OF HIGH SCHOOL and the promise of a full four-year curriculum, Bunkerville felt the need to improve its appearance. The townspeople were called in for public discussion as to what might be done to improve the living conditions. First, the swarms of flies and mosquitoes must be eradicated, and that could be done only by a united effort. In the fall the hordes were at their worst; we would design effective traps for the flies, and cooperate during the Christmas–to–New Year's holiday to see that every corral and pigpen in town was cleaned out and the contents spread over the alfalfa and grain fields.

Why not give some consideration for a town swimming pool? Since those that needed it most were the least able to pay, families could contribute either in labor or cash.

Another new idea was that the husbands might do the family wash. This had never been done! Girls were usually hired to provide extra help, or Indian women if they happened to be in town. But Erastus Romney spoke very frankly about it in the Priesthood Meeting. His wife was pregnant, and was not strong even when she was well.

"If you men think your work hard, just try to do the family washing. With all the barrels full a day or two ahead, you still must lift the heavy bucketfuls to the boil tub, the rubbing tub, and the rinse tubs. By the time you've handled all the sheets and pillowslips and towels, not to mention the underwear, scrubbed them on the washboard, stomped them in the boil tub, lifted them out into another tub to rinse out the soap, and into the blueing tub, you have handled every piece five times before at last you hang it on the line. That's real labor, not to mention taking them in, ironing and folding and putting them away. So I'm going to continue to help with our weekly laundry, and even take it over entirely if necessary."

While the eight grades all had their rooms, with an extra for the library and principal's office, the high school classes were held in vacant houses in town. The Lee house had two large rooms on the ground floor which made good classrooms. The band met in the empty Jones house east of the school building. The sewing class met in our upstairs bedroom. With the hall doors closed, the girls could enter without disturbing the family. There were six sewing machines, a long table for cutting out the patterns, and a supply box of threads, tapes, pincushions, marking pencils, and scissors. Mrs. Kelly was an expert, a perfectionist in every sense of the word, and every girl who worked under her came out with fine articles. Some of the women in town thought that this sewing class was the most important part of the school. The whole community was impressed with the dresses at graduation time.

There was no equipment for a cooking class, but in the class called "Homemaking" Mrs. Kelly taught basic principles so effectively that the girls never forgot them. "Anyone can boil an egg, but no one ever ought to do it," she often said, and to prove it she subjected an egg to such high heat that it became absolutely inedible, the white almost as tough as leather. This homemaking class was also permitted to travel by train to Las Vegas, and there go through modern homes and shops. The girls saw the furnishings and equipment in modern homes, such as some of them might later occupy.

In spite of all the difficulties, there is no way to measure the value of the high school to the whole community. It brought a new standard of cleanliness, in and around homes, along the public sidewalks, in corrals, and in garden plots. People became more clothes-conscious. And as the final two years of high school were added, a decided improvement was evident in all phases of public gatherings. There was a great change in recreation. The theater took on an added significance; even the Halloween programs seemed more thrilling and frightening.

Behind it all was the determination of Mr. Kelly that those who graduated from this little school would be prepared to enter any college in the country.

When school opened in the fall of 1914, I was in the third year of high school. The town wanted to impress upon the state officials that ours was a fast-growing high school without a home, rather than a few students doing post-elementary work, so we moved away from the elementary building entirely and set up our headquarters in the old rock church, two blocks away. The church officials had arranged to hold services in the largest of the grade school rooms, and to turn their building over to us.

The church building was inconvenient for a school; it was large, high-ceilinged and hard to heat. One classroom was built by the expedient of lowering the curtain which had been used for theater, and hanging the side drapes. Thus the class on the stage was cut off from view of the main hall, but the teacher's voice was quite audible from the farthest corner. With one class in session on the stage and another around the stove in the center of the hall, the students at the few study desks in the back of the building had to exercise all their powers of interest and concentration to make their preparations.

In addition to the church house, we had a school room upstairs in a nearby home, where long tables and a blackboard accommodated the algebra and geometry classes in the morning.

Our English class was held in the woodshed outside. Though the corrugated tin roof would keep out the rain and the sun, the walls of mesh chicken wire were small protection against the wind, and the door was merely an opening between two cedar posts. We met daily here at one o'clock, by which time the sun had usually warmed our classroom so we didn't need our coats. Being outside, there were often diversions: Inquiring sparrows hopped about; blackbirds settled in undulating swarms in the tithing office yard across the street; when the warm days came, there were lizards, little gray ones with beady eyes and wide mouths and turned-in toes, and black-collared bull lizards whose green bellies, covered with a thin wash of gold, glistened in the sunshine. Still later, a nest of flying ants broke up one of our classes. By any standard, a poor classroom, yet many of the most profitable classes I ever attended were held there. We were introduced to Hamlet and MacBeth, to Adam Bede and Silas Marner and David Copperfield, to Portia and Jane Eyre and Christabel.

Because of the conditions inside, we took up our study hall on the woodpile or at the base of a cottonwood tree, or on the back steps. I had my own private place in the tithing hay shed, where the faithful farmers had brought every tenth load of hay and filled the open barn to the rafters. I hollowed out a place on the south side near one of the large uprights, where by curling up a little I could keep my back to the afternoon sun and my book in the shadow. Here I read my history and economics and German assignments. Here I lost myself completely in the books that were suggested as outside reading in English.

One day I became so absorbed in *Ivanhoe* that I did not hear the bell that marked the change of class, and came to myself only when the shadows were long and I was cold and the book finished. At another time, Mr. Kelly, evidently noticing that a wide board had been broken from the fence and that it marked the beginning of a well-worn trail leading to the barn, discovered me. I was in some far land, weeping copiously over the ill fortunes of some character, only dimly conscious that Mr. Kelly had walked past. He pretended not to notice me, but later asked me if I didn't think that I should study where I could hear the bells, and not miss my economics class so often.

The whole arrangement was not so haphazard as it sounds, and for me it was a very good school, with every day full of something challenging and new. Never before had I read with such omnivorous delight, getting at books that had meat in them, something to set the teeth into, rather than the mush and custard that had formed my reading diet so largely before.

It seemed that all my life and interest were tied up in school. I ate at home and slept there; I helped with the morning and evening chores; I did my share of the washing and ironing and housecleaning. But my heart was not in the home work. For the first time it seemed that the margins of the untravell'd world had opened and expanded and stretched away to something comparable to what the Outsider had suggested by the manner in which he quoted the lines I had never forgotten.

I never lacked for partners or fun at the dances, but I had no regular, steady beau, perhaps because no one had singled me out for marked attention, and I had not set my heart on any particular boy. Perhaps Pa's admonitions were responsible in part, for without seeming to do so, he kept me conscious of my relations with the boys by occasional comments made as we stood together at the corral fence or waited for a horse to finish his grain. (With all my growing up and my school interests, I still kept in touch with the animals.)

"I wish you could have heard the talk on the ditch today," he once said. "I'd hate to have the fellows discuss my daughter like they did one girl this afternoon. If she knew the things the boys say about her, she'd be less free with her favors.

"Nobody wants a girl that everybody can handle. She's like a peach. After a few have squeezed it, it gets soft and rotten and nobody wants it. If a fellow respects you, he may learn to like you; if he doesn't, he'll still respect you."

Without elaboration, without further preaching, Pa dropped such remarks and changed the subject, leaving me to ponder them as I might.

The first graduation in 1915 was a stirring thing for us. Seven of the original fifteen students completed four full years of high school and received their diplomas. The graduating exercises were held in the old rock church, and the graduates had class rings and printed programs. The members rendered musical numbers and gave the class will, the prognostication, and the valedictory address to a much impressed audience. We all felt that the town of Bunkerville had passed a milestone.

The fall I entered my fourth year of high school, we were still holding classes in the rock church, but we had a promise from the state of a new building. One afternoon in mid-winter we were in class on the stage behind the curtain, the most desirable of all the "rooms," warmer, smaller, not too well lighted, with no view out of windows. Suddenly there was the sound of running feet up the body of the hall, Lem's head between the main curtain and the side pieces, and his voice like a trumpet shouting, "We've won! We've won! The boys are the champions!"

We all came up as by an electric shock, our bodies and our voices rising at the same instant. It was too good to be true! It just couldn't have happened to us! Our little school, with scarcely enough fellows to make a team, had won the basketball championship of all Nevada! We hurried out of the room to scatter the good news throughout the town.

The word had come by mail, and the boys would be close on the heels of the letter. We must all go out to meet them and escort them in with the ceremony befitting such heroes.

The boys would be coming in by car, not the mail car which had taken the place of Pa's buckboard and trotting ponies, but a private car which they had used to reach the railroad station. With feverish haste we made ready, teams and wagons, one car decorated with bunting and flags for the boys to ride in, one for the Bishop and school officials, one for the band, now lessened in numbers because some of the team usually played in it. We all traveled together out onto the road to the top of one of the hills three miles from town. There on the barren slope, in the midst of the sage and cactus, we waited.

Again and again we told each other that this could not be true. We had all thought Mr. Romney was a little extreme when he got the fellows out to practice basketball on the outdoor court at daybreak every morning. Parents complained that boys who normally could not be dragged out to do their chores now went to bed at dusk and got up without any call other than the ringing of the bell before daylight. They would have started their practice earlier, but they had to wait until it was light enough to see. For an hour they played, to come home all reeking wet with sweat, rinse off in a wash basin and sponge off the best they could, do their chores, eat breakfast, and go back to school. They might doze in the afternoon classes, written assignments might be copied or skipped, but nothing could interfere with this morning basketball schedule. Now it had paid! *How* it had paid! The smallest school in all Nevada the basketball champions, a school without a building to its name, in a town that at least 99 percent of the people of the state had not known existed until now.

We talked it all over among ourselves, the parents who had objected most to the training schedule now being most puffed up and proud. Finally the fellow on lookout signaled that the car was coming. The band struck up a tune; Mr. Kelly and the other members of the faculty stepped into the middle of the road and stopped the approaching car, transferred the boys into the decorated one. After another band number, we proceeded in triumphal procession to the meeting house, where we heard the report of the trip.

The fellows, shy and awkward and self-conscious on the stage, spoke briefly, but Mr. Romney told us what we wanted to hear. The boys were not used to bright electric lights and slick floors and big crowds, he said, but they knew how to find the hoop, and they were in perfect physical condition. Since none of them had ever used tobacco or liquor in any form they could simply run their opponents down. Surely now the state officials must recognize the fact that we had a high school; surely now they would not deny us a building.

When it came time to graduate that spring of 1916, I felt my whole world falling apart. I was through high school. I could not come back here and study, and my crowd was scattering. I felt sure that I could not go away to school, for with nine younger children, Pa had all he could do without financing school for me. So my graduating day was a miserable one for me. Behind me were four happy years, years of achievement and growth and happiness. I felt as though I stood on the edge of a cliff, unable to go either forward or back.

Things certainly did have a way of working out, however. The basketball team had drawn attention to the Virgin Valley, and at the same time that we hoped for a high school building, Mr. Kelly announced that we were to have a Normal Training Course established in Bunkerville. Students who completed the training would receive a certificate to teach two years in the elementary schools of the state. In a burst of pride, Nevada had realized that she imported practically all of her teachers, and had resolved that if any native sons or daughters wanted to qualify to teach school, they would receive help. From our class and the one that had graduated the year before, there were eight who signified their desire, and so a teacher was assured.

Pine Valley Summer

How should I spend the summer? Pa was quite set against any of us going to Las Vegas to work. Ella Hafen had been living with us this winter; now she would like it if I would come with her to spend a couple of weeks.

We had a puzzle that we sometimes confused our friends with regarding the relationship of Mother, Aunt Rosina, and Ella: "Mother and Ella are sisters; Rosina and Ella are sisters; but Mother and Rosina are only cousins." Sounds crazy, doesn't it? Mother and Ella had the same father; they were Hafen girls. Rosina and Ella had the same mother, who was married to Grandpa Hafen after her first husband, Henry Blickenstorfer, died. Grandpa Hafen, in accordance with the doctrine of polygamy, took five wives, these two among them. Aunt Rosina's mother was married first to Henry Blickenstorfer, and had two children, a son named for his father and Rosina herself. Then came a plague among the young men and Rosina's husband and brother died within days of each other, leaving her the only one with the Blickenstorfer blood in her veins. She then married Henry Gubler, by whom she had two sons, Archie and Clement, and who later died in a similar plague. After some fifteen or sixteen years, Rosina was married to Ben Blake, whose wife had died leaving a large family, several of whom were married. Rosina gave Ben Blake three more children: Hazel, Ina, and Cecil.

With this setup, Aunt Rosina didn't need company, but when we wanted to go to the ranch at Pine Valley, we were more than welcome. After many summers at the ranch, the older Blake girls wanted no more of it, but Marie was glad to be wherever her father, Aunt Rosina, and the younger children were. Both Ella and I thought it would be right romantic to go to the top of the high mountain and to help with the work at the ranch, including the chores of milking and making butter and cheese. Ella had some fancy needlework items to finish, and I smuggled in a copy of *Oliver Twist* which I had only started before I became involved in graduation routines.

The ranch at Pine Valley was always referred to as the Blake–Gubler Ranch, because the two men had joint ownership of the spring, using the irrigation water in turns. Their homes were about a half-mile apart, with a deep swale between them, the corrals of both on the side farthest from the other. Both raised large fields of alfalfa, potatoes, squash in several varieties, corn, and small garden stuff for their own tables, with carrots to last far into the winter.

When we arrived in May, the potatoes, squash, and other garden stuff was thrifty. The Blakes were milking eight cows, which meant butter, cottage cheese, and some few small pressed cheeses to ripen for winter. Here is where I made myself useful, for I knew how to milk and how to handle the calves. Clem appreciated my help, whether anyone else did or not, for the bulk of the milking fell to him.

Royal (Ral to us) was there, too, but he was working on top of the mountain, getting timber out, long pine poles which he would drag by team to the edge of the cliffs that encircled the mountain top. He pushed them over, end-wise, and "snaked" them down the steep incline to the bottom, where they would be loaded onto regular lumber trucks and taken to the sawmill.

Our trip to the top of Pine Valley Mountain was a most thrilling experience. I had read about "This is the forest primeval, the murmuring pines and the hemlocks . . ." but now — right here it was! The tall, tall trees, the grass and flowers in the clearings, the pools of water newly-melted, and all more beautiful than could be put into words. At "Further Water," a spring bubbled out which went to the eastern area below, and the earth fell away and stretched into eternity toward the Virgin River and Zion Park. I could absorb it, but there were no words with which to describe it. Not for anything would I have missed this experience.

A few nights later, Brother Mart McAllister came to visit. He was a forest ranger, having to do with the amounts and kinds of lumber taken off the mountain. Seeing the organ, he seated himself and struck a few chords. Soon he was singing "Bonnie Annie Laurie" to his own accompaniment, but he seemed unable to make the right changes. Then seeing the song book *101 Best Known Songs*, he leafed through it and turned to ask if I played the organ. "A little," I told him. The fact was that I knew them all, and could play them well.

He began with "Bonnie Annie Laurie," went on to "Drink to Me Only with Thine Eyes," and on to almost every song in the book. He sang well, too. He was tall and big-boned, without any middle-aged sagging in front. In his day, he must have been a really romantic figure, I said to myself. Though I saw him once more, I never played the organ for him again. I went home. All because of "the Cedar Post."

Early in the season Uncle Ben and the boys had fenced in the large garden spot, including the potatoes and squash. They had used cedar posts set quite far apart, with a coarse net between, large enough for cats or rabbits to go through but too small for pigs or dogs. The pattern of chores was to turn the cows out in the morning and drive them to the east and north, where there was water and fair feed. In the evening and again early in the morning they would be fed hay.

The calves were driven along the garden fence to the west and south where there also was fair range feed. Sometimes they would work their way back to the corral by milking time. On this day the sun was getting low, the pony was saddled and bridled at the hitching post, so when Clem suggested that I go down and round up the calves, I was quick to take the chance.

If I had followed my own inclination, I'd have pulled the saddle off and ridden bareback, but I thought that maybe her back would be all wet with sweat. The saddle was big — high and heavy in front and built for a man with a much fuller figure than mine. The stirrups

[191]

were too long, so I fitted my feet between the straps on top of them. They were now too short. Again I considered taking that saddle off, and was about to do it, but up here girls didn't ride bareback.

Though the calves were scattered, I soon had them rounded up, a herd of about twelve, for some were yearlings that wanted the evening feed of hay. They had made a beaten path running along the wire fence, and I noted that while the wire was fastened onto the large bottom pole with staples, it was laced to the willow poles along the top with baling wire going round and round only inches between.

The calves had trotted along ahead of me, while I stopped to adjust one foot in the strap, and to fasten my hat more securely under my chin.

Suddenly, right in front of me, was that top willow pole out three feet at least. Instinctively I braced my feet, threw out both hands and grasped it firmly. A split second and a loud CRACK. The cedar post broke at the ground level and went down easily, relieving all the pressure and setting me free. I was weak and spent, as though in that instant I had drained every ounce of my energy. I was troubled, too, about the broken cedar post.

I rode over to where Clem was, near the corral.

"I'm afraid I'm in trouble," I told him. "I broke off that cedar post on the corner, right down to the ground. Come over and see. I didn't mean to; it just happened."

Clem immediately climbed up on the corral fence and called Ral, who was already on his way. Then he pulled out his red handkerchief and waved it to attract the attention of Mart McAllister, who was going toward the house. Mart evidently passed the word to Brother Gubler, who also came.

"Let's not move anything until Dad gets here," Clem suggested.

"Well, I helped to set that corner post," Ral said, "and we wanted it to stand till the Millennium. Dug the hole deep and tamped it in solid. It's a new post, not touched by bugs or rot. Funny how all those little splinters in it stand up so straight." Ral seemed to be talking to himself.

"I'm sorry," I said. "I didn't mean to do it."

"Sorry! Sorry and be damned!" Ral broke in. "You'd better fall on your knees and thank God you're alive to tell it. Where would you have come out if that pole *hadn't* give way? Just turn that over in your mind!"

"Well, if you ask me, either your pituitary gland or your guardian angel, or both, were on the job. There's more here than meets the eye." That was Mart's conclusion.

"Your hundred-and-ten-pound weight and them skinny arms of yours'd need some reinforcement from somewhere . . . to break off a post of that size," Clem added.

"We've witnessed a miracle here this day," Mart McAllister said solemnly.

When Uncle Ben came, he didn't try to reason. "I was looking at that willow pole just last night," he said, "and thought then that it might be a deathtrap for someone, but I thought I'd need the saw instead of the ax. I had the ax with me, too, to sharpen the ends of the bean stakes, so I should have cut it off then, but them long willows is so tough that you can't faze 'em without a solid block under 'em. Now that it's down, we'll cut it off right here, and then lift that post into place again and brace it a little higher."

It seemed all quite simple. I knew that I wasn't needed here, so I said I'd go on over and put the calves in the pen.

I decided that I'd not say anything about this to Aunt Rosina; she would get all stirred up, and so would Ella. Instead, I suggested that I'd like to go back to town with Ral when he took his lumber down. I just might get a way back home to Bunkerville, and maybe go on to the Muddy Valley.

I studied about the cedar post most of the night: If I had followed my own promptings, I'd have taken off that saddle. Then when I came to that pole, I'd have no doubt grasped it just as I did and let the horse run on without me, and then have just dropped to the ground unhurt. But in that saddle, I was perfectly helpless. The short stirrups were my salvation, though, for they braced my whole body and gave the needed leverage to twist off the post, a fact which I could hardly believe myself even though I had experienced it. My guardian angel seemed as good an answer as any.

Miss Mina Connell

MISS CONNELL WAS SLENDER AND TRIM, carrying her long braid of auburn hair around her head like a coronet. She had with her boxes and boxes of material which she had shipped by express ahead to use in her work. These had been taken directly to the Relief Society house, which we were to use this winter. Miss Connell wanted us to be apart and away from the high school entirely, and the Relief Society sisters figured that the rent offered for the building would far exceed any that they could raise, no matter how many quilts or pieces of fancywork they could offer for sale in a bazaar.

So it was that Miss Connell, fresh from Columbia University, took over a week before the term began, and had the place really attractive before the school opened. The year before there had been eight high school graduates, several of whom joined our class of five to make a total of eleven. We each had an individual desk, besides a drawer in which to keep material that we wished to save for our work the next year.

Our first assignment was to write a personal letter to Miss Connell, telling her anything about ourselves that we felt she should know — our aims, our weaknesses (if we thought we had any), and the areas in which we would like to work after we had finished the course.

She had made it clear in her introduction that the state would guarantee employment to every person who would be graduated.

This, of course, could not be determined until the end of the year, for too often potential teachers got cold feet and decided that teaching was not for them. She insisted that the standards here should be equal to any other training school in the state, or even in the nation.

I had applied for and received the janitor work for the winter. Miss Connell was to have as long as two hours after the class was dismissed in which to work unmolested, which meant that I would go home, get a bite to eat, change my dress, and be back by five o'clock. Usually she was still there when I arrived; often it seemed that she waited for me to come, for there were things she wanted to ask about. First, she was not interested in the Church; her whole business was to conduct a school. But she was interested in our folkways and in our speech patterns. When I saw that she was making a collection, I became interested, and helped her fill in her little book.

MISS CONNELL'S BUNKERVILLE-EZE

Sun-up and *sun-down*, instead of *sunrise* and *sunset*.

Drug, used as a verb: they *drug* off dead animals.

Kittern, to cut diagonally cross-lot.

To *grain* the horses, *slop* the pigs, and *strip* the cows. *Stripping* used instead of *milking* meant laborious work to get the last drop.

Spondulix, hard money, silver coins

P D Q, Purty Dam' Quick.

Pike-away, Indian for get-the-hell-outta here; be gone! Pronto! in all haste!

Yake-away, Indian for "he is dead," permanently gone.

Don't stand there like the fifth calf! A cow can accommodate only four calves at a time. The fifth calf is simply doomed unless someone comes to his rescue and forces each of the others to surrender his place for a few minutes, at least.

A person in too much of a hurry would be admonished: *"Don't get your shirt off!" "Hold your horses!" "Don't get into a sweat!" "Don't get all hot and bothered!"*

The word *Petered* was used in many connotations. I'm "Petered" if I'm completely worn out, without one drop of energy left. A program begun with great enthusiasm and zeal, and then dropped, *peters out*.

[195]

The reference is evidently to Peter of Old who was so zealous in his love of Jesus that he cut an ear off a soldier, and then later, when he was accused of being a follower, said, "I know him not."

Chuck-ne-bucks, tall tales which everyone enjoys, but nobody believes. The more ridiculous, the better.

A woman in anger at her husband might *Give him a good dressing-down, A Scotch Blessing*, or *a raking over the coals*.

Paid in chips and whetsones refers to men who in good faith cut trees and dragged them to the lumber mill, expecting to get their pay in lumber, but are left with the leftovers, chips, and whetstones with which to sharpen their axes to cut some more; to be beaten in a bargain.

Certain titles were applied: *Windy Bill* spoke at great length, many words but little matter; one man given to laying down the law was called *"You tell 'em, Moses"*; another, *"Cut it fine; stir it well; spread it thin!"* for by the time he was through, there would be no time for anyone else.

Helping Zeke: Zeke was one of several unfortunates who went to work in the mines at Delamar, and got "Delamar Dust." This silica-loaded dust lodged in the lungs, and meant slow but certain death. In the meantime they constituted what we called the *Spit and Whittle Row*. A farmer passing one day asked Zeke, "What ya doin' today?" "Nawthin'" was the answer.
"What you doin' today, Soapy?"
"Helpin' Zeke."

One story said to have originated in Bunkerville concerned an athletic coach. Smoking was forbidden by both the Church and the athletic rules, but he always was able to manage one in the privacy of the outhouse; perhaps he had several if he felt the need.

Aunt Vina Bunker ran the hotel-boarding house in Bunkerville, for she was an excellent cook and an immaculate housekeeper. One day she washed her living room drapes in gasoline, hung them on the line, and poured the dirty gasoline into the hole of the outhouse. Later, the coach, comfortably settled, lit a cigarette and flipped the match into the hole beside him. The instant explosion lifted the building off the ground and tipped it over several feet away.

No damage was done, except to the reputation of the coach, who explained lamely, "It must-a been something I et!"

As for Miss Connell, she put in long hours at the school, but she never left the house for walks or to attend meetings of any kind. She played the piano well, both for her own entertainment and to accompany any of the guests who enjoyed singing; she wasn't given to talking about herself, so that Aunt Vina had very few items of interest. What could you tell about a lady who kept her own room clean, and locked it whenever she went out, if it was only to run over to the Post Office?

But she did talk to me — not about herself, of course — but of some of our folkways, remedies in sickness, practices in planting the plants that mature underground during the dark of the moon, those whose fruit is above the ground in the light of the moon, or during the growing moon. I myself did not believe in all these things, though I had seen the brand on cattle grow to a great size, said to be because it had been put on during the growing moon.

As for her, her one driving aim was that this class would measure up to the standard expected of teachers, that they should leave as well equipped to meet the problems of the small rural schools where they would be employed as she could make them.

For some time I had been organist in Sunday School. My cousin, Bert Leavitt, was called to be chorister. Although we lived just a block apart, I hardly knew Bert to speak to him. He was in an older crowd. Now, in this first public call, he felt that he should come early every Sunday morning to select the songs and run through each enough to get used to the tempo and pitch. We — or he — would decide what we would sing, and I always agreed. We would walk over together early to see that everything else was in order.

Then after several months, the ward organist, Ivie Cox Leavitt, became pregnant, and the folkway in our town demanded that after a woman began to "show," about the fifth month, she did not appear in any public program. She might attend, and usually did, but she remained seated in the audience; she did not give a lesson or stand in front to be conspicuous. This meant that I should be organist in meeting, too, for the next six months. After that she would return, for this was her position, and she was much better prepared for it than I.

This also meant that we ran through the songs the choir would practice, and since this was at night, Bert would come to go through the songs as usual, and then walk me home at the close. Before we realized it, we were going steady, and becoming altogether too fond of each other. Our two fathers were brothers: that is, Uncle Ab was a son of Grandma Maria Huntsman and Pa's mother was Thirza Riding. That was better than if we had been descended from the two Huntsman sisters, but even that was too close.

Our two fathers evidently decided that we should be separated before it should become more difficult. Some of the local boys had volunteered to go to the army; one or two were drafted, but Bert was called on a mission, which would mean a full two-year absence. Few romances could survive that. I always felt that the call came as a result of a suggestion to the Bishop from either my father or his — or both.

As I remember it, Bert left for his mission in late March or early April 1917, and though for a while I was very lonely, I soon adjusted. So many things were happening to be excited about. For instance, a company making the Arrowhead Trail came into town, called a public meeting, and told us of the new highway to connect Salt Lake City with Los Angeles. Here we would be less than half a mile from this great thoroughfare. True, the Virgin River would have to be bridged, but that would come in time, and until it did, they wanted a reliable man with a good team to camp at the river and haul the cars over. Most of the time the water was shallow, but the bed was of shifting sand, and most people would prefer to pay a reasonable fee to be taken across than to risk driving. Somehow Pa and others secured that job for Uncle List. As travel increased, it became so lucrative that other teams took over for part of the time.

Our school work became more interesting, too, as we began the "practice teaching program." Mr. Kelly was now County Super- intendent, which made him directly responsible for hiring all teachers up to the eighth grade. Uncle Roy — "Mr. Hafen" to us now — helped to select the teachers who would work with him in the high school.

I was so pleased that Priscilla Leavitt was appointed to take first and second grades in Bunkerville, while I got the third and fourth grades when the time came to place the Normal School graduates. I don't remember who had the other positions, but I think it was teachers who had been there and were permitted to stay. However that was, Miss Connell's promise was kept. Every graduate was signed for a school somewhere.

Then, too, when Mr. Kelly interviewed me, he suggested that I borrow money if I needed to, to take me away for the summer. I would have a change, and it would be better all around. Did he know that Uncle Roy was planning to go to Berkeley for a part of the summer session there?* However it happened, my cousin Leah Leavitt and I were hooked to go with the Hafens to share expenses and housework and baby care, and take some courses at the University of California.

We would drive the Hafen car to Salt Lake City and leave it there in the garage of a friend, while we rode the train to Berkeley. I had been to Salt Lake City once before with a group of Mutual Improvement Association girls to Conference, but we didn't get far from the Temple Square Hotel or the temple grounds across the street. Now we visited the railroad depot, and the University being built on the elevation far to the east of the city. Every minute was exciting.

Our train ride was more exciting because it took us across the Lucin Cutoff, where the elevated tracks rattled us along on the trellis above the water, literally water, water, everywhere, nor any drop to drink. Beyond the lake was a long stretch of the Nevada desert. To arrive at Carson City and Reno was to repeat among ourselves the stories of our basketball team, trained by before-sunrise practice on the ground, and leading every team in the state in scoring and sportsmanship.

Most impressive of all was the road through the mountains with the giant trees, one so large that the train ran right through it, leaving enough timber on both sides and in the top to insure its life.

How we secured our living quarters, I did not know. The Hafens evidently had friends who had at least two places available that they might have a choice. My memory is of a two-story house, the lower one facing the street in front and coming up four or five steps to the

---

*Uncle LeRoy Hafen later became director of the Colorado Historical Society and a distinguished scholar of Western American history.

street level, while ours upstairs opened to the back with a closed-in deck at the entrance and stairs down to a trail which was a cut-off to a lower street directly to the campus.

We split all expenses four ways: rent, food, utilities, and shared the work in turn, all cooperating on the whole family wash, ironing, and cleaning. Every Saturday we tried to finish most of the routine tasks so that we might spend Sunday sightseeing. This meant riding the ferry across the bay to San Francisco. If we thought Salt Lake City awesome, we were frightened by San Francisco's narrow lanes between walls that reached up and up.

We all preferred the open parks in Berkeley where Norma could run, and we could sit or sprawl on the grass. One Saturday afternoon we had been shopping in a little market nearby, and as we were on the way home, I saw two young men across the street. Instantly I knew they were Mormon elders.

"Let's watch them," I suggested. "At the last house, the shorter one rang the doorbell and gave his little speech to the landlady. Next time the taller one will take his turn."

It took only the one time more to convince us, so we brazenly cut across to come out just ahead of them on the next stop.

"Aren't you Mormon elders?" Leah asked.

"What makes you think so?" the taller one asked.

"You looked the part, and you seemed to be carrying on the business of tracting according to the plan."

We introduced ourselves and told them we'd like to come to church if we could find it. At this, they each gave us a name card with the Articles of Faith on one side, and the elder's name on the other, along with the address of the chapel.

"We always catch the bus at six o'clock. There's one every fifteen minutes, so you can get there OK. We take this because it is early and it gives us time to greet the people as they come. Some go on the earlier bus, but most come on the one later — don't make much difference so long as you get there."

So we set out the next Sunday night, but we didn't catch the six o'clock one or the next one either. When at last we got out, we didn't know what direction to go; as we stood in indecision we heard the strains of "How Firm a Foundation," being sung by an audience in an upstairs room. We found the steps and slipped into the room as quietly as we could. For the next hour, we would be truly home again, with the familiar songs, the sacrament service, and the extemporaneous sermons. As the members of the audience greeted us at the close of the service, we promised them and ourselves that we would come again. But we did not; we spent every other Sunday sightseeing. There were only a few left, and there was so much to see.

We learned about the Market Square and took our half-gallon glass jar to get peanut butter. The nuts were ground and ran directly into the jar while we watched and waited. It was simply delicious, especially when mixed with the fresh honey which we took away by the two-quart bottle.

We visited the area of the past World's Fair, where some buildings were still standing, and where a theater was presented in an out-of-door auditorium. We saw Fishermen's Wharf, but we enjoyed as much as anything an afternoon at the park where our cousin, Laman Leavitt, joined us. Laman was tall, dark, and handsome; he looked impressive in his uniform. Ann's cousin, Irvin Harmon, and his wife were also a part of the group, and we made plans for other activities.

When we left California, we didn't know that Stake Conference was being held in Panaca on the last weekend of August. I had been notified in the spring that I would be expected to work in the M.I.A., so I should be in attendance. I at once telephoned Brother Ira Earl, Stake President, and he said he could take me in his car — one of the brethren had decided at the last minute that he could not leave. My parents were to be there, and I would go home to Bunkerville with them.

Panaca was a distinctly Mormon village, with uniform square blocks with picket fences and open ditches bordering the sidewalks, supporting poplar trees or cottonwoods. The lots were each a quarter-of-a-block, which made room for corrals and outbuildings, a vegetable garden and some fruit trees — not enough to be called an orchard, but enough to supply a family.

The public square held the Meeting House, made of brick and in the regular New England pattern, with a set of ten to twelve steps up to the main auditorium, long windows and a stage with pulpit, sacrament table to one side, and recorder's table on the other, the choir in tiers at the back. Classrooms were in the basement.

The Meeting House was the heart of the block, with its tower and steeple and bell, and its imposing size and structure. To the side and back was the Relief Society house, a smaller one-room auditorium, with storage space of shelves and built-in closets for quilts and quilts-in-the-making — blocks, linings, cotton batting, etc. And in accordance with the advice at the time, they had a smaller storage room in which were bins for gleaned wheat and barley, dried fruit, almonds, and sometimes a few pumpkins or squash. It was the duty of the sisters to have items for the poor in the ward, and to be able to raise money at dances by selling pies made from their own store.

Thanks to the energetic sisters in Salt Lake City, who traveled and preached preparedness for any emergency — earthquakes, floods, pestilence — these precautions were taken; some of the houses still remained in the rural wards. And Panaca was one of these.

Since my parents had been sent to Bishop Edwards' home, I went there, too. I could sleep with the family girls upstairs.

Brother Edwards met the evening train, but there was no Apostle on it.

"It's just as well," he said at supper. "Apostle Smith is a good man on doctrine, but he is not an inspirational speaker. Our folks here say that Harvey Sprague is second only to Melvin J. Ballard in his ability to hold and move an audience. Some say that Harvey is better. I only know that I've traveled with Brother Sprague, and I've never heard him repeat a speech. Every one is different; each one is for that particular audience. Every one goes home to every person in the house, as though it was meant for him. I, for one, am not at all disappointed not to have a speaker from Salt Lake City. We'll get along just fine."

Saturday's meetings were for the officers of the various auxiliary groups: Sunday School, Primary, Mutual Improvement Association, in which the winter's program was discussed and the necessary manuals and texts were handed out. These meetings were conducted by the Stake officers.

The evening was a get-acquainted social and dance. Our wards were so widely scattered that the young folk were all strangers to each other. The main objective here was to help the young people get acquainted. Brother Dan Heaton was in charge, and since the object was to get to know each other, he had two tables, with an adult at each provided with three-by-five-inch cards and heavy marking pencils. Each person's name and home town were plainly written, large enough and black enough to be read at a distance, and pinned on his left breast.

When the crowd had gathered, Brother Heaton called for all to arise, and for all the girls to form a circle, holding hands, in the center. The boys, also holding hands, formed a circle outside. The music struck a lively tune; the girls were to go clockwise, the boys counterclockwise. At the signal from the whistle they all stopped, and the boys, still holding hands, threw their arms over the girls nearest them, broke their hold, and took one for a partner. Since there were more girls than boys, the extra girls remained in a group in the center of the hall, where they should remain until the whistle signaled, and then each might tag a boy she wanted, while his partner might tag someone else. After a few rounds, the whistle sounded again and everything stopped. Now Brother Heaton said that each person should get acquainted with someone new, learn where he came from, and what he was interested in.

From this time on, they should address each other by their first names; they should keep these fancy cards and wear them at tomorrow's meeting, so no one would be embarrassed to speak.

The Sunday morning meeting was regular, with special musical numbers to improve the tone of it. My interest — after listening to Bishop Edwards — was in Harvey Sprague. He had grown up in the lot just east and across a narrow lane from our first brick house. Since he was nearly ten years older than me, I really had no memories of him at all. I was a child when he and his older brothers moved to the Muddy Valley, and Brother Edwards' evaluation of him as a speaker was the first word I had of him. His mother was Pa's sister, Anne, oldest daughter of Grandpa's Indian wife.

Harvey Sprague was not a large man, but of medium height and square build. Nor was he handsome; his skin was dark, his hair black and straight. But his eyes were expressive and his voice almost a musical instrument in its variations. Today, he told us, we were using the account of Jesus Christ as written by St. Mark, the shortest book of the four Gospels, but the most vivid and exciting. This book was Jesus in action, without much preaching.

In Harvey's hands it all came alive. The flow of his language, the vivid comparisons, the relating of Jesus to each of us in our personal lives was masterful. Never before or since have I been more stirred by a sermon. The whole audience was caught up in it, and as he came to his conclusion, with a personal appeal that each member of the audience seemed to think applied to himself, the "Amen" was spontaneous, the air so charged that the Bishop hardly knew where or how to proceed.

We could all understand how congregations listening to this man would be glad to pay him $5,000 to $7,000 a year to preach Christianity to them. I felt that perhaps he had cheated himself for not accepting a pulpit. He could have had a comfortable home and surroundings, while here he was earning a miner's wage, working like a mole underground in the shafts, getting out ore — at a mere subsistence level. Within our own Church there would be no chance for an appointment for which he would be paid; he had not the right name, and his wife was not from one of the right families.

I think I was attracted to Marjorie Brown by the fact that we happened to be sitting near each other, and both reacted to the sermon in about the same way. She had been at the dance the night before, but with all the activity we had not met to talk together.

Seeing my name card, she asked if we were going home to Bunkerville after meeting, and if we might have room to take her along. She was eager to get to St. George; she had an invitation from a new boyfriend, Clarence Cottam, to come up for the Washington County fair and the rodeo. The Dixie College would begin its session on the following week, and she planned to stay if she possibly could. But Panaca was off any direct route: she could go to Modena by train and down on the mail rig which ran three times a week, or she could perhaps come to Bunkerville with us and catch a ride up with someone who would be going. I would have a little time on my hands, so I invited her to crowd in with us — we already had four, and all three of the others were large people. If she could stand it, we could.

We were late getting home. The other girls were still in Las Vegas; the bedroom upstairs would be hot, but we could manage for one night. Before breakfast was over, Pa came in with the word that one of the neighbors was going to Washington for some piece of farm machinery that he had bought, so he could take passengers up, but not bring them back. The fare would be three dollars; we would have to ride on a quilt-covered plank behind the cab. Could we make the trip under those conditions?

Yes, we would go, and it seemed that three other men were going also, one to sit up front with the driver, the two others on another plank behind ours. Marjorie felt that we were most fortunate; we would tie our floppy straw hats on with wide, bright-colored scarfs to save us from getting too sunburned; with any luck we should make the sixty miles in four to five hours, the roads being what they were, dusty and full of chuckholes. We had to stop and put water in twice along the slope, and each time the radiator cap was removed, a geyser of boiling water shot up two or three feet.

We had passed the summit and were making good time along the Ivins Bench, when Marjorie started to pound on the back of the cab motioning for the driver to stop. Thinking that she needed a rest stop, he pulled off the road. The men on the back plank, knowing the rule, "Gents to the right, ladies to the left," jumped off and hit for some squawbushes down the slope to the right. The man in the seat followed them, but the driver remained in his place, eager to be on the way. We jumped down to the left where the vermilion bluffs were glowing in the slanting rays of the sun.

"Isn't that lovely!" Marjorie exclaimed. "No wonder people from all over the earth stop to view this scene. How purple the shadows are! And it changes every minute."

By this time the men were back. The driver, just a little nettled, said, "This young lady stopped us to admire the scenery. Tell me, what do you think of it?"

"Purty poor pickin' for cattle," Windy announced.

"Maybe some silver hid in some of the crevices," another observed. "It's a lot like the formations at the Silver Reef."

"If an artist could capture it just as it is, no one would believe it.

They'd think it just couldn't be that vivid," Marjorie said. "It's such a scene as you will see only once in a lifetime."

"And if we don't get movin', we'll not get there before all the stores are closed." The driver couldn't quite hide his disgust. He must make extra good time from here on.

Arriving in town, he stopped at the tabernacle corner. "Maybe you all better get out here, unless you want to stay on and go over to Washington. I got no time to deliver you-all now."

"Let's see if we can check our suitcases here at the Dixie Drug, and walk down," I suggested.

That didn't appeal to Marjorie at all. "I'll telephone to somebody; if I can't find one, I'll try another."

Before long Clarence Cottam was there in his car, ready to take us both, for I was right in the way they were going.

"I'll be seein' you," Marjorie said. "Thanks for everything. And thanks for supporting me in that stop on the Ivins Bench. I wouldn't have missed that for anything, even if Mr. Driver was put out."

I think that was the last time I got to talk to Marjorie. I heard or read of her marriage, and of her husband's activities in the field study of migrating birds. But I have always been grateful for that brief stop on the Ivins Bench, which made me conscious of the beauty of that vivid scene.

At Las Vegas, Leah's older sister Betsy and Uncle Weir's daughter, Thirza, were living together in a nice apartment, while my two sisters, Charity and Aura, shared a small house owned by Mina Hanson Stewart, another cousin. Though I had a teaching position assured in the fall, right now I needed cash as badly as either of them. So they moved over and made a place for me.

But let Aura tell it as she remembers it after all these years:

You ask about our years in Las Vegas.

Charity and Velma Waite went down there first to work in Lambert's Cafe. Soon after arriving, they wrote for me to come — Lambert needed a dish-washer. I was young, but strong, and tickled pink to think my parents would give consent for me to go.

Pa warned me and talked to me about going to that wicked place — for me to hold my head and not get taken up with flattering words of men — that was just laying around Las Vegas to entice young, green girls to listen to their tales.

[206]

That year Hazel Waite came down to Las Vegas, too. She was pretty and very attractive to all. It was not many days until Lambert put me on the early morning shift, waiting table. I made good money on my "tips" alone.

Melvina Leavitt came, too — she fell in love with Lambert, and they were married. Lambert was very good to her. She could do as she pleased, she even "bossed" him sometimes.

Charity and Velma came later in the day to work. They were there for the noon rush and for the evening.

I went home early and embroidered or sewed or went to the Old Hall cat-i-cornered from the cafe, and practiced on the piano.

Ira Earl was Bishop or Presiding Elder for the Branch. They asked me to play for Sunday School. Church was held in that old dance hall. On Saturday nights they danced until midnight or later. The place "reaked" with tobacco, and empty bottles were strung around. Before church could be held there they had to do the janitor work and air out the place.

Hazel Waite coaxed me into quitting at Lambert's to go to work with her at the cafe in the Overland Hotel, just on the other corner from Lambert's. The wages were better, and the service more elaborate. We often carried meals to the patrons of the Hotel — political leaders, church leaders, community workers . . . .

So here I was a Susan-come-lately into this industrious crowd. I knew that I would be no good at all at waiting tables, so I was glad to get into a small bakery. My wage was set, and not nearly as much as any of the others, but neither was the work so demanding.

This bakery was run by a German man, his wife and two young sons: For the next month, I took the place of the wife, and doing chores that the older son could have done just as well. I came at seven in the morning, and began my day by breaking a dozen eggs in each of six large bowls, being careful to rub the inside of the shell with my forefinger. Otherwise one-seventh of the eggwhite would be left in the shell.

By this time the morning baking of bread would be ready to wrap. I was shown how to take the paper from the pile with one hand, set the loaf onto it with the other, wrap the paper around, doubling in the ends just so, and push it through a little heated contraption which sealed the ends. The oldest boy stood on the other side to take the loaf and set it onto a rack. As the cupcakes came out of the oven, I put on the spoonful of icing and arranged them on trays. Then I served the customers.

I was taken on in the first place to give the wife and the younger boy a month's vacation, and kept on after they returned to give her a chance to do fall housecleaning and other household chores that she had wanted to do, but had not time if she were tied into the front of the shop. So I was kept on until time to go home for school, just a month.

My work was humdrum compared to that of the other girls. Charity told of one experience. Two men, evidently cowboys who had been fortified with a drink or two, came in and ordered prime beefsteak — rare. When she brought it in, one fellow cut into his and motioned her back. "Tell 'em to 'rare it' again," he said, handing her his plate.

She took it away.

When she returned, the other cowboy had cut into his steak, and seeing the red blood run out, slipped it from his plate onto the floor, stood, put his boot heel into, twisted, and said, "Beller, damn you! Beller!"

His companion told Charity quietly to bring another serving medium-well-done, which she did. In the meantime she picked up the steak from the floor, and mopped up the mess.

They found the second serving just to their taste. The sober man left her a silver dollar tip; his companion pulled out a roll of bills, peeled off one and put it under his plate. It was twenty dollars!

She said not a word about it until the next morning, when she showed it to me before I left for work. I rejoiced with her, but said nothing, leaving her to tell or not to tell as she wished.

The Little Schoolteacher

DURING MY OWN LAST YEARS IN THE GRADES, OUR SCHOOL had taken on a very military tone. The half-hour-ahead big bell was rung, then at three minutes to go, the hand bell was rung and we must run promptly and take our places in line. There were four long lines formed, two for each room, each room having a separate door. The lines must be straight; the students must stand at attention, then mark time and at the order "March!" they filed into the room and down the aisles, each to his seat. "Turn!" "Sit!" And everyone was in his place and supposed not to move out of it without permission. This military order held for at least three years.

By the time I came to teach, Mr. Kelly was supervisor, and he did not like this military regime. On the other hand, there must be some order; students must not come in pell-mell, shoving and pushing and wrestling. There should be a place where each could hang his hat and jacket. There must be order in passing out pencils, paper, or other work material, so that the actual class work and study time should be maximized.

The teacher was expected to make her room as attractive as possible with plants or pictures or occasional displays of various kinds. But the essential business of the student was study, doing assigned tasks at the time they were assigned, and reciting or participating in discussion at class period.

I had third and fourth grades, and one grade was to make preparation while the other recited. In general, we had a wholesome attitude, the youngsters responded and things went well. As always, some students would finish before others; some would not get through at all. I remember one boy, Stan. He was always trying to pick a fight by slapping or shoving or generally disturbing. One day as students were leaving for the noon recess, he stuck his foot out into the aisle in front of a student and tripped him. He knew that I saw him and was watching, as he stood, caught another boy by the arm, tripped him, and then shoved him to the floor, so that the youngster skinned his knee and went out crying.

By this time I had Stan by the arm and held to it, twisting it just a little. The others were passing out as they always did after they were excused, but I held Stan until the last one was gone and the door closed.

I was angry when I caught him, and became angrier the longer I held him, until when we were alone I began slapping him and cuffing him about as hard as I could, telling him at the same time that I had put up with his foolishness as long as I was going to. He was crying hard before I turned him loose and ordered him to go home and not to come back until he could behave himself.

I was trembling and weak as he left, and sank into a desk about to cry; embarrassed, ashamed that I had become so angry; humiliated, both for myself and the boy. I waited to compose myself before I left the building, resolving that next time I would try another way.

Stan lived just a half-block beyond my home, so I waited until I knew he would be out of sight. As I walked down the street I saw Mike Leavitt — a cousin about my own age — grinning at his gate.

"Stan just passed a while ago. I could see he'd been bawling, so I said, 'Looks like your teacher had to git after you.' 'Hell! She didn't give me a bit more'n I deserved,' he said."

When Stan came back that afternoon his face was washed, his hair slicked down, and he carried a beautiful red pomegranate. From that day on, he was on my side. I immediately appointed him to be monitor to gather up the papers. Not only did he behave himself, but he tried to help keep some of the others in line.

[210]

Charley B. came into school a month or so late. His family had moved about a great deal, and he had not had a full year of school anywhere. His father came with him at first and explained that he would need to start in the third grade. Charley was large for his age, so he seemed out of place with the third graders, but from what I could see of his reading ability, that's about where he belonged. His father inferred that he had had trouble before, but that if he made any here I should report it and he would see that the boy was punished.

I could see that Charley had trouble applying himself to his reading assignments, but that during the fourth grade arithmetic class, he was paying full attention to it. We were drilling in addition, and he was following this instead of working his own assignment.

One afternoon just at closing time, I saw him lean forward, pull out the neck of Rhodella Abbott's dress just in front of him and drop something down her back. Instantly she jumped and screamed and began to cry. I hurried, stuck my hand down her back and pulled out a wild bee, which I dropped onto the floor. Unbuttoning her dress, I saw the red blotch with the stinger in, knocked it out and wet the place with a little spit.

"Charley, what made you do that?" I asked.

"I didn't do nothing," he said innocently.

"You run across to Aunt 'Rell's and tell her to put some soda on it," I told Rhodella. "That will make it stop hurting."

"You stay where you are," I said to Charley. The others had already been excused, but slowed up at the sound of Rhodella's scream.

Again I was furiously angry. That a big boy should drop a bee down a little girl's back! Where had he gotten the bee? He hadn't moved from his seat. He must have had it in some kind of a container and just kept it until closing time before he placed it. And then to look so innocent and say, "I didn't do nothing!"

I closed the door behind the last student, and then instead of coming directly back to Charley, I picked up an eraser and began erasing the blackboard, rubbing them down hard to work off my anger. How to deal with this? I didn't think; I just kept at the boards until both were clean, then I came back to the sulking, defiant boy.

"Charley, how would you like to be promoted to fourth grade?"

[211]

I heard myself saying. That was not what I had intended to say. I had felt that I should have censured the boy more for telling the lie than for putting the bee down her back. But that was what came out. I could hardly believe myself.

Charley was caught entirely off guard. He was braced for defense, for defiance.

"I have watched you during the arithmetic class," I went on, "and I'm sure that you can do fourth grade arithmetic as well as any in the class — better than most of them. But you must study your geography and language. You must learn to read better. You are smart; you can learn it, but you haven't been trying. Now if you will pitch in and really work, I think I can graduate you from the fourth grade in the spring."

Charley was braced for censure, not kindness. He couldn't believe this; he couldn't take it. He didn't want to cry. His throat tightened, he blinked back his tears, but he couldn't answer.

"Come, now, there's an extra desk, a large one down the hall. Why don't you go get it and put it at the end of the fourth grade row? It will fit you better than the one you are in. Move your things into it, and sit there from now on."

I didn't want Charley to break down and cry, either. Getting the desk and bringing it in saved him. From that day on, he worked at his books, graduating near the head of his class. I might add that he went on to school, became an honorable citizen, married well, and had a family. And more and more I was grateful that for this rare time I had acted wisely.

I was glad to teach my first year in the same room in which I had sat out my fifth grade under Aunt Martha Cox. In many ways, I have considered that one of the most profitable of all my early school years. I had an advantage over Aunt Martha, though, for while she had three grades, I had only two. Mr. Kelly was strong in the conviction that a teacher should be able to know her students well enough to be conscious of their personal problems and home background.

I grouped my two classes with an extra space between them, and reserved a place for a long table at the back of the room for what I called "nature study." The students might bring interesting things to place on it or to hang behind it. We had a pasteboard box colony of doodlebugs; we had three or four of last year's birds' nests, a wasps' nest, and a mud dauber's nest, all hanging on the wall, and assorted pretty rocks in piles on the table.

I had pictures mounted on stiff cardboard which were changed to fit the class schedules. Much of this sort of thing I must credit to Miss Connell, who had stressed the surroundings.

On Mr. Kelly's first visit, I was a bit worried when I noticed that he was making notes. I needn't have been, because most of them were laudatory, and he mentioned them in his conversation after the students left.

"Don't be too troubled about the slow child; so long as he is doing the best he can, praise him. But don't spend too much time with him, either. Be more conscious about your quick students; don't waste their time. The idea is that each does his very best, and you have some here who can do much more than you must assign to the average of the class. These are to be given time to read; be sure you have a library shelf available to them."

But this was too short-lived. During the night of December 20, 1917, the school building was burned to the ground. No clue was ever found, for the fire wasn't discovered until the building was nearly gone.

But school must go on. We might have a little longer Christmas holiday, but school would open on the Monday after January 1. The whole town was canvassed for vacant rooms and adequate ones found. The State made an extra appropriation for new desks, books, and necessary items. I was glad that I had kept my basic supplies at home. I had even taken down the Christmas decorations, and nearly all of the Christmas things, expecting to get the New Year's new arrangement up before January 1.

As far as my own class was concerned, I tried to make the change as slight as possible, so I substituted the yard in front and beside the house for the indoor nature study area. We would rake and clear the weeds, save the perennials, prune the bushes, and plant some few new shrubs. On the other side of the walk, one of the boys got his father to plow, clear, and furrow a nice place for a vegetable garden. As a result, we had enough so that each child could carry home radishes, turnips, carrots — most of the peas were eaten raw. Some of the older boys took the responsibility for irrigating the yard, and took pride in keeping it beautiful. One lad, a slow reader, and troubled by his times tables in arithmetic, gained the applause of the whole class as "the farmer of the year."

When it came time for the next year's contracts, Mr. Kelly spoke well of my work, but said he wished to transfer me to Mesquite, where they still had to have three grades in a room. The expense of our fire had made it impossible to make many of the improvements he had hoped to make there. In view of this fact, he felt that the teachers there should be given higher salaries — at least the equivalent of an extra teacher divided three ways. These were computed on the number of students. Teachers who attended summer school also had a small allowance.

So it was that during the summer of 1918 I attended the University of Utah, living at Carlson Hall. I was a total stranger, but soon met a few who were friendly. One of the most interesting of all was a little Japanese girl. She was so thin and emaciated that she looked as though she might have just escaped from a prison camp; the fact was, she came from a wealthy home.

We were often in the serving line together, and she would heap her plate high with everything that was offered, and reserve a muffin or other items of food on my plate to eat between meals. She explained that her basic metabolism was so high that she simply had to eat almost constantly. Her specialty seemed to be to work with numbers. Once she demonstrated. She had me write three numbers over three other numbers and multiply them. She had the same numbers in the same order, but turned her back to me and looked at them for a few minutes, and wrote the correct answer, without ever touching pen to paper. We tried this several times; it was always the same. She said that playing with numbers was a part of her mental gymnastics to keep her mind in trim. I've often thought of her since and wondered.

Another interesting lady had gone to the Navajos of southeastern Utah, married an Indian man, and now had a teenage son, who was proud to remain Navajo, as she also wished for him to do. She made no effort to be identified as a white woman. Her work was as a school teacher, teaching the Navajo to read basic English, and to speak enough English to be able to trade with white men and live in their world.

By late August I was back in Bunkerville, ready to plan my living quarters in Mesquite. Should I just board with some family, or should I set up housekeeping for myself? I did not like to "batch it" alone; neither did I want to live in with a family. So I suggested that I get a house or an apartment and take the two little girls, Daisy and Eva, with me for company. This would relieve Ma a little, and the girls would be just as happy there.

They were quite enthusiastic about the change; yes, indeed, they would like to go to Mesquite. I found an apartment in the home of Brother David Abbott—a large room which I divided with furniture and a curtain. It was just a short walk to the school house. The little girls would not come over until school was ready to start.

In the meantime, I had been there to two Sunday services. One of the first persons I met was Brother Nephi Johnson. I was greatly attracted to this patriarchal old man, with his sharp black eyes and long beard. I shook hands with him and sat beside him during the opening exercises of Sunday School that first Sunday, and always afterward went out of my way to greet him.

On the Sunday just before school started, my cousin, Donetta Leavitt, asked me if I would like to go with the crowd of young folks into the fields in search for melons after church.

"Well, not in these clothes," I told her. "I'll run down and get into something else, and be right back. But don't wait for me. I never know who I'll find when I get there. So don't wait."

Just before I reached my gate I came up with old Brother Johnson. He had heard me coming and had stopped.

"Hi, Brother Johnson," I said, expecting to go around him into my yard. But he held out his cane and stopped me.

"I want to give you a Patriarchal Blessing," he said.

"Well," I stammered, "I'd like to have a Blessing — I've never had one, but . . ."

"My book is here just across the street in Brother Walter Hughes' house. His daughter Afton is my scribe," and taking my arm, he steered me across the street and into the house.

I thought of the Ancient Mariner, who ". . . held him with his glittering eye," for I had no way to get out of the situation.

We opened the door and went in. (At that time no one in the valley had a key to his home. It would be an insult to his neighbors.) Brother Johnson pointed to the big ledger on top of some built-in shelves, and I climbed on a stool, pulled it out, brought it down, and opened it at the place where she had left a marker.

So I wrote my blessing as he pronounced it, his hands heavy on my head. It was a good blessing, not so wordy and elaborate as some I have read, but with promises that I would be a leader among the sisters; that I should have a family; and that I must always be mindful of my Father in Heaven, to take my problems to Him and to accept His answers.

He had just finished when the family came in from church. I was so glad to meet the wife, Aunt Lydia, for I had heard her name mentioned but never met her before. Afton was about my own age, but we had not met.

In the visit that followed, I learned more of the goings-on in Mesquite than I had heard in the whole week that I had been in town. Ernest Pulsipher had not come home from his mission early because of his health; it was because the construction outfit at the Virgin Narrows had abandoned their project and moved away, and the check they sent to the Pulsipher family for $1,500 had returned with a big NO FUNDS written on it. Their whole summer's work for nothing! They had made purchases on the strength of that check.

Yes, earlier in his mission Ernest had been very sick, but Brother Melvin J. Ballard, his mission President, had administered to him and he had been healed, and was going about his work as usual, when this word came. The family needed the help of every member to pull themselves out of the predicament they were in financially.

The one person who was happiest was his little girlfriend; it had been hard to stay faithful for a year and a half.

I had known the Pulsipher brothers chiefly as baseball fans, who boasted that if the four of them could be on one team, their opponents could have their choice of all that were left in the valley. With their own pitcher, catcher, first baseman, and shortstop, they'd chance it; yes, they'd put money up on it, Lew especially. The others were all less loud and aggressive. But it all added to the excitement for the crowd.

I prepared for my school in Mesquite with the help of Mrs. Emma Abbott, who had taught there for several years. She suggested that I fit up a little area in the back storeroom where the children would have a place to clean up. Though there was no water in the room, she had kept a large bucket and a dipper on the washbench. The janitor would fill this every morning. A large wooden bucket on the floor would hold the slops for the day, which would just be thrown out into the graveled backyard every afternoon.

I hardly had put my books down on the first morning before a little girl came in, all out of breath from running. Her feet were bare, her dress unbuttoned, her hair uncombed.

"Aren't you too early?" I asked. "Does your mother know that you are here?"

"No. Ma's sick and the others all getting theirselves ready, so I've come on up here."

"OK. Shall I button you up?"

She turned her back, and I could see that the only article of clothing she had under the calico dress was an underpiece made of blue denim, evidently the back of the legs of her father's cast-off overalls. The front extended almost to her knees; it buttoned down the back, and the dropseat panties were fastened on each side by large white buttons.

I met the rest of the students at the door, admitting the third grade first and letting them choose their seats within the area set apart for them. The fourth and fifth grades then proceeded to their areas. Every seat was occupied.

"Just find a seat in your area for now. If we want to make changes, we'll do it at recess. Now let us all sing 'America.' Everyone should know that song. I'll prompt you at the beginning of each verse; this is a song which every American should know."

I gave them the pitch and started them. How they could sing! Through all four verses — full of vigor through the first three verses, and with a reverent softness at the beginning of the fourth. I was happily surprised at their responsive reaction to my leadership and the quality of their voices.

"That last verse calls for a word of prayer. This morning I'll offer it, and then you may each have a turn."

The brief prayer over, I told them that I heard some very fine voices in different parts of the room. Now we'd take time to sing just for the fun of it.

"I want two of the best singers in each grade to be our lead choir in singing some rounds. Tell me, fifth graders, who are two of your best singers? Two from the fourth grade and two from the third."

With six to lead out, we sang once in unison the whole round: "Are you sleeping? are you sleeping? / Brother John, Brother John / Sabbath bells are ringing, Sabbath bells are ringing / Ding Ding Dong, Ding Ding Dong." Then we broke it into its parts, and got such good harmony that I was pleased and a bit surprised.

"Wonderful! Just wonderful! Now we'll know what to do if we are tired or bored. We'll sing a round or two."

The students liked that so well that they called for another: "Three Blind Mice," which went off equally well. I was happy to be off to such a good start. Here I had spent sleepless nights wondering what I could do to develop some kind of an *esprit de corps* in my room, and here it was on the very first day!

I went on to tell them how pleased I was to find such a wonderful group, all eager to learn to read well, to capture from a printed page all the wonderful, exciting stories. To read well was one of the very first essentials to an education. There are those who could draw and paint well, and others that had different interests, but there was no substitute to reading well. Each student had his reading book and arithmetic book on his desk; each should write his name in his book in pencil, because this same book would have to serve someone else next year. "I'm sure such fine students as you know how to study," I assured them.

I immediately assigned the fifth grade to the first lesson in their reading book; the fourth grade were given an assignment also, before I turned my full attention to the third grade. Here each child was given a chance to demonstrate his ability to read aloud.

Finally, finally it was four o'clock. I was relieved and happy that I was off to such a good start, but by night, I was almost exhausted. I stood at the door as the students passed out and said a good night; from most I had a hearty response, but a few walked away in silence. This troubled me; I tried to identify them, for I felt I must learn more about each. I knew I must find some way to get through to them.

Both Mr. Bowler and Mrs. Abbott congratulated me on getting through the first day so well, as they felt it was an indication of what would follow. Now I wondered if having my two sisters, Daisy in the fourth grade and Eva in the third, was not also an advantage, for they, I knew, would give me full support, and already they were making friends among their classmates.

I looked forward to Saturday, when I could relax. I was hesitant about going to the dance that night until Donetta and another girl called for me, saying that if I stayed home, I'd hurt nobody but myself. The dance would be the best place to get acquainted; boys who wouldn't ask you to go to the dance might ask to take you home after it.

As soon as I was seated, Alf Hardy came for me to dance with him. He said it would be a shabby cousin who would let a girl sit on her seat. After that, dances came easy, and once, as the music stopped, we stood near Ernest Pulsipher, standing on the sideline.

"Who's yer new girlfriend?" Ern asked.

"You couldn't guess," Alf bantered, "but she's a real dancer! Try her and see."

Ernest could hardly refuse that challenge, for this was the last half of the waltz. We started off and were going very well when he said, "The thing I can't understand is where you have been all my life. How come I didn't see you long ago?"

"That's easy. I was in Bunkerville, and you were too busy here in Mesquite."

"That's right, I guess," Ern admitted. "And I'd better be on my way or the girlfriend will think I've deserted her."

He took me to my seat and hurried out. I knew his girlfriend only slightly, and had no idea where she lived. The Pulsipher family home was a good three miles west of the dance hall. The boys would come into town on horseback, unless, perhaps, they would use the light buggy to bring the girlfriend in, if she lived far from the dance hall.

It seemed that everyone arrived at the dance at once, for soon the floor was crowded, and I was on every set. I noticed that Ernest and his group of about six couples were in the northwest corner of the hall, and were exchanging dances. The musician played every dance twice, so that each person could try every kind: waltz, quadrille, polka.

Ern waited for a waltz before he came to dance with me again. I had been doing a polka and was quite out of breath, so I welcomed the slower pace. We didn't talk much, but danced together with perfect rhythm. As the music stopped and we turned to walk to our seats, he stopped to say, "I'm pretty well tied up until after the holidays. After that, you'd better look out!"

"I just might have something to say to that, too!" I bantered.

"I'm just giving you fair warning, that's all."

"OK. I'll remember."

Winter of Courtship

THE FALL DAYS WERE PLEASANT, the air just sharp enough to be exhilarating. We had no freezing before Christmas. The little girls, Daisy and Eva, were really enjoying this experience, for they made friends easily, and being sisters of the teacher seemed to give them a little prestige. They would be glad to go home for Christmas, but expected certainly to come back.

We came home on Saturday, and on the following Monday morning I went up to the store to look for some little Christmas gifts. The clerk at once asked if I would be interested in helping them out here; they could manage quite well in the morning, but by afternoon they were crowded — so many were coming from Mesquite with the word that Uncle Abram Woodbury had not stocked any Christmas toys at all. Since I was slightly acquainted with most of the people, perhaps I could help if only to visit with them in a friendly way.

Late in the afternoon the Pulsipher boys, Ernest and his cousin Bill, came looking for gifts for family and girlfriends. At sight of me, they seemed a little flustered, at least Ernest did. Since that first dance with him in September, I had hardly seen him to speak except briefly at Sunday School or church, and to dance with him once at every dance. Always it was a waltz, and always there was some little banter or suggestion about the coming of spring. The little crowd of which he was a part met weekly, whether there was a dance or not. Saturday

[221]

night found them at one home or another making candy, having a quail supper, or just playing rook with an accompanying cake and punch.

The boys were looking through the collection of cheap jewelry, the few wrist watches, beads, and fancy scarfs, but nothing seemed exactly what they wanted, so they each took a box of chocolates, gift-wrapped.

Evidently they did not think that this was enough, for when I went to work on Monday afternoon, the clerk hastened to tell me that they had arrived early that morning, and each had bought a piece of jewelry — she didn't know exactly what, for she didn't serve them, but she was sure that it was jewelry. So runs gossip in a village.

The Christmas weather was perfect. With the spread of the flu, there could be no meetings inside, but outside sports went on as usual.

Before the holidays were really over, the epidemic of the Asiatic flu was sweeping the country. We were all aghast at word that Brother Erastus Romney, our favorite teacher, had died of it at St. George. It seemed impossible. He was always so full of vim, such a "leader-outer" in all the improvements in the town: cleaning ditches and sidewalks; bridging the ditches in town; getting the swimming pool finished, filled, used, and drained for clean water. Most of all, he had been coach of the basketball team that had won the state championship two years in succession. He had played the male lead in *East Lynne*, one of the better plays ever staged in Bunkerville. Because of him, Bunkerville was a changed town, a better town. Now he had just been made President of Dixie College in St. George, and had not even served out his first year. The pity of it!

We had no cases in Bunkerville, nor did they have any in Mesquite up to this time, but the body of Jay Huntsman was shipped home from Las Vegas. Ralph and Jay were the sons of Uncle Solon Huntsman, who had married Aunt Theresa, Pa's youngest sister. This made it a family affair for us. We all liked Jay for his bounding good nature, his willingness to cooperate in whatever project was under way. But he thought he needed cash money, and Las Vegas was the place to get it. He had found work and was doing well, but was stricken and dead before anyone at home even knew that he was sick.

The body was sent back to Mesquite and taken directly to the meeting house, where the casket was placed on two sawhorses and opened. There would be no services, but relatives and friends could come and view the corpse. They would then go to the cemetery where the grave had been prepared, and where a short service would be held: a song by the choir, a few words by the Bishop, and a prayer before the grave was filled.

Two weeks later another young man was brought home in a coffin. This was Dolph Burgess, whose parents were George and Florence Pulsipher Burgess, the only girl in Ernest's family. Dolph had also been in Las Vegas, and his family did not hear of his sickness until word came of his death. Dolph was very popular in his set of young folks at Mesquite.

The same pattern was carried out: the open casket at the church, the brief ceremony at the cemetery. The boy's father was not present — he had probably not heard of the death — but the Pulsipher boys were all there: Lewis, Stanley, Ernest, and Howard. Their mother, Florence, was prostrate with grief, and the father remained home to be with her and to take care of the telephone business.

The flu took only one person in Mesquite, little George Bowler, a fourth grade student of mine. I didn't learn of his death until school opened and I faced his empty seat. It was really quite a shock, for he was a favorite — so bright and cheerful and willing.

Since there had been no flu in the Virgin Valley, and school had been ordered dismissed for two weeks, Doctor Donald McGregor of St. George wrote to the Bishop or the principal — someone who had influence — and suggested that, since the tonsils almost always needed to be removed, he would bring his nurse, Miss Mary Whitehurst, and if they got as many as thirty patients, they would give the wholesale price of $5.00 each for removal. A bargain! Since the general belief was that the tonsil was almost always a nuisance which should be removed, thirty-three families responded. At least that number could be guaranteed.

The teachers were expected to be on hand to help, and I was glad to be present. The recreation hall was cleared, with the benches around the walls. Each parent brought a quilt and pillow for each patient.

[223]

It seemed that most of the patients were from my room; there were few over the age of twelve, and fewer under the age of eight. The doctor set up shop in the Bishop's council room, with its large table. The child, accompanied by his parent, would walk into the room, and after a relatively short time, be carried out and placed on his own quilt and pillow. Poor little shavers! They went in well and happy, and came out miserable.

Things seemed to be working well. The tonsils were deposited in the wastepaper basket to be taken out at the end and buried. Then, we outside were conscious that there was a problem in the operating room — a tense time, when the father of a badly bleeding boy was called in by the alarmed doctor.

Everyone was relieved when it was all over. All felt that a good thing had been done that afternoon, a step toward better health. So in ignorance we deceive ourselves!

By the last week in January the apricot trees were in bloom, while the plums made the whole air fragrant. Some wild flowers were starting in the hills, and spring was in the air.

Now Ernest Pulsipher and Woodruff Potter, Donetta's boyfriend, planned an outing up to "Elbow," a place in the canyon to the east. Donetta and Wood had been keeping company all winter, and it was generally believed that they were engaged to be married in the spring, though there was no ring or announcement.

We went in a white-topped buggy, with Ernest driving the team. He was glad, I think, to have his whole attention on the team and outfit, for the road was very primitive, and very steep.

We stopped at a grassy spot by some quaking-asp trees. Here there were several little pools, the watercress was thrifty, and the mountains high. Everyone was hungry.

I had brought a pan of baked beans with smoked ham, a covered dish of potato salad, and some Boston cream candy with walnuts. Donetta had sandwiches, boiled eggs, and a custard pie. As an afterthought, I had put in some bread-and-butter sandwiches of homemade brown bread, and a small bottle of jelly.

We spread the tarp on the ground, folded a campquilt on it, and spread a white tablecloth on that. I thought we had a nice, tasty lunch. Wood piled his plate high with some of everything. Ern took tiny samples of everything before he took a serving of anything.

The baked beans and the plain bread-and-butter sandwich appealed to him; the potato salad he picked at gingerly. Finally he had asked what it was. He had never eaten potato salad — never even seen it before — he insisted. His potatoes were always served hot: fried potatoes and onions, mashed potatoes with butter and cream added, or served with meat and meat gravy. But cold potatoes! And raw onions and sliced boiled eggs and radishes and lettuce leaves! Cow feed!

I put the lid on the dish and wouldn't let him touch it. Where had he spent all these twenty-seven years and never tasted potato salad? I was in a humor to tell him to go jump in the creek!

At last the food was put away and Wood sprawled out with his head on Donetta's knee, while she combed at his hair. Now Ern had an idea.

"Let's go exploring. We might find something very nice farther up."

We rounded two turns and came to a gigantic rock with its point high above our heads; while the little stream washed by it on one side there was a grassy knoll on the other, a perfect place to stop. Ernest pulled me toward him, "I've waited six long months for this," he said and gave me a kiss that I thought would smother me. Then into my hands he slipped a little velvet case. A diamond! An honest-to-goodness diamond! Not very large, but genuine!

"I told you what to expect the first time I danced with you. Remember?"

I had no voice. I could hardly get my breath. I was caught between laughter and tears.

"Remember?" he insisted.

"Yes. Of course I remember. But I didn't quite expect this. Not today, anyway."

"Well, this is the fastest I could pull it off, even to getting the size of your finger. Sometime I'll give you the whole story."

We soon returned to show our ring and air our plans. Maybe early September when the fair was on in St. George; maybe earlier. He must get this — whatever it was that was giving him this pain in

[225]

the neck — under control. It wasn't so bad that he couldn't take it, but still a nagging, persistent pain.

In a small village, news travels fast. A few of my students had heard that I had taken a diamond ring from Ernest Pulsipher, and were so curious and eager that I had to show the little ring and assure them that this would make no difference whatever in our relationship. What was really different was that we now had lost five students from our room: my two sisters had been kept home because of the flu scare, little George Bowler's empty seat would be moved out, also. Then there were the two boys who had been living in the covered wagon across the Big Wash; their parents had moved on out to the Arizona Strip. Seems that several years before they had been called to settle in Arizona, and had gone down into the Salt River area somewhere, but couldn't make a living. Their call was specifically to Arizona, so they moved out to be over the line. I was sorry to lose these two eager, earnest students; I wished that I had sent some books with them — library books that they might read and return, perhaps, or an arithmetic book.

Moving out five desks did make the place seem much less crowded, and there were plenty of bright ones left to fill in. Best of all, Santa had brought new shoes to some of those who had been barefoot before, along with new shirts or dresses and an occasional new sweater.

The school morale was high, so that when Mr. Kelly happened in just as we were starting on our round songs, we did three for him, as a sample of our work in that line. The pictures on the walls were student work, too. His visit was too late for the arithmetic classes and the reading classes, but he might call on individual students if he cared to. That would not be necessary, he said. He was well-pleased with the general atmosphere and student response. His theory was that children learned more rapidly in an atmosphere that was pleasant, and where their efforts were appreciated, even if they were not the very best.

During the winter, I had made it a point to speak to Old Brother Nephi Johnson at Sunday School and Church; occasionally I sat beside him. I was not disturbed when he came to my room one day just before closing time. The students were all busy in a drawing lesson. "Don't pay any attention to me! Go right on with your work," he said as he tapped his way to my desk and sat down in my chair. The children were well-behaved, so things in the room proceeded normally until the bell sounded, when they hurried out, but in good order.

I came at once and pulled a chair up facing Brother Johnson. This was what he had been waiting for. Leaning with both hands on his cane, he said impressively, "I want you to do some writing for me. My eyes have witnessed things that my tongue has never uttered, and before I die, I want them written down. And I want YOU to do the writing."

Silly, foolish me! Why didn't I just reach for a pencil and pad, settle myself and say, "Go ahead?" Instead I hedged.

"Oh, Brother Johnson, I'm afraid I couldn't do much this evening. It's after four o'clock, and I have an officers' meeting before Mutual, and we could hardly get started. But I do want to do it, and I will do it. We can make a start on a Saturday, and then go on into Sunday if we need to."

He was a little reticent. He had come prepared to talk now, but when he saw that the sun was really getting low and Maggie was across the street with the buggy, he brightened up.

"OK, then," he said. "We'll do it another time. Maybe if you could come down to the ranch after school has closed."

"I'll remember," I said. "I'd really enjoy hearing about your life."

School closed in the last week of May, and by the time I had moved back home and got adjusted, I had forgotten all about Old Brother Johnson. One evening Lew Pulsipher, Ern's eldest brother, called at the house.

"Nita," he said, "Grandpa Johnson is down. He's really quite sick — looks like he might not get up again. But he keeps calling for the little schoolteacher, all the time. He is looking for the little school-teacher."

"I'll be right over the first thing in the morning," I said. "I'm ashamed. I did promise him that I'd do some writing for him, but you know how it is — the nearest thing gets the attention."

The next morning before sunrise I was at the lower ranch. I left my horse with the reins over the hitching post, and hurried toward the house. Maggie had seen me, and came out.

"I'm so glad you came," she said. "He's been so restless about what he must tell you."

She led me into his bedroom, the lean-to room that had been built against the side of the original home. It was a large, long room, with a slanting ceiling which was painted a bright blue.

"The little schoolteacher is here, Father," Maggie said, putting her hand on her father's forehead. "She has come to do your writing for you."

Brother Johnson stirred and opened his eyes.

I took his hand, leaned down and put my cheek on his forehead. He closed his hand on mine, smiled, and said, "Good! good!"

"Rest awhile, and then we can talk," I said. "I'm going to stay right here and not go away."

He seemed greatly relieved.

"He'll be all right now, I think," Maggie said. "I'll go in and put breakfast on for the brethren. They came at two o'clock, and have had a long stent."

I could smell the hot bread and bacon, and hear the pause while the blessing was being said, and the low voices. Then I looked at Brother Johnson. Horrors! He had died! His mouth had fallen open, his eyes rolled back in his head, and his throat rattled. Instinctively I jumped and called Maggie, who came quickly, patted his face, lifted his head up, and fanned him. In just a minute he caught his breath again, and seemed to rest.

"He'll be OK now," Maggie said.

I was shaken by the experience. I had never seen a person die; in my confusion, I went out to walk in the yard. Uncle List came out and talked to me in very strong terms.

"What is the matter with you, girl? Ain't you got any nerve? Ain't you got any sense? Why couldn't you let that old man die? He's been ready to go for two or three days, but was waitin' for you to come. Then he relaxed and could have gone. The next time that happens, you hang on to your shoelaces, and wait — and wait — and wait, quietly, and then come in and say, 'He's gone.'"

Brother Johnson lived through another day and well into the

second night. He seemed troubled; he rambled in delirium — he prayed, he yelled, he preached, and once his eyes opened wide to the ceiling and he yelled, "Blood! BLOOD! BLOOD!" At first I thought it was the blue of the ceiling, but the word *blood* was repeated too many times.

"What is the matter with him?" I asked Uncle List, who waited outside. "He acts like he is haunted."

"Maybe he is. He was at the Mountain Meadows Massacre, you know."

No, indeed, I did NOT know. I had read and been told our standard story: that some emigrants had been massacred at a place called Mountain Meadows, far away from the Mormon settlements, but it was the work of Indians. They were stirred up because some of their number had been killed by these emigrants, and they wanted revenge. A few of our people who lived in the area had tried to restrain the Indians, but were able to save only about seventeen children, who were sent back to their relatives in Missouri.

So Brother Johnson had been at the Mountain Meadows! That was what he wanted me to write! Clearly that was what he meant when he had said that his eyes had witnessed things that his tongue had never uttered! Fool, fool that I was, not to have taken the opportunity to write it when he was eager to talk, all ready to tell it all!

Brother Johnson lasted into the second day, and I remained to the end, hoping that he might become lucid enough to tell something significant. But I had missed my chance.

After he finished his chores, Ernest rode down and joined me. There was nothing either of us could do in the house, so we sat on a log out near the corral. We had not seen each other since school closed, and we had many things to discuss.

About eleven o'clock Uncle List came out and said that it was over. Brother Johnson didn't rally enough to say anything positive or coherent about the massacre, but it was on his mind right to the end. The record says that he died 6 June 1919, aged 86.

There was no use for Ernest to ride all the way to Bunkerville at this time of night. We rode out the half-mile to the end of the lane, where we stopped long enough to kiss good-night without getting off

[229]

our horses. I would be back for the funeral the next afternoon, and we would have more time by ourselves.

We sat together during the funeral, and then rode to Ern's favorite place in a corner of the field, where there was shade and seats, and we could talk about our hopes and problems.

Ernest loved this large farm. Here we were on the high ground near the red sandhills, and we could take in the full expanse of green, so large and beautiful. We would build our place on the higher land, where we had a magnificent view, not only of the farm, but of the distant mountains.

The Cabin Spring

I SPENT MOST OF THE SUMMER AT OUR TENT HOUSE AT THE CABIN SPRING. It was not so far away in distance, but because it was so high in the mountains, there was some travel to it. Following our short time together at Brother Johnson's funeral, I had no word from Ernest, and nearly a month passed before he came to see me. The moon had been full the night before, so he said that he had cut the hay during the night. His neck hurt so bad that he couldn't sleep; anyway, it was cooler at night, and so would be easier on the horses.

Although he was taking four or five aspirins at a time, he still was suffering pain in his neck. It seemed to be localized on the right side, down from his ear and inside his collarbone. He remembered that long ago, before he had gone on his mission, he had been hit on his neck with a baseball. During his illness on his mission this pain had not been a problem; anyway, President Ballard had given him a blessing, and he had been healed. This thing would have no connection, he felt sure. He would wait until this crop of hay was up, and then go in to St. George again, and maybe have them take out his tonsils. He couldn't find anything else to blame the pain on.

It was August before Ernest came to the mountain again. No, he hadn't gone in to St. George yet; he had found some salves and liniment that he was rubbing his neck with, and it seemed that exercise like pitching hay didn't hurt it any — at least it wasn't any worse.

I gathered that he wanted to not only get his hay cut and baled, but enough sold to be able to pay for the operation. Seems that the honey crop had been extra good; alfalfa honey was always first-rate, and they had a very good sale of half-gallon and one-gallon cans. And they had secured the paste-on labels which insured quick sale in large lots. Now he would go in to St. George and have his tonsils out, and be able to pay the bill before he left.

Not only the doctor bill. A young man getting married must pay for the license, a few necessities like a new shirt, maybe, or a frying pan for the kitchen. He always had a clever turn, a surprise. And now, another thing he must be able to afford would be a good treat of wine for Uncle Pidge Barnum, so he'd play extra good music at the wedding dance!

A group of families from Mesquite had taken an annual vacation to the mountains over the last few years to gather pine nuts. They had always spent at least one night on the way up just across the creek from our place. We had put a dam across the canyon, which backed up a lake large enough and deep enough to swim in, and this is where they camped.

This group would continue by horseback up the canyon to the large pinions which bore the best fruit. There they built pits for roasting the cones, and followed the Indian pattern of covering them with ashes and coals and cooking them overnight. If the frost had hit, they would pick the nuts from the ground. From them we learned that Ernest Pulsipher had gone to St. George, where Dr. McGregor had taken out his tonsils.

The next day Pa sent Melvin up on horseback to tell me to come home. Warren Hardy's wife, Leila, had died of a heart attack, and since Warren was a cousin, Pa knew I would want to be there. Besides, they might need me at the piano.

Leila was about my age, but she had married young and had had two beautiful children, a boy and a girl, and the report was that she had become pregnant again. Whether or not that was true made little difference — she had developed a bad toothache in one of her upper back molars. Brother James Abbott was the nearest thing to a dentist in town, although he had no equipment except a pair of forceps which he had used a few times on children's teeth. He didn't volunteer his services, but if people came for him, he would do the best he could.

This operation had been a real ordeal. The tooth was broken off and only a part came out. The pain was excruciating, and Leila's heart was running away — at any rate, she died before morning of a heart attack. And following Pa's request, I went home on horseback.

The funeral was held September 27, and I was there to play the piano. I had a hard time controlling myself; I wanted to cry out loud at the tragedy, for the two beautiful little mother-less children and the heart-broken husband. I was still upset when Lew came to talk to me.

"Ernest got home late this afternoon. He had his tonsils out, all right, but he is real miserable. It will be several days before he'll be able to come over to see you. Why don't you get your horse, and ride over with me?" he asked.

"Maybe I will," I said, "but you needn't wait for me. I have a few things I need to do here before I leave. Thank you for suggesting it, and I think I will come. But don't you wait."

It was dusk when I stopped at the Pulsipher ranch. I threw the reins over the hitching post, made a little noise with my feet on the wooden porch, tapped the door slightly, and opened it before anyone came. Father Pulsipher was still at the corral, and Mother Pulsipher was in the kitchen.

Ernest had been lying on the couch, but raised to a sitting position as I entered.

"Don't get up," I said. "I'll just sit right here by you," and I kissed him and sat down.

He thought I would still be at the mountain; they hadn't even heard of Leila's death and the funeral. But he had been home only an hour or so, and just hadn't caught up with all the current news. He seemed weak, so I pulled the big high-backed rocking chair around and sat in it, while he stretched out on the cot. It seemed hard for him to realize that a tonsil operation for an adult was something serious.

I held his hand an stroked it, and tried to find something to talk about. He raised into a sitting position again, and said, "I don't know whether I should tell you this or not. But all the way home from

[233]

St. George I've been troubled, wondering if we should go on and get married. I had about decided to tell you that we should break off until I can get myself in better shape than I am in now; break off, and let you take the teaching position there in Bunkerville. Then just as you came in — you couldn't have been more than getting off your horse — I saw you sitting in that chair, just like you are now, and you were holding a white-headed baby boy in your arms. It flashed into my mind: 'One year from now, this will be yours.' Funniest thing! That instant you opened the door and came in."

This seemed the answer, crystal clear. What more could we expect? We would act accordingly, and go back to St. George. Together we went to Dr. McGregor, and told him our story.

"I am not a well man," Ernest said, "and I don't want to tie this girl up to me if I am not going to be able to take care of her."

"Did you come intending to be married?"

At Ern's affirmative answer, the doctor said, "Well, then, why don't you go to the temple and be married? After two or three days come in again, and we'll see what we can do about it."

We went to the temple on October 10, 1919, went through the whole ceremony, and were sealed to each other at the end. We went to Aunt Rosina's house, but it didn't seem much like a celebration. I was not well-impressed with the ceremony — later I would talk it over with my mother, who was shocked and saddened by the fact that parts of it seemed medieval and repulsive to me. Ern was plain miserable; he walked around most of the time because he couldn't stand still. He went right back to the doctor the next day; there was no point in waiting.

Doctor McGregor cut into the diseased place and found a white, fibrous growth, so hard that he couldn't cut it with the scissors. From this center, long tentacles were growing in all directions. These he tried to follow and remove. Instead of staying in St. George two or three days, we were there three weeks, and then Ern went in to Salt Lake City, and I went home.

The teacher of the seventh and eighth grades in Bunkerville had left her post after less than two months. The school board called me by telephone on the same day that Lew was there to take Ernest in to

Salt Lake City: Would I be interested in taking over, at least until they could secure someone else? Both Lew and Ernest thought I might do well to go down and take the position, for we were almost out of cash.

I had no trouble at all with the students. They were just a little ashamed of their conduct and the bad name they had given the school. They knew I was there only in their interest, and, knowing their background, I would not call them "ignorant Mormon brats," but would expect superior work from them because of the fact that they *were* Mormons. I taught them five weeks, and left them with a different attitude toward schoolteachers, while I had $125 to help with expenses.

Ernest was staying at the home of a cousin, Zillie Laub Earl, whose husband was Perry Earl. I never did understand exactly how Mrs. Earl was Ernest's cousin except that there was a common Grand-mother Huffaker somewhere in the background. I knew only that we were here in a rather small home in the northeast part of town, above the Ensign Ward chapel and across the gully east of the State Capitol, and because of their relationship, the family had taken Ern in.

I learned that eight doctors of the L.D.S. Hospital had examined Ernest carefully, and then said to him, "Young man, we don't want your money. We won't deceive you. What you have is malignant, and we know nothing with which to combat it. We understand that the Mayo Brothers in Rochester, Minnesota are experimenting with radiation, but we have no assurance of its effectiveness. Your life span will be from six to nine months."

So that was that. Ernest next learned of a cancer specialist who was treating malignancies, and had many cures to his credit — from warts and moles to some ugly and disfiguring growths. He examined Ernest's neck and assured him that it could be cured, all right, but it would take some time and would be most painful, because it was much deeper. By the time I arrived, the lump on one side was removed and the doctor had started on the other side. I kept a little journal in which I told the story as best I could:

> He used a salve that contained some strong acid, that burned and killed all the flesh it was put on until it became black and hard. Then he put on another salve that would draw this dead flesh out in a solid piece.

This was terribly painful, and he had to take morphine, and then it was almost more than he could endure.

He had three pieces drawn from the right side of his neck and one piece from the left, each from a half inch to a quarter thick and nearly as big as a saucer. This took three months, and a terrible three months it was. . . .

. . . They said that he could not live, but he would only answer that he had been promised by the servants of God that he would live and overcome this disease, and he knew that he would.

Time and again we had the elders in, and usually Ernest got some relief; a number of times he had experiences in which he thought he was out of his body and in beautiful gardens and among many people, but I felt that perhaps the morphine was responsible for it.

One incident I did not record in the book; instead, I wrote it in a letter to my folks. I couldn't believe it; I couldn't understand it. But it happened.

We were alone in the house. The Earls had gone to spend the holidays with a married daughter and were away nearly two weeks. I sympathized with them; it must have been very hard for them to have this sick man occupy their livingroom.

On this evening Ernest seemed much worse than I had ever seen him before. What could I do? I knew no one to call. We had no neighbors to go to — no relatives. No one.

Then there was a knock at the door. I answered it, and a man took off his hat and said, "Is there any trouble in this house?"

I choked up until I couldn't speak; I just stepped aside and pointed to the bed. The stranger walked over, looked down at Ernest, put down his hat, took off his overcoat, and went into the bathroom to wash his hands. Then he picked up the bottle of olive oil on the stand, and proceeded to anoint Ernest with a drop, and go on with a blessing. Before he had finished, Ernest was sleeping quietly. The brother told me his name, which seemed a strange one to me. "Verens" stays in my mind, but I can't be sure.

He told the most incredible story: He lived way down on the Wasatch Boulevard, or above it. As he sat relaxed in his chair, he had such a strong feeling that he was needed somewhere that he got his overcoat and hat and started out. He caught the first streetcar north to North Temple, changed to another for the high Avenues, got off at the stop near the Ensign Ward church, and walked to our little house.

He was not a large man, but thin and wiry, with a heavy head of hair which had once been dark, but was now thickly mixed with gray. He wore it parted in the middle. He was a convert from Wales, he said, and had been in this country for some time. One eye had been lost in an accident, the eyeball punctured had drained out and shriveled. He told me that he had been promised that this eye would be restored, but I thought it would have to be in his next life; it couldn't possibly in this one.

As he sat and visited, I became all the more impressed and astonished that he should have come here without someone telling him about the young man with the cancer, or perhaps seeing us sometime. It was neither, he insisted; he knew that he must go somewhere to someone in great trouble, and he found us here.

Ernest slept well the rest of the night, and awoke refreshed and renewed. For about a week he seemed so much better that we built up hope that he had made a start toward complete recovery. For months he had not been so near his old self as he was the next few days; I myself came to feel more like a wife and less like only a nurse. Surely, surely, this turn for the better would be continued.

At our next trip to the doctor he told us that he had done all that he could for the present. He had removed three large cancers; now he hoped that Ern's body would be able to heal itself. The mild climate of the south would help.

We arrived back home at Mesquite on February 6, 1920.

Birth and Death

THERE WAS MUCH TO BE DONE ON THE FARM, but Ernest was not able to do more than walk around the place. Day and night the pain continued; nothing that we could do seemed to make a bit of difference. We had only God to turn to, and we couldn't seem to get through to Him.

Then someone suggested that we go to the temple in St. George, with the idea that in that holy place, with the faith and prayers of others there, he might be healed. We had heard several stories of others who had been healed of their infirmities, some of them very bad indeed.

So we gathered ourselves together, took such supplies as we had, and Lew took us to St. George, stayed with us until we had secured the Charles Walker home to live in, and, I think, paid the rent. I know that he saw us well-supplied with groceries and arranged for us to have milk delivered daily.

We went to the temple, but it was soon clear to us that this was not the answer. Ernest was so weak that the constant changing of clothes, the getting up and sitting down — the whole procedure — was too much for him. Before the first week was out, he became very ill with a fever and a rash which the doctor said was erysipelas; this he warned me was very contagious. Ern's body was fiery red all over, his temperature was high, and his skin itched. I followed the doctor's instructions, and I also sent word to Uncle Francis Bowler, who was in St. George at the time, asking him to come. With our combined efforts the rash cleared within a few days.

Now Ern had violent nosebleeding, which it seemed would drain his body. Dr. McGregor taught me how to dip a cotton roll into steeped green tea and insert it into the nostril. The tannin in the tea would coagulate the blood and stop the bleeding. All in all, Ern was miserable, sick beyond my help.

One night I will never forget. Ernest was sick; the room smelled of fever and medicine. But there was a moon outside high and bright, the fragrance of fruit blossoms on the air, and one little bird that sang all night. With that for company, I found peace and resignation. I had done all that I could.

By June we were back on the farm, for by now I knew that there was a baby on the way, and I must make preparations. In this I was helped most by my friend and cousin, Vada Hardy Pulsipher. Her mother and my father were full brother and sister; her husband, Bill, was Ernest's cousin and best friend. Her little daughter was more than a year old; I could use her baby shirts, belly bands, pinning blankets, and tie-in the-front gowns, and return them when my baby would grow out of them. I could get flour sacks from the two families, enough to bleach and hem for diapers.

Ma had started saving her flour sacks soon after I was married. She always did unravel them, open, shake, soak, and bleach them if only to use them as lining for quilts or as dishtowels. The bleaching process took such a long time; sometimes the print would never come out.

As for me, I could only help Ernest to dress and to take his pills and nourishment regularly, for now he was living chiefly on a liquid diet. For twenty-four hours a day he rested at short intervals as he could, but mostly he walked himself to exhaustion. Hardly a night passed that we didn't walk the road out toward Lew's place, and pass by the turn and go on to the end of the fence and back again. By that time Ern would be weary, and so would I, for the child I was carrying was becoming active. I always referred to "him" when I mentioned the baby, until the folks worried a little for fear I'd be disappointed, and get a girl.

I knew in general that the child would be born in September, but I was not sure of the date. I seemed so large, and he so active, that I thought we should go to Bunkerville about the tenth, so we packed up and went. Just as we stopped the buggy at my folks' house, Warren Hardy came along. I stopped him, and asked the date of a memorial service for Leila.

When he said that it was to be held September twenty-seventh, I knew that we had come too early. We stayed overnight and went back to the farm in the morning, to wait out the time.

We returned in the forenoon of the twenty-seventh, and I went into labor that afternoon, but it was long, and I wasn't as brave and hardy as I should have been.

Strange how one forgets the pains of childbirth. But though the memory of the pain grew dim, that of my complete helplessness before the great creative force did not. I was not I. I had no control over me. I was only an atom in the hands of some mighty power. I was walking — walking, restless, fearful, worried — but totally powerless. (I remembered the government bulletin for rural mothers which assured me that 95 percent of all babies would be born *almost* as well without a doctor as with one.) Then the rhythm of the pains came harder and more often. (A friend long ago had talked about butcher knives under the bed to cut the pains. I thought, Well, she was right about being willing to try anything.) I could not lie down; the bed was too soft. Quilts were folded on the floor with sheets and a rubber protector over them; my baby was to be born here before the fireplace.

At last I became so weary with it all that I would fall into a semi-coma between pains. As though from a great distance I heard the midwife say over and over, "Help me! Help me! Bear down! Bear down!" But I couldn't help her. I couldn't bear down. I couldn't help it when the pains began going the wrong way, or scattered their force without doing any good.

"We must do something," she said at last in a panic. "We must do something quick or we are going to lose them both. Get someone on the way to the doctor! Go see if the Bishop's car is in running order!"

Numbly, I thought that the doctor was ten hours away by the fastest car we could get over the road. There was no telephone here, no other way to reach him. Ten hours would be a long time to lie like this. The pains were running the wrong way, I could sense that, but I couldn't make them behave, and between each I would relax into a brief sleep.

Then Pa's hands were on my head, hard and rough, but cool. He had just washed them, I knew. He always stopped to wash his hands before he placed them on any person's head to ask God's blessing. As if from a distance I heard his voice, clear and strong and deliberate: "Rebuke the power of the Destroyer, cause that every part of her body shall perform its proper function, that the muscles shall react properly, that the bones shall be flexible, that her heart shall be equal to its task, that all things shall be governed by the power of light and life and shall work in harmony to the end that this child shall be born well and normally . . ."

As though by the force of his will, by the very weight of his hands on my head, I felt a blessed relaxation, and then a lusty cry. My son was born, white hair and all.

The day after the baby was born, we had word that a Salt Lake City doctor had secured radium, a new miracle cure for cancer which was being used by the Mayo Brothers. Though the reports were fragmentary, we were willing to try anything. Ernest felt sure that God's Hand was behind it all, and this would be the answer. This must not fail; this had to be it!

After the baby's eighth day, we returned to the ranch, I to take over matters there, and Mother Pulsipher to go with Ern in Lew's new Buick. Through all our trouble, Lew was the one always on hand to take us where we needed to go, always with a road-worthy, reliable car.

Ern's spirits soared. This would surely be the long-looked-for cure. "Mang," (the pet name of the whole family for their mother) would go with Ern, while I would stay on the ranch, prepare the meals, keep the house, do the laundry, and help Grandpa John-David with the chores.

Most important was the duty of acting as "central" in Lew's telephone system. The central office was in the front room, and I must place all long distance calls: those between Bunkerville and Mesquite, and those of either town to Littlefield on the east or St. Thomas or Overton or Logandale on the Upper Muddy Valley on the west.

Grandpa John-David was a pleasant, quiet old man. He found in little Ern a constant delight, trotting him on his knee, chanting rhyme songs and fitting folk games with his fingers and toes. But Grandpa had many duties besides entertaining the baby; he must feed the horses, milk the cows, separate the milk, and take the skimmed milk and bran back to the pigs. He also answered the telephone when I was busy.

Little Ernie grew and developed normally, a happy little spirit, good-natured and responsive. The older he grew, the more his grandfather delighted to hold him, rock him, or play with him, seeming to enjoy having the baby get his hands tangled in the white beard that was so thrifty, and such a novel thing for a tiny baby boy.

During the three months of his stay this time, Ernest didn't write a single letter — just a line on the bottom of his Mother's. Hers were brief, and without the note of optimism which I longed for. This treatment was different: the results could not be immediately visible, but the doctor held out hope. He would plan the treatments so that Ernest could come home by Christmas Eve, and remain to see the effects, which should be favorable.

I don't know what I expected, but I was totally unprepared for the emaciated, weak husband who got out of the car with so much effort and assistance, and had to be helped unsteadily into the house. He was only a shadow of himself. No. Indeed, he was not better.

Early the next morning we helped him into the big white rocking chair which had played an important part in our lives. I had the baby dressed and Ernest asked to hold him, but he just couldn't do it. I held the child up to show how healthy and happy and rosy he was, but that was all. After a light breakfast, Ernest wanted to go to the corral to see how his horses were faring. He leaned heavily on me, but he did make it down, rested against the pole fence in the bright sunlight, and seemed to be glad things were as good as they were. Slowly he made his way back to the bed, which he never left again.

From his first night at home, some of his quorum brethren came to sit with him during the night: two to stay until two o'clock, the next two to remain until breakfast. There were times when Ernest would talk to them clearly and in full possession of his faculties; at other times there were only snatches, disconnected phrases, or single words.

On the morning of January eighth he called me to him and talked like his old self, clearly, and with love and appreciation. He was hungry, he said; he'd like an egg and toast and hot milk. I was just starting to cook when his mother came down and went to his bedside. He was unconscious. All day he remained thus — silent and still as death, but with the heart still beating. With the sunset it was finished — on January 8, 1921.

What followed is a blur in my memory. Somehow one lives through these crises, walking in a daze through the crowds that come, all eager to be of some assistance, sitting through the meeting with its songs and talk-talk, hearing the sound of earth being shoveled into the open grave. It all blends in the memory as a drama in which I was a spectator rather than a part of the cast. I had with me of my own family only my brother Melvin to lean on. My parents were on their way home from Alamo, Nevada, where my sister Charity was teaching school.

I took my baby back to the ranch house and to the room I had occupied all the time I had been here — except the last night, when Ern's body was laid out there ready for the coffin, and I slept fitfully on the livingroom couch.

The morning after the funeral Mang announced that she was going back north to Idaho with some of the relatives who had been visiting in the area. They had been in Mesquite a week and were ready to start back home. She needed to get away a little while after the strain of the three months in Salt Lake City, and this last week here. That left Grandpa John-David, baby Ernest, and me, right where we had been the past three months. We were all well-oriented; we were congenial. There was no criticism or complaint.

I wondered at the time if the basic reason for her going was that she had never been able to reconcile herself to having me in the house. She had never been cordial with me from the first time we met; we never talked to each other as women normally do. There had been the time when Ernest called for her to come in, and asked her in my presence to have my name put on his life insurance policy as beneficiary. This she promised she would do, but did not do, nor did either of us ever mention it again.

I knew of all the Pulsipher family reverses, but of the finances after our marriage I knew nothing. I had spent my savings on the rent and living costs while we were in St. George at the temple. My parents paid the midwife for her work at the birth of the baby, so I was without cash and with no way then to earn any. But I had decided to remain here. All that my husband had worked for all his life was here; we had walked so many times along the top of "our forty." Ernest liked to look at the width and length of it and of the lush growth of alfalfa. This was the source not only of hay, but of honey, which had come to be a good cash crop. We had — just one time — climbed to the top of the knoll where we would build our home.

If Mang had ever discussed money matters with anyone, it would have been with Lew, who was really the financier of the family. He was always so generous, so ready to take us where we needed to go, and with no mention of cost. It was he who finally told me that Mang had received the insurance money; she never said anything about it, and neither did I.

The whole problem was that we did not talk to each other. She would make breakfast for herself and Grandpa while I bathed and dressed the baby. Then I'd go in and get something for myself, for I knew that I must eat and have plenty of good food if *he* were to thrive. I felt no guilt about eating anything there was, especially eggs and milk and vegetables from the garden. All these were plentiful. And I always cleaned up after myself. Always I waited until they had finished their meal before I went into the kitchen to get my own. I was most taken aback when she told me that I would be expected to pay for telephone calls to my family! I who had served as operator all those months!

While Mang was up north before Ernest died, I had found the diaries of Grandpa John Pulsipher, and was so much impressed with them that I decided to copy them. I got an old Remington typewriter and a ream of paper, and worked at them at odd times, when there was nothing else to do and the baby was asleep. I still think that this record is the most eloquent and detailed of any I have seen, made in

[244]

1857 during that time of suspense, when the Mormons were faced with an army, approaching in spite of all their efforts to stop it. This was the time of the battle song, "O ZION, DEAR ZION . . . land of the free . . . On the necks of thy foes thou shalt tread. And their silver and gold, as the Prophets foretold, shall be brought to adorn thy fair head!" was being sung in the great tabernacle, while young men like John Pulsipher were freezing in the mountains. Only because of their foresight in digging or enlarging caves, where they had fires and some shelter, did any of them survive.

John Pulsipher wrote eloquently and in some detail, and I copied it all carefully. But that was during Ernest's treatments with radium, and though I talked some about it to Father John-David, I talked little about it to anyone else. I thought that it was worth doing and that I should make use of the opportunity.

Then someone told me that Laura Abbott had the diary of her father, Uncle Myron Abbott, but it was so old that she thought it was of no value, and was going to use it for paper to start fires in her kitchen stove. I promptly called her on the telephone and told her I'd send her a brand new Sears Roebuck catalog in exchange for it. Ern's brother Stanley made the exchange for me, and when I showed him the typed copy of Grandpa John's record book, he became interested in this Myron Abbott one. It was most important because the writer was the watermaster on the Bunkerville ditch during the early years of that settlement. He had recorded every flood, and the number of loads of rock and brush and days of labor it took to get the water back into the ditch. Since every man was supposed to share this work, it was important that the account be complete and detailed. Years later, government officials who came to study the conditions of the Virgin River settlements said that this volume was literally worth its weight in gold.

My chief interest was that the town of Bunkerville had a moving population. Every year several families would leave, their empty homes sometimes taken over by newly-married couples. Why was I concerning myself with this kind of thing, here on the farm? Why couldn't I find things to do like needlework or crochet or patchwork quilt blocks? For one thing, I hadn't a dime with which to buy a spool of thread.

[245]

In the meantime, my parents had been having troubles of their own, so many and so bad that Ma remembered it as the one dark, dark time in all her married life. She always counted this "disaster" year from the midsummer of 1920 to midsummer of 1921. It really began, of course, with my engagement and marriage to a mortally sick man, but was more closely brought in to her when I came home to have my baby and they saw Ernest's suffering at close range.

Dudley's ordeal was perhaps the most traumatic. He was just past his eighth birthday, and had gone in the morning to take the cows to the pasture along with two of his little friends, new to the river. All forenoon they splashed and swam and had water fights, until when he came in as the family was at dinner, his face was red, his hair stiff with silt, his eyes bloodshot, and his whole body tired out. He ate a fairly good meal, and went to lie down. No one paid any special attention to him as he slept, until Ma noticed that he was whimpering a little.

When she went to look at him, his eyelids were red and puffed up like inflated red balls. She at once bathed them in a cool epsom salts solution, for they were too sensitive to bear the weight of a cloth. For a week they tried every remedy they knew, but he grew steadily worse, running a fever, his eyes so sensitive to light that the room was kept darkened all day.

After several days, during which he was no better, they decided to take him to St. George to Dr. Woodbury, who had to put the child under ether in order to examine his eyes. He wore a serious face as he reported his findings: one eye already blinded, the other in great danger also, with the chance that the infection would reach the brain and render him an imbecile for life. He suggested that they keep him here in the dark the rest of the day and take him home during the night. Upon arriving home they should keep him in a dark room until there was a drastic change in his condition. There was little anyone could do.

Ma felt that she would rather bury the child than to have him go through life a grinning idiot — he who had always been so sharp, so alert to everything. If that were the answer, she would prefer death.

They got back home Saturday and the Bishop sent word out asking all members of the ward to unite in a fast all day Sunday for this child, that he should recover his health. How many took this seriously there is no way to know, but in every public prayer there was a petition for a special blessing for him, that he might retain his sight. Sunday evening at dark a group of about ten of the men who held the priesthood gathered at the home, at Pa's invitation, their purpose to hold a prayer circle in which they would unite to pray that Dudley be restored to health, or if he were appointed unto death, that he be taken.

Ma sat holding Dudley in her arms in the center of the circle, while the brethren kneeled. The prayers were short but sincere. Sometime during this, the child fell asleep, and at the end they all slipped quietly out.

All through the week Dudley had slept on a folded quilt on the floor; it was cooler on the floor, and he had a great fear of falling. He slept well this night; he was still asleep the next morning when breakfast was ready. The family knelt around the table as usual so that they would not disturb him. Francis was to stand by, or lie beside Dudley in case he should want anything.

Breakfast was just being served when Francis came running in, calling, "Dudley can see! Dudley can see!"

He had opened his eyes and asked, "What they got that old shawl hanging over the transom for?" Then with his finger he traced the design in the linoleum on the floor.

Such excitement! Such joy! Dudley wanted to hug everyone; he wanted to look and look at everything. Where was Griz? He must see him, too. Ma could only weep for joy. "Someone call Juanita," she said, and at the ranch I took down the receiver to hear the happy clamor.

"Dudley can see!" "His eye is bright and perfect — the good one." "He's all perfectly well!" came in different voices over the wire.

"The Lord's a good man, ain't he," was the child's way of acknowledging the transformation, for to him something more than salves and medicines had combined to make this miracle come to pass.

With Dudley made whole, the family was all in good health ready to carry on, each his appointed task, every one with a new fervor. The Fourth of July was just ahead, and this family could really celebrate, not so much in doing different things but in putting new vim into old ceremonies — raising the flag, reading from the Declaration of Independence, entering into the competitive sports of the afternoon and the dance at night.

I thought of all this, alone with the old folks and my baby on the ranch.

The Twenty-fourth

SOME OF THE PULSIPHER FAMILY FROM GUNLOCK HAD COME DOWN TO CELEBRATE THE FOURTH OF JULY AT MESQUITE. They brought word from Aunt Florie Truman, Mang's sister, to bring me back with them to Gunlock. From there, she would take me to her ranch on the Mogotsu, a lovely place with cool weather, mountain water, and plenty of fruit. They'd be glad to have me for as long as I cared to stay.

Would I like to go? Would I! To me it was the hand of God extended. What I would do at the end of the visit on the ranch, I didn't know, but I'd take every scrap that belonged to me when I left here. That wasn't hard; I had nothing except my scant wardrobe, the baby's things, two quilts, a pair of blankets, and two sheets and extra pillow cases for my two good pillows. I filled my two suitcases and put extras into a new "gunney-sack" that the folks had left on their Christmas visit after the funeral. Mang was not at home when we pulled away.

The Truman team was in Gunlock when we arrived, so it was only a matter of moving from one wagon into another. The reality was so much better than I had anticipated; it was so wonderfully cool and pleasant, the water like ice, almost, the fresh vegetables and early apricots at their best. The weather was nippy in the early morning and pleasant all day. I had such an appetite that I was ashamed of myself; the baby was happy and hungry, and I was glad that I had him weaned. At ten months he was not yet walking alone, but could pull himself to his feet and walk around a chair, sit down, and get up again, as if he were in training.

In the backyard there was an iron bedstead set up, which I used for a playpen. The baby didn't crawl under to get out; he used the sides to walk along. One day I found him sitting on the ground, holding his hand out as if to touch a large red racer snake, which in turn was watching him closely. I cried out, but approached carefully lest the snake strike. In the back of my mind I knew that this was not a poisonous snake; its bite would not be much worse than a wasp's sting, and what a beautiful little picture they made! What a snapshot this would be! A snake and a baby, strangers trying to get acquainted!

Sensing my presence, the snake turned and slithered away into the grass. The family thought I was strange not to follow and kill it, but I explained that it was not dangerous; it lived on gophers, field mice, and insects, and was considered by some farmers to bring good luck.

Soon the family began to plan their trip to Enterprise for the Twenty-fourth of July celebration. Our national holiday was important; all were proud of the founding of our great nation. But to us, the entrance of the pioneers into the Great Salt Lake Valley was more significant. Our own grandparents had often recalled the long trek, whether by team or handcart, and the thrilling arrival in the Valley.

We traveled in a covered wagon to Enterprise. The climb from Mogotsu Creek north to the Mountain Meadows was steep, but suddenly the country opened onto a broad plain covered with sage and greasewood. So this was the Mountain Meadows where the massacre had taken place — the crime which had troubled Brother Nephi Johnson on his deathbed. Far across this valley, nestled among giant lombardy poplar trees, was the Burgess ranch house, with a large orchard behind it. In 1857 this had been the site of the Jacob Hamblin summer home; he had used the same spring of water. But he also had a rock house with a shed and corrals on top of the hill to the east, the outlines of which I had been told were clearly visible. Perhaps on our way back we might detour and go around that way, but for now our destination was Enterprise.

The town was larger than I had expected, not so much in the number of houses, but in the fact that they were more scattered, with each home taking a half-block. I had expected to headquarter in the wagon, but a lady insisted that I stay in her house, which I learned was the home of Amm Truman, the man who had kept my little pony, Selah, so many years before. I finally found courage to ask about her.

"Oh, so you're the girl that had little Celia first," his wife said. "She was surely a blessing from heaven. If ever there was a perfect kid-horse, she was it. I never thought an animal could be so much loved and petted as she was. As Bill grew up, he wanted a bigger horse that he could use on the cattle drive, so Celia became Betty's. They were great companions, though Betty didn't really ride her too much; she liked to pet her and take her apples cut up into quarters. Finally Celia stepped into a gopher hole as Bill was running her hard chasing a calf and broke her leg. They had to shoot her. Betty was a long time getting over that."

It was a relief to know about my Selah, and a relief to know that she was gone, and quickly. I didn't want to even talk about her to Betty; I had grieved too much for her. I assumed that Betty also was sad at her passing; the experience had best be left without discussion. Evidently Pa had made it a point to tell Amm the pony's name.

When Amm came in, he asked at once about Pa, and how he was getting along. I was glad to report that he was well, but not the athlete he had been as a boy. He had to lead his horse to a stump to mount now, I told him, and to Amm that spoke volumes.

In a small town one cannot remain anonymous. To the oldsters, I was the daughter of Henry Leavitt, the first Leavitt to break through and marry a Santa Clara Dutch girl. After that, all three of the other Hafen sisters had married Leavitt men, all descendants of Dudley, who himself had taken on an Indian girl as one of his plural wives. That branch of the Leavitts was sure mixed up!

To most of the village I was the widow of Ernest Pulsipher, the boy who had come from his mission with a cancer that couldn't be cured, though the family had tried everything under the sun in its treatment. Strange there on a mission this thing should get hold of Ern; you'd think the Lord would have more concern for men who were out preaching His Gospel. But who were we to question?

So, his widow was here with the Bert Truman family. She had taught school in both Bunkerville and Mesquite; she'd likely be okay on the dance floor.

Rodney's sisters were encouraging him to loosen up and dance, and not just stand on the sidelines and look on. He had insisted that nobody wanted to dance with a kid that didn't know how. I joined in with his sisters, and when he demurred, I bet him a candy bar that I could teach him to schottische in one time on the floor, if he'd stay on for one full round. When the music set up the right tune, he came to test the wager. We got into position, and I set up the one, two, three, skip, routine, and before he knew it, he was in perfect time and execution. He was almost breathless when the music stopped, but said "You win!" Now on the second half, he would try the variants in footwork during the pauses between those one-two-three steps. So in his first time on the floor he had become so confident that he would try most anything else.

This little demonstration was good for me, too. If I could teach a youngster to schottische, I ought to be able to waltz or two-step. At least it would not be too big a gamble for a fellow to ask. So I hardly missed a dance the whole evening through. I was glad that I had worn my one nice dress, and the new shoes that I hadn't put on through all the months of my marriage until the funeral. Before the dance was out, they were well broken in.

The morning program on the Twenty-fourth began with a parade. But this was something to take part in, not to watch; the celebration would include everyone in town who could possibly join in the pageant of the pioneers. The families who made up the emigrant train were to gather at the edge of town, but the band of young men who were to represent the Indians kept their hideout a secret.

When the line formed to enter town, a white-topped buggy led the way, with an elder, representing Brigham Young lying on a bed in the back. Behind this were the covered wagons drawn by oxen or by mismatched teams of horses, mules, and cows. All the wagons had torn, sagging covers of old canvas or worn quilts; all had hardware and furniture tied on the outside; some had poles out the back upon

[252]

which were boxes of chickens or rabbits or little pigs. Most of the men walked beside the teams, while women holding babies sat on the spring seats, and children's faces peered from beneath the covers. Behind the wagons came the handcarts, some with children riding on top, all fitted up as for a long journey.

At the top of a slight incline the buggy pulled out and came to a stop. Raising on his elbow, Brigham Young looked out over the imaginary valley and said, "It is enough. This is the place! Drive on." Another short pause and he climbed out of the buggy, gazed upon the desert valley, and climbed back into the seat to ride the remainder of the way beside the driver.

The participants knew in a general way that somewhere en route the Indians were to attack, but they were hardly prepared for what happened. With a sudden whoop the band dashed out of a narrow lane, yelling and shooting into the air. They looked fierce and real, with their brown bodies bare, except for their breech cloths, their faces streaked with red and blue paint, and feathers stuck into the bands around their heads.

Up toward the wagons they dashed in a cloud of dust, while the white men shot back valiantly. One Indian slid from his horse as though wounded, crawled behind a bush, and kept up a steady fire at the train. Another snatched a little three-year-old girl from the top of a handcart just in front, and was off to the hills at breakneck speed. Though the child knew the Indian was her brother, her crying was real enough.

One team stampeded and ran into a fence, tipping the wagon over. The drivers of others were kept busy at the bridles, calming their animals, until all were relieved when the Indians had galloped past, and the train could move on again to the camping place. The circle was formed beside the meeting house, and the women set about getting breakfast, frying eggs and bacon, and putting out such dainties as real pioneers never saw.

Before the meal was served, white scouts returned from the hills, bringing with them the stolen child and all the Indians. Brigham Young greeted them all with dignity, and motioned them to form a circle, where the white men joined them to smoke a pipe of peace. It was all very impressive and interesting, but to the breakfast-less children it was too long and drawn out. The smoking ceremony over, Brigham Young made a short talk to the natives. The chief grunted approval, and said a few words to his followers in a strange language, to which they gave assent. Only then was grace said, one blessing on each separate table.

At ten o'clock the crowd gathered in the meeting house for a program. Brigham Young and the other pioneer men of the train sat on the stand; on one side the Indians squatted on the floor, and on the other some of the old folks had a place of honor. The first song would have to be the song of the plains, "Come, Come Ye Saints," the hymn which had sustained every company of emigrants on their long and arduous journey.

Brother Brigham was the orator of the day. There were some who thought he looked and sounded like the real Brigham, as he told the stories they all knew so well, stories of what their parents had endured for the Gospel's sake. He told of the dark days in Missouri and Nauvoo, of the mobbings and whippings and burnings, and of those who had left their homes and farms to camp with the fugitives in the snow across the great river. He went on to tell of the journey to this dry land, this place where the Kingdom of God was to be established in the tops of the mountains and exalted above the hills. Though it had cost so much in human suffering and sacrifice, it should never be torn down or given to another people. As he closed, there was an ardor throughout the audience that was almost electric.

After the closing song and prayer, as the audience rose to leave the building, the organist began to play again softly the music of the opening song, "Come, Come Ye Saints." Through all the greetings and visiting, this melody ran like a subconscious expression of hope and faith. Where at the beginning of the service it had seemed to look to the past and to express the trials of the pioneers, now it was forward-looking and optimistic, a do-and-dare challenge.

Games and contests of various kinds on the square filled the afternoon. Everyone joined in, whether threading needles with the men, or racing three-legged with the boys. And another dance and picnic would close the celebration, with pies and cakes auctioned off, and free lemonade provided by the committee.

I wore the same dress that I had on the night before, but with a strand of beads, and a fancy comb in my hair. This time three other young women with babies agreed to hire one girl to sit with them all, and would take mine in, too. So this night I started with Rodney for the first dance and hardly missed a set the whole evening. It seemed such a long time since I had done anything just for the fun of it; I felt almost young again. I'd try to join in like this more often.

On the way home we went to the Burgess ranch, climbed the hill to the east, and were surprised at the distances to be seen in every direction. This was the Mountain Meadows that extended over the Great Basin Divide, the water on one side draining to the Great Basin, and on the other to the Pacific Ocean. Moving objects could be seen miles away, and a company of wagons camped within three or four miles would be clearly visible. I felt that Brother Johnson's last visions of "BLOOD, BLOOD" had surely been seen in life at close range. But men did not gather here by chance or mere hearsay. If they were here, they had come because they were ordered to come. And whatever went on was done because it had been ordered, not because individuals had acted upon impulse.

Dixie College

Aunt Florie took me down to Gunlock to the home of Uncle Charles and Aunt Kate. Though the family were all very cordial with me, I couldn't help remembering the old adage: "Guests are like fish; after three days they stink!"

After church on Sunday, several of the family met at the home of Uncle France, who had been so kind to us in St. George. He had come often to see us, and several times I had gone to ask him to come to administer when Ernest was especially bad. In the families everyone said that Ernest looked more like his Uncle France Bowler than like the blonde Pulsiphers. Both had dark brown hair, and neither was as tall as the Pulsipher men, but more agile and quick.

On this afternoon their Grandpa Holt was visiting. His wife had recently died, and he couldn't stand to stay in the big, empty house alone and do for himself.

"What are you intending to do this winter?" someone asked.

I had to admit that I didn't know, unless it would be to go back to the ranch at Mesquite. There were no teaching positions vacant in the Nevada district, and I didn't know whether I could qualify in Utah or not. I really felt I ought to go back to school another year, at least, if I hoped to teach outside of Nevada.

Grandpa Holt made the proposition: "Why don't you go to Dixie College and live in my empty house there? I've got at least three grandchildren that should be in school at Dixie — Erma and Stella Bowler, and Emma Hunt — and there may be others. You needn't pay any rent, if you just keep the place clean and take care of the furniture. There's plenty of wood all cut to last the winter, and I'll pay the utility bills. You would be in charge."

Before we were through we had agreed that Lillian Jones should go along, too. One or two more would make little difference in the utility bills, and they could furnish their own food; I would also need my sister Aura, who had graduated from the Bunkerville high school, to help with the baby. She was an excellent manager in the house, a good cook and an immaculate housekeeper. She'd be worth her cost anywhere.

So it was that the very next day we went to St. George, taking Grandpa Holt, with Uncle France in charge of the outfit and his wife and Erma along to assess the situation. I could move into the house at once and do what I found necessary, but first of all I must get word to my folks about our plan, so that they could bring Aura up and some supplies for us both. I might have to sponge off Aunt Rosina Blake for a couple of days.

It just seemed too good to be true! I could hardly believe it myself! I hated to admit, even to myself, how I dreaded to go back to the memories at the ranch and to Mang's too-evident disapproval.

My folks were even more delighted than I. They lost no time load-ing — in addition to Aura and her things — bottled fruit, dried figs, apricots, molasses, honey, flour, cracked wheat cereal, ham and bacon, homemade soap, and bedding, towels, dish towels, and dishes.

They came straight to the place, and I was out to meet them. Like me, they were humble before this good fortune. Having both of us in school and still not having to neglect the baby seemed the answer to their prayers. The Lord certainly had a hand in this, they thought.

"You have taken on quite a responsibility here," Pa cautioned. "Use your best judgment, but don't be too quick to dictate or question. Expect that the girls will act like ladies; don't have any rough stuff, even in fun. Some sort of a curfew should be set up. Remember that this good man has put into your hands the home he spent a lifetime building and improving; you should not have to remind his grand-children of this." Nor did I. The grandchildren were very strict that nothing be defaced or broken or left dirty, a fact which I appreciated very much.

Behind the home a short distance was a stone half-cellar, some four feet deep and eight feet above the ground, an exceptionally good place for storage, with shelves for fruit, bins for potatoes or squash, and a screened milk cupboard for dairy products: milk, butter, and cheese. Though all the buildings were old, they were well-preserved and functional, the best of that older period.

We girls had a long session in which we planned our procedures and divided our responsibilities. My first care would be the baby; my sister Aura would share this. The others need be not concerned about him at all. We divided our home duties to work in teams. The two Bowler girls would work together; Emma Hunt would work with Aura; Lillian Jones and I would make the third team. Responsibility for the meals would last one week, during which the two girls would provide all the food, prepare and serve it, clear up after it, and wash the dishes. It was a big order, but it seemed to work out better than to try to divide the kitchen tasks. The Bowler girls prided themselves on having good food well-served. Aura was a home economics major who also was a good cook and liked to manage, while Emma was more than glad to take the orders and help as she could. Lillian was the strong one of our team, but among us we got along very well indeed, without an argument or serious disagreement.

As the two wagons from Gunlock were unloaded, I thought I could serve best by keeping from under foot; each girl knew her own things and had some idea of where she wanted to put them. Because of the baby, I had already taken charge of the front bedroom, which was really the nicest in the house. Aunt Rosina had brought a baby bed with a let-down side in from storage — just the thing for little Ernest. This was only a loan; Aunt Rosina was in the baby business, taking in mothers for delivery and ten-day care. She insisted that the little new babies were better off in their little lined baskets, which each mother furnished, in order that the baby would have no adjustment when it was taken home.

We polished up the wooden bedstead and put our bedding on the mattress, after turning and cleaning it; laundered the curtains, and cleaned out the closet before putting our things in. We had already cleaned an area in the rock cellar in which to store some of the items the folks had brought up, hanging a ham by its leather string on a nail, putting all the other things in a small area. When coming to the last of the items in the wagons from Gunlock, Uncle France came pushing a little two-wheeled cart, sturdy and new, saying, "Where did this thing come from? Who put *it* in?"

Nobody knew. Nobody had seen it loaded into the wagon — the one which carried Emma Hunt's and Lillian Jones' clothes and supplies. It had evidently been put in before the real loading commenced. It was collapsible, and had a piece of heavy cardboard between it and the boxes of bottle fruit. Clearly, it could not have been meant for anyone but Baby Ernest — and his Mother. In all my life I have never received a gift more needed, more appreciated, than this. Too young to walk and too heavy to carry, Ernie posed a real problem. This would make his transportation a pleasure. I felt sure that Uncle France had put it into the other wagon so that his own family would not know, or even suspect it would come to me.

I wondered at the generosity of Grandpa Holt in giving us living quarters, lighted and heated at his expense so that we had every opportunity to devote our time and thoughts to our studies. I tried to take full advantage of it; for the most part the other girls did too.

Aura and I planned our classes together, arranging them so that one or the other of us could be at home with the baby. During the fall quarter Aura went early every morning, and had two classes before ten o'clock. By that time I would have Ernie bathed, dressed, and fed, ready for a trip out-of-doors. I would put him into the little cart and start toward school, usually meeting or waiting for Aura in front of the public library. It was a good place to meet, for we could pull him to shelter under the entrance. Rain or shine, it was the same. There was a cover of sorts on the cart, and we had a waterproof hood–jacket combination for him, with woolly mittens for the cold weather.

From her first piano lesson, Aura resolved to have the honor award which was given each spring. After all that she had gone through earlier to take piano lessons, nothing here seemed hard. True, she wouldn't touch the piano at home if any of the Gunlock girls were there; but when the house was empty except for the baby, she would play with a right good will. The college kept a piano in the basement of the tabernacle especially for students who had none at home or who wanted to practice in their free time at school. Miss Thurston helped them make out a schedule, but if one failed to use the piano when she was scheduled, she would lose her right to it.

Miss Lucy Phillips taught an English class slanted for teachers in the upper grades, which meant, essentially, a review of formal grammar. My work in Nevada had given me a good background, as had my experience in teaching.

At the close of class one morning she stopped me and asked why I didn't arrange my work so that I could participate in the debate program. (I was correcting papers for 25 cents an hour.)

I had not time, I told her. I must work to pay off a note I had signed for part of my tuition. I'd really enjoy it, but couldn't work it in.

The very next day I was called into the president's office.

"Miss Phillips says that you cannot debate because you must pay off a note for your tuition. How much do you owe?"

"About twenty-five dollars, I believe. I signed for thirty."

He called to his secretary and asked her to look up Mrs. Pulsipher's note and bring it in to him. He glanced at it, tore it into strips, and threw them into the wastebasket.

"Forget that note," he said. "Go ahead and debate. You're worth more than that on a debate team."

I could not trust myself to thank him properly, but never, before or since, has twenty-five dollars seemed so large a sum.

I don't know how the debate teams were made up — whether they just decided among each other those who would like to work together, or whether Miss Phillips paired them off. I only know that I was assigned to work with Paul Thurston, an enthusiastic nineteen-year-old, tall, lanky, all arms and legs and hands and feet. He was intense in his interest, though, and willing to spend any amount of time digging out information. I'm not clear on the wording of the question, but it had to do with the establishment of a World Court.

We worked together on our general outline. He would speak first and establish three points, I would follow, establish only one new point, but reiterate and strengthen his and summarize the case. Several times in the course of our preparation he came at night, threw a pebble at my window to waken me, and as soon as I had the window propped up, he'd begin: "Look, I've got an idea . . ." "Where did you get that citation you used the other day?" "What do you think about this answer to . . ." In this vein we would sometimes talk far into the night, though his file box was already crowded full.

My most pressing problem was what to wear. I hadn't had a new dress in the last two years. My philosophy was that a dress may be new to the society in which you move if the people hadn't seen it before. I had talked with Aura about doing something with one or another of my old dresses, but she couldn't see the slightest possibility.

I don't know just how she got it, but she came home with a length of "Factory" long enough for a dress. Evidently she and Arthur K. Hafen's wife, Orilla, had been talking. I suspected that one of the Ladies' Club members had learned that I was to represent Dixie College, and I needed to make a decent appearance.

Aura did sewing for Mrs. Hafen, making shirts for her family of boys; they evidently discussed my dilemma. This "Factory" was so named because it had been woven from local cotton into fabric at the local factory. It was a heavy piece — not as heavy as a wagon cover canvas — but heavier than most of the fabric which was used to line quilts. It was a rich cream, bordering on yellow, and had a sheen on the right side — a satin finish.

Thus fitted out I went forth with new confidence. My dress might not be stylish, but it was different, and from the stage in the assembly hall, it just might not be too bad. I confess that I was shaken when my opponent from Cedar City, Miss Clara Farnsworth, came onstage in an expensive tailored suit, the style and quality eloquent of price.

The two teams had much in common: two inexperienced young men and two mature ladies. All were well-prepared; indeed, the three judges in different parts of the room would be taxed to say who won.

As the debate progressed, we could see that we had met our equals, perhaps our superiors, for their speeches were well-organized and memorized. But in the rebuttals, Paul had a card which answered very neatly one argument which they had stressed. Miss Farnsworth came back with evidence that Paul's main source had changed his mind on a point, and had thus destroyed his whole basic argument — or maintained that she had. By the time I had a chance to speak again

[261]

I had to restrain myself — there were so many little contradictions that I wanted to point out. "Easy does it!" flashed into my mind, and I remained calm and collected, made my point, and picked up or turned a phrase or two which brought a definite response from the audience.

The chairman collected the decisions of the three judges. As he studied them, I felt a great uncertainty, for our opponents had indeed presented a strong case. But when he finally read the cards, and every one of the three had voted in our favor, the audience went wild. Walter Smith, the new student body president, jumped up onto the stage to be followed by the crowd. The judges did not confer; their points of interest were not always the same, but in the end, each gave Dixie, clearly and emphatically, the decision — but by a narrow margin. I wondered if the decision might have been different if the debate had been held in Cedar City.

Paul was overjoyed, but so disappointed that none of his family had come out to hear him, that he went home and shaved the dog, leaving the hair only on the head and shoulders and on the tassel on its tail, as visible evidence that something important had happened that night — something to be remembered.

This year at Dixie was especially hard, for the legislature had provided no money — or not enough to carry on the regular activities. Last year's yearbook had been beautiful, indeed. It was large, well-illustrated with hand drawings and many photographs, but now the students must do with only limited funds — so limited that they could have only group pictures, small and poor at that.

Things came to a crisis on "D Day," when the senior boys gave the D on the hill above town its annual coat of whitewash. The climb was steep, the letter large, the buckets of lime heavy, so that the workers were worn out by the time they had finished. The two Miles boys, Henry and Wyatt, did not appear, though they were leading seniors. Their classmates later caught them and held them down while an expert with a pair of clippers ran a line on each from the base of the neck in back over the top of the head to the forehead, and another over the head from ear to ear, leaving a large bare cross on top. A Pectol boy was also caught; a "D" was put in the middle of his forehead with a brown solution of mild acid.

In the Virgin Valley

WITH THE CLOSING OF SCHOOL, we all cooperated to be sure that we left the house and yards in good condition. The four Gunlock girls were all going home; Aura would go directly to Las Vegas, where she knew that she could find work. I had secured a contract to teach fifth and sixth grades in Bunkerville. After my brief experience with the eighth grade two winters before, the townspeople seemed glad to have me back. I would spend most of my summer at the Cabin Spring.

Charity had received a call to go on a mission to the southern states, the first girl of Bunkerville to receive a mission assignment. This really worried Pa, for another flood had wiped out his farm entirely, and he had no regular income. One day at the dinner table the subject came up, and I volunteered: "I'll send you forty dollars a month for the first year, if you'll give me half the blessing." I kept that promise; every month she received her check promptly, and always expressed her gratitude.

The ward followed the regular pattern for sending out their missionaries: a special dance, with picnic and sale, a quilt to raffle off, and a few other items for auction. At any rate, they raised more than enough to pay transportation to her field of labor.

The first month I set up my plan for spending my salary: to Charity, $40.00; to Mother for board and baby care, $30.00; to tithing, $8.00, which left me only a measly $42.00. How could I ever

[263]

save enough to get through college at that rate? But when I went in, at the close of the year, to settle my tithing, the Bishop said that he must list me as a "part-tithe payer." I should have paid my $12.00 tithing first, he said, and then do whatever I wished to with the remainder. I insisted that the $40.00 went first to the Church, leaving me only $80.00 to use for myself. But he would not be convinced.

"I'll have to put you down as a part-tithe payer," he insisted. "Would you like that on the records?"

"I'll argue it out before St. Peter when we get there," I told him. "I believe he'll agree that I'm making quite a liberal donation to the cause."

I said nothing to the folks about this, but evidently the Bishop talked to Pa about it, thinking to get more. But Pa only said that I was an adult, and could manage my own affairs.

My summer at the cabin was pleasant; in addition to the chores of garden and fruit, I was looking through the text for sixth grade history. *Old Europe and Young America*, it was called, and it began with Alexander the Great and followed events down to the French and Indian Wars, ending just after the capture of Fort Kaskaskia, near the confluence of the Missouri and Mississippi rivers.

I went down the mountain to talk to Mr. Kelly, now superintendent of the district, and we agreed that I should have for my room a large, unabridged dictionary, a relatively large globe, and a five-volume encyclopedia, *The New Practical Reference Library.* We also wanted to order copies of other books the State board recommended for the coming year.

This history course later became so interesting to the sixth graders that many of their written assignments for English class grew out of it; and some fifth graders neglected their own assignments to listen to this exciting story. Among my history "helps" were large cardboard-mounted pictures of the Colosseum, the Colossus of Rhodes, a mosque, the three Great Pyramids, the Great Sphinx, and many other examples of the Ancients' engineering skills which our modern civilization could not match.

As in other years, we had a section for interesting nature study: birds' nests, wasps' nests, a turtle (which we set free after a few days), and several lizards of different varieties, each of which was taken across the Big Ditch and sent off, without a rock being thrown! One thing we wanted and never did catch was a bat, but since they were geared to night activity, I thought perhaps it was just as well. The bat was the mortal enemy of the mosquito and any other night-flying insects, so we felt it deserved to be free.

Best of all was our music class. I had some good voices in my room, and how they did love to sing, especially when directed by Mr. Karl Fordham! In all my experience, I have never met a person who could get as much music from a group of youngsters — especially when he had a potential like I had in this room. The children looked forward to his coming the last period of the day on Monday, Wednesday, and Friday, and would always clap their hands in welcome.

During the term he found occasion to have the room sing in public: at a Parent–Teachers' meeting, at a missionary farewell, and on the Sunday after school closed, in a Sunday afternoon Testimony meeting. But in the daily practice he had a way of selecting a group of three to six and having them sing special verses, with the whole group joining in the refrain. He was careful to give everyone a chance. Some would prefer not to be thus singled out, while others were eager for it.

The weekend before school closed, Ernest's brother Howard called on me. What were my plans for the summer? Would I be interested in going with his family to the Gyp Camp in lower Nevada? Myrtle's mother, Mrs. Granger, would be running the boarding house. She had one girl employed, but she needed another to be "second cook." There were approximately one hundred men, about eighty Mexicans and twenty Americans. Howard and one or two others lived in temporary homes with their families.

I was more than glad for this opportunity, though I well knew what it would be like: bareness, heat, long hours. I still do not know where the water in the big tank came from, but it was clear and wet and plentiful. The desert stretched out in every direction, with the scrubbiest of little scrub brush the only vegetation. Two brave little cottonwood saplings were trying to exist below the taps where we got our water for the kitchen, and another was outside the bunkhouse where we lived. Except for the mill, the dining–kitchen complex, and the home of the manager — in this case Howard's family and the Grangers — the only dwellings were tents set on wooden floors with four-foot lumber walls. The midday heat was terrific, but the nights were cool. My salary was one hundred dollars a month for three months, paid by the company to my position of "second cook." The waitress was Mabel Truman. Beside her, I looked like a study in slow motion.

The policy was that the men should be well-fed — good food, and plenty of it. Breakfast was always cereal for any who wanted it, with packages on the tables. So few called for mush that we learned to suggest that those who wanted it should always sit together near the end of the table, where they could help themselves from the long-handled kettle. Four or five men took large bowls of cooked cereal each morning. Everybody had hotcakes; everybody had eggs, as many as they wanted; potatoes, boiled in their jackets the night before, were peeled and diced in to brown with bacon and onions. The general idea was that men who have had a good, satisfying breakfast would not only work harder, but be better-natured.

Their lunch consisted of two sandwiches, one of ham or beef and one of tuna or salmon, an iced cupcake or three cookies, and an orange. Coffee was taken to the quarry in large thermos bottles, and each man had his own tin cup.

The dining room was kept locked until everything was ready. Then it was my chore to unlatch the screen doors and step outside to ring the bell that hung in a rack. I had to stay close to this rack or I would be knocked down and run over. The men reminded me of hungry pigs, pushing and jostling — that is, some of them came just drooling. Others, knowing there was plenty of food and plenty of time in which to eat it, stood aside and smiled at the eagerness of others.

We slept in the bunk house, Ernie in the lower bunk, and I above him. We had a little chamber pot for him, so that we were not troubled about bed-wetting. He usually slept until the men were off to work and I was free for a little while, long enough to bathe him and help him dress. We had our breakfast together, and then he went over to Howard's to play with Berniece, who was nearly a year older than he. They really got along well together.

My work was varied. I usually got the lard out of the big barrel and assembled the ingredients for the cakes, scrubbed a big potful of potatoes to boil for tomorrow's breakfast, and carried out the canned foods that we would be using.

One man Mabel and I called "Judas" between us, for we both disliked him heartily. He would want to pinch her or get hold of her whenever he could. She avoided him like the plague and so did I, though I must admit that he had never yet had an opportunity to get near me. On this forenoon the place was empty; I had taken Ernie over to Howard's. Mrs. Granger and Mabel were both resting, and I was in a small supply room digging out lard for the day's cakes. It was in a large barrel, and was down more than half-way, so I had a long butcherknife to cut out chunks. I thought I heard something behind me so I pulled myself up and at the same instant heard him say, "Oh-ho! So now I've got you just where I want you! You'll not get away so easy this time!"

I turned around quickly, the butcher knife still in my hands, and faced him.

"Damn your dirty heart!" I said slowly, "You dare to touch me, and I'll split you from stern to gudgeon!"

"By God! I believe you would!" he said, backing off. "I just believe you would!" And he walked away.

I don't know where I had heard that phrase or what it actually meant, but I find from the dictionary that it was exact and appropriate. Whatever it meant to him, it was effective enough, for he never approached me again, and I studiously avoided him.

Salas was the Spanish interpreter, the go-between in all differences and dealings, for it was he who had persuaded the Mexicans to come in the first place, and he wanted to iron out any misunderstandings. He protected them in their rights so far as the wage and working conditions were concerned. True, they worked in the quarry in the hot sun, but Salas persuaded them that they were better off than the men in the mill who must wear goggles and respirators, and would come out so covered with the white dust that it was hard to even tell who they were.

Everybody came to breakfast clean and fresh. At the evening meal every Mexican had showered and shampooed and changed clothes, as carefully almost as if he were going to spend the evening out with a date. Some of them played at different games; others played guitars or banjos and sang, making the evening perfectly delightful.

Most of the Americans worked in the mill; most were married but living alone here, so that they were not nearly so careful and clean as the Mexicans. One or two were extra careless, coming to dinner in their work clothes, with as much of the dust out as they could brush off, and only their hands (to mid-elbows) and faces (to the hairlines) exposed to soapless water. Their companions' comments were sometimes frank enough to be insulting, but they made little difference.

Several of the Mexicans played at card games; some competed in sports; some sang to guitar accompaniments; but in general all were good-natured about whatever they were doing, as they relaxed in the evening. Salas talked to the management, asking that there be some move to help the Mexicans learn to speak English, to count out their money, and to read their own contracts. A warehouse room was nearly empty; why couldn't they clean it out and fix it up to be a schoolroom, where the men could learn English, at least well enough to read newspapers?

The management consented, provided the men would keep the room in good shape; in fact, it would secure a large blackboard, chalk and erasers, and put in a table and chairs, so that they could practice writing English, too.

Next Salas talked to Howard. The little lady with the baby — had she not taught school? Could she not help the men with learning English? If each man paid 20¢ a night for five nights a week? He would help them too, after hours.

Actually, Salas was a more effective teacher than I, but between us the men were pleased with their progress. The County school board gave us permission to use a box of first grade and beginner's books, and we used also the day-old newspaper that came into camp on the mail rig. Each man would pay one dollar a week for six night classes

[268]

— twenty cents a night for five classes, and then a free one at the end of the week, where each could have a turn privately to sum up and show the teachers how much he had learned. They really looked forward to this session, which began early — right after supper — and lasted until nine o'clock or later, until every man had his turn at reading.

The next week would begin with twenty new men. If there were not that many who wished to start, Salas would fill the number with men who were eager to continue from the last week, for they called it "a dollar well-spent." For me it represented twenty dollars a week for four weeks — a real financial lift.

I needed to leave on the first of September in order to prepare for school in Provo. I would not go back home, but would take the train at Moapa. The only disadvantage was transportation from the camp to Moapa, for "Old Judas" drove the mail truck and there was no other way to go. I hadn't told Howard of my experience with this man, nor indicated that I had any reason to be afraid of him. Traveling in midday, with the little boy along, and for a less-than-three-hour trip, I felt I should be safe enough.

We were started when Old Judas began to tell me that it was his custom to take one short rest stop on the way out; there was a fine little grassy area with a forest of old, spreading mesquite trees and a pool around a slough with flags and grass and blackbirds — a very pleasant stop. And this time he didn't mean to be cheated as he had been once before. Had I forgotten what an exciting experience it was to "have connection"? I had been married; I ought to know that some sex experience was necessary for good health. It was the finest, most genuine thrill that life could offer.

This time I had no defense; I did not care to argue or discuss this matter; I could only pray silently: "Dear Lord, God help me!"

Little Ernie had gone to sleep; he was lying between us, his head in my lap; it would be easy to slip out and slip a cushion under it, but I had no intention of doing it. I would remain where I was; he would have to drag me out.

The place was really an oasis, with many ancient mesquite trees whose thorny branches twisted as though with every growing season they had hardened into fantastic shapes by winter snow, sometimes so low that cattle could not stand under them, protecting the food for the little chipmunks, squirrels, and rodents of the area. In other places there were inviting grassy areas where the limbs were higher. But today there was nothing for me outside the car.

"I'll put some water into the carburetor," Judas said, picking up a gallon brass bucket from the back. "It's nearly empty, and we might want to get off in a hurry."

Before he had the cap screwed back on, help came. A man leading a limping horse rounded the base of a knoll just ahead.

"How lucky can I be!" he called out. "To find water, and a man with a bucket, besides. We were jogging along when she reared back, and wouldn't put her foot to the ground. I haven't been able to examine it; the ankle is not swelling, so it must be something in the tender part of the foot. You wouldn't have any tools with you that I could use — a hammer or pincers, would you?"

"No." Judas was short in his answer, though he did permit the young man to take the bucket to carry water to the mare. With the bridle off, she drank deep, but still would not put her foot to the ground.

"Looks like I'll have to leave her here and go on to Moapa with you. My brother lives there; we'll have to bring his truck and some tools, and then see what is wrong, or haul her to a vet somewhere!" He didn't ask permission; he just assumed that he could go along with us.

He took off the saddle, which had some fancy tooling on each side, and the bridle, which had silver medallions on both sides.

He acted as though there should be no question about his going with us, but when Judas stood in sullen silence and evident resentment, he continued, "You see my predicament. I might have to stay here all day tomorrow before another car would come along this road. And you are certainly *not* loaded."

Judas was still silent, so I stood up, and he saw me for the first time, while Judas was out of range. I nodded to the young man, and motioned for him to come, and quickly sat down again. I felt that if it came to the worst, I'd rather get out and take my chances with this young man than to ride the rest of the way with Judas.

"Will this make any difference?" the young man said, taking out his purse and pulling out a ten-dollar bill. "It's only twenty miles to Moapa from here."

Judas took the money. "Git in the back," he said.

By this time Ernie, now fully awake, was standing in the middle, looking through the window and repeating, "Big man out there, Mother. Big man out there." He would never understand what comfort I had in that knowledge.

We traveled the rest of the way in silence. Sensing that Judas was annoyed by the baby, I took him on my lap, found a cookie and a pint bottle of milk in the satchel, and tried to find other entertainment for him.

When we arrived at the station, I pulled out my purse.

"That'll be five dollars," Judas said. "There's the kid, and the luggage."

I had heard him tell Howard that the regular one-way fare was two dollars, and he'd not charge for the little feller, but I did not question. I was just too happy to reach Moapa, which had not changed much since I had been here so long, long ago.

At the BYU

THERE WERE FEW PASSENGERS IN THE CAR I WAS DIRECTED TO. Three men were playing with cards near the rear of the car, a man and his wife were several seats in front of me, and across the aisle was a lady traveling alone. Whether it was the letdown of tension or the swaying of the car, I became motion sick, and I was just so miserable that I couldn't hold Ernie; it was all I could do to sit and keep myself together.

The lady across the aisle, sorry for my whimpering child, slipped over into the seat beside me, and took him onto her lap, where he settled down and went to sleep.

"Where are you going?" she asked.

"To Provo, to go to the BYU," I answered.

"Do you have anyone to meet you? Does anyone know you are coming?"

"No. I have never been to Provo before. But I assume that there will be cab service and hotels where I can find lodging for one night, or maybe until I can find something permanent."

"I have reservations at the Roberts Hotel," she said. "You may go there in the same cab that comes for me, if you like. It's a very nice place to stay."

"Thank you very much. I'm ashamed to be like this, but I can't help it. As soon as I can get my feet on the ground, I'll be OK."

"Where have you spent the summer?"

"Working in the dining room at the gyp mine out on the desert."

"Do you have your school wardrobe?

"No. I didn't leave the place all summer. I made pretty good money but didn't have any place to spend it. I thought I'd get here and settled before I set out to shop for clothes."

"Clothes are my business. Let me give you a little advice. Get *one* good dress. Don't go to Penny's or the little shops; go to Dixon–Taylor–Russell and get yourself one *good* dress, an all-wool, hard weave, navy blue, that fits well, and then get several sets of accessories: different collar and cuff sets, at least four. Then you can wear just a pin or some beads for a change. But you will always be well-dressed. If you give the dress good care, it will last the whole winter long, and you'll look better than if you had three cheap dresses."

She was so right. I followed her advice. I've wished that she had told me her name or given me her card, but she did not. Evidently she didn't want any further association with me, for she didn't ask my name, either.

I awakened early, but decided not to stir until Ernie had his sleep out; this day might be harder for him than for me. My greatest hope was that I might get settled in one day, and not have to come back to the hotel to sleep. Somewhere in this big town there must be a place where we two could live happily together and I still be able to go to school. We would begin with a generous breakfast, and I'd carry a snack besides in my bag for mid-morning; if possible, I'd try to make my head save my heels.

We were five blocks from the University. After a hearty breakfast, we set out in high spirits, going directly up the west side of the street. For the first three blocks Ernie did right well; on the fourth, he slowed down, and by the middle of the fifth, he was dragging his heels. As we neared the last house on the block, we saw a little boy playing on the lawn with a red express wagon, so Ernie turned in at the gate to examine it and just maybe get it for his own.

The other lad wasn't about to hand it over, so the two mothers came in on the business. I told the lady my name, and explained my problem. She was Sister Watts, and perhaps she could help me.

She knew a Mrs. Edwards who lived five blocks east and took in students; why didn't I come right in to her house and use her telephone?

Mrs. Edwards did take in students, I learned, but she did not want children; her cousin, Mrs. Geneva Larsen, lived on Fifth West at Seventh North, and she might be right glad to take me. Her husband was waiting for her fifth child to be born before he could leave to go to Paris to study art. The baby was overdue, and his schedule close. It might be well to call Geneva, or better still, go out and talk to her.

I explained to Ernest that I'd have to go seven more blocks, but I'd be back for him as soon as I could. In the meantime he could play with the little boy here, and if he got tired, take his nap. I would come back as soon as I possibly could, but seven blocks out and seven blocks back would be a long walk. He must not fret even if I seemed to be gone a long, long time. He should lie down with his new little friend, and both take their naps together; he must show these fine people what a good boy he could be, and make his own mother proud of him.

The hike was long, but Geneva and I liked each other immediately. We agreed that Ernie and I could live in the back bedroom. I would help with her children, and during school hours she could take care of Ernie. We would cooperate on the housework, I cleaning on Saturday and being responsible for the ironing. I would pay $20 toward home expenses each month, beginning today — I made out a check then and there. Bent, her husband, was at school with the car, and probably would not be home until well after dark, so I decided to go back and join Ernest at the Watts home.

I reached the Watts home just in time to see the husband come into the driveway with the car. After I told his wife how happy I was with my arrangements for the winter, she insisted that he take us down to the hotel for our baggage, and deliver us to the Larsen home. Surely the Lord was on my side this day, I said over and over, for here I was all settled, and had gained two wonderful friends in Brother and Sister Watts.

Bent still was not home when I unloaded my things and took possession of the back bedroom. Never in all my life had I been so utterly weary as I was now; though it was not yet dark, I undressed and rolled into bed. Ernie had eaten at the Watts home, so he joined me. I knew nothing more until sunrise the next morning.

[274]

Mr. Larsen had prepared himself to dislike me, for during the night his wife had given birth. How could I have slept through this, with only a door between Geneva and me? She had made plenty of noise; there had been activity and hurrying about. But I had not heard a sound.

I did get up early, though, before anyone else was stirring, took a quick bath, and put on a gingham house dress. Then I slipped back into my own private room until I should hear someone else begin to stir. Everyone was excited about the new baby boy who had arrived during the night. "B. F.," as his wife called him, was ready to leave early in order to make the right connections all the way to Paris. Since Geneva couldn't drive him, and none of the children was old enough, his good friend, M. Wilford Poulsen, came to take him to the station. They had come from the same town together to enter the BYU, had gone through and graduated in the same class, and were now both on the faculty, Bent in Art and M. Wilford in Psychology. The homes were about as far apart as they could be and still be in the same town: Larsens' in the far west, and Poulsens' in the north-east. But they kept in touch, the wives by telephone and by going together to the BYU Women's Club, and the husbands by seeing each other on campus.

So Bent left before the family had breakfast.

Before classes started that fall I wrote home to tell the folks that I had found living quarters and was very happy about how things seemed to be working for me. Would Ma collect my winter dresses and pack them in a box or in an old suitcase that I had used once before, and send them up with anyone coming to Provo?

I registered for Miss Effie Warnick's "Quantity Cooking" class in the home economics department. This met daily from ten to eleven o'clock, at which time I would go to my new job of cooking at the school cafeteria during the noon hour; my meal was part of the reward.

My schedule came to be an eight o'clock class and a nine o'clock class, then cooking and serving school lunch, with a half-hour recess between that and my afternoon classes. I had one study period every day, which I always spent in the library. I wore my wool dress to the classrooms; then changed into a washdress for cooking and serving the food; relaxed on a couch in the ladies' room for about thirty minutes; and then, properly clothed, went to my two afternoon classes. I was usually back home at the Larsens' before the children came in from school.

I enjoyed this very much, indeed. My working partner at the cooking lab was little Verna Decker, a perfect doll. She was engaged to a boy who was doing graduate work at Columbia University, Hal Bentley, such a wonderful young man. She wanted to be prepared to manage a home and cook good meals, as she had not had much experience.

Miss Warnick was also cordial with me. "You don't know what that *Mrs.* will mean to you in a career. I'd give a lot if I could put it before my name. It gives a sort of prestige," she told me.

It did put me into a class by myself, as I knew it would. For example, one of Geneva's nephews returned from a mission, and came to stay with her until he could get registered and settled. He rode a bicycle, and twice took me before him and delivered me at the school.

"I could really go for you if you hadn't been sealed to another man," he said in all seriousness.

"I'm not at all sure that I would be interested," I answered quickly.

Professor M. Wilford Poulsen taught Psychology 72, a required course for all students, so his room was crowded. I liked the way he had planned his class. We were seated alphabetically; his reason was not only to save time, but to give each member of the class an opportunity to express himself. In a class this size, the student would not have a fair chance to show his abilities in an open question-and-answer period. But if each was given fifteen minutes in which to write on some phase of the assignment, the teacher could better form an idea of his potential and his preparation.

To me, Mr. Poulsen was B. F. Larsen's friend who had taken him to the railroad station, and who was the only faculty member to come to Geneva when the newspapers headlined *Brigham Young University professor in a riot in Paris!* in large black letters.

The article in the paper explained that in a demonstration in

[276]

a public plaza in Paris, the American flag was carried in, along with the flags of other nations, to be set up as part of the program. A man, knowing that B. F. was an American, called loudly, "To hell with the United States of America!" and spat at the flag, whereat B. F. slugged him in the face, knocking him down and rendering him unconscious for a short time. Bent was taken into custody, but released.

All who read about it knew that it was merely an incident, but Mr. Poulsen made it occasion for a call on Geneva. He told her that he was going to take his wife and children up the canyon that afternoon, and would gladly take her family, too. The leaves were turning, and were so beautiful. Geneva accepted eagerly, but said she would leave all the children at home. The baby was too young to care, and too large for her to handle well. The older children could stay home and take care of him. It would be a relief to get free of them all for a few hours.

As he was leaving, he met me coming in, and asked if I also would like a ride up the canyon this afternoon, since it was Saturday. They were taking a little picnic, and would be glad if I would join them. I was glad to, but added quickly, "May I bring little Ernie? I'm away from him so much, and I know he would enjoy it."

He later used this illustration in class as a discussion of the relationship of parents to children — or, more definitely, of mothers to children, and invited the class to talk about the "unwanted child" situation.

I took no part at all; there were many students eager to discuss the problem. The teacher had a very warm respect for the mother who would ask to take her son along. But might there be a danger later that the child would become too tied to his mother's apron strings? And was the first mother not justified in asking that she go alone, or take only the child just older than the baby? Of them all, he might need a little more attention, especially just now.

I tell all this to show that there was a friendly relationship between us. He could pay me a bit of a compliment without anyone suspecting it. Later in my life I worked closely with M. Wilford Poulsen in the collecting of early diaries, letters, and records of any kind, and I respected his meticulous accuracy in copying from originals.

[277]

In mid-April Ronald came home one evening with a flushed face and a bit of sore throat. His mother had him gargle and go to bed early, but the next morning he was red as a beet with measles — from head to foot — just covered. She put him into the small bedroom which had been the youngest ones' special place, and we all tried to keep the others away, even the ones who had long ago had measles. I was concerned for Ernest, because a little earlier the two boys had been building castles with their blocks, getting them up and up and then jumping with glee when they all fell down.

Ronald came through them just fine after three days in the darkened room, and I told myself that Ernie would perhaps escape them. Friday night he was restless; I got him a drink twice in the night, but when I got up he seemed to be OK.

I set up to do my regular Saturday morning chore, the cleaning of my serge dress. I liked to get it over with immediately, so it would be ready for Sunday and the week. One thing about it, the dress always looked better enough to reward me for my work.

Most of the girls had already come out in spring dresses, and with Easter only a step away, there would be more. I set about brushing, sponging, and steaming, when Ernie started to fret, and I called out that I'd be there in just a minute. I pulled the front placket of the skirt into place and spread the damp pressing cloth over it, set the iron on end, and went to get the baby.

He was a solid blotch of measles, fiery red. He needed to go to the bathroom, so I wrapped a blanket around him, pulling it securely around his shoulders, and folding the bottom over his feet and legs, arranged him so that he could be independent of me, as he always wanted to be when he was well.

I was hardly back to the iron when I heard a sound, and there he was, pale as a ghost and slipping down into the toilet. I dropped the iron, ran to him and picked him up, crying out for Geneva. Seeing the child white and limp in my arms, she ran to the door and called to Brother Fielding, who was just passing on his way to work. He turned and came in as fast as he could, for her voice told him we were in trouble.

Ernie lay in my arms as white as chalk and limp, and it flashed into my mind that Ma's younger brother, Wilford, had died when the measles "went in" on him. Geneva was holding out the bottle of olive oil. Brother Fielding pulled the high stool over and had me sit on it, the baby in my arms. All the time I was saying over and over in my mind, "Dear Lord God, help us! Save my baby!"

Brother Fielding put a bit of the oil on the forehead and prayed to God to restore this child and spare his life. Why did it take so long? It seemed an eternity to me before some faint color began to appear, the child caught a deep breath, and the body processes were in motion again. To me, it seemed as if he had been literally snatched from the grave.

But that smell! My wool serge dress! The iron had burned through the damp pressing cloth, through the dress, through the ironing-board cover, almost to the wood itself. I could never wear that dress again, nor could I salvage enough of that expensive material for any good use. Aura could perhaps scheme some way to take it apart and remake it, putting the burned place to the side and covering it with a ribbon bow. But Aura was teaching school somewhere out in Nevada.

Just before noon, the mailman came. A package for me? A letter attached from Mother to say that she had seen this fine fabric and liked it so much that she made me a new dress for Easter out of it. Hoped I would like it.

It was indeed a fine zephyr gingham in inch-size squares of lavender and yellow, and it fit perfectly. Geneva was loud in its praise; I wouldn't ever need to apologize for this dress. At this time of year, it just couldn't be more appropriate. It looked like Easter morning, and was like "the loving hands of home."

I knew that Professor Poulsen wasn't trying to embarrass me when I came into class on Monday morning, and he said, "Why, Mrs. Pulsipher, how delightful to see you in a different dress!"

I could only take my seat in utter confusion. I knew that he was not being malicious; it was his own bungling way. But during the class I studied how I might come in tomorrow in still another dress.

Geneva told me that students and faculty had the free services of Dr. Carroll for their families and suggested that I take Ernie for an examination, so as soon as his measles were cleared, I did just that.

The doctor studied the card I made out for his file, which told my story and that of the baby quite fully, and told me to take off all his clothes. He said nothing until he got to the feet, and then he seemed almost angry.

"What in the world are you doing to this child's feet?" he asked. "You'll ruin his toes and particularly his toenails! If you can't afford a pair of shoes for him, make some moccasins, or, better still, cut out the toes of his shoes." Then he picked up an instrument and proceeded to cut the cap off the end of each shoe, so that the toes were free to stretch as far out as they could.

I was embarrassed and ashamed that I had been so ignorant or insensitive, but we had always made a game out of putting on his shoes, with Ernie joining, and the shoes were not badly worn at all, too good to throw away.

The older boys and Celia got ice skates for Christmas; Ronald's were roller skates. Ernie had no skates, but after he came home with his "new" shoes with the ends cut out, we called them his "running shoes." He was proud to demonstrate how quick he was on the start, and how very fast he could run. "Roller skates for Provo boys and running shoes for Dixie boys," he would say proudly.

When school closed in the spring, I found a ride all the way to Mesquite with David Abbott. His wife, Emma, had come up for the first quarter of summer school, and he had brought her in their truck. He would be traveling back alone, and so was glad to take Ernie and me with him.

The Red Maxwell Racer

IT WAS DURING THAT YEAR'S SPRING ROUNDUP IN BUNKERVILLE, when the yearlings were branded and marked, the males castrated, and buyers visited with owners. Youngsters watched from the top of the pole fence, or sat a little distance away on their horses. Melvin was among them.

"You're Hen Leavitt's boy, ain't yu?" George Strasser asked, coming up to the horse's side. At Mel's affirmative nod, he went on, "I've owed your Pa thirty dollars ever since I was married. He staked me to that much for my wedding expense. At the time, I thought I could pay it off by fall, but I just couldn't make it. Now that more than two whole years is past, he's probably give up ever gettin' it.

"If I take these bills home, I'll never git my hands on 'em again. Here, take these three tens, and git 'em to your Dad as soon as you can. Tell 'im that I didn't add no interest. He'll likely be glad to git this much."

Mel smoothed out the bills, folded them carefully, and pushed them into the bottom of his shirt pocket. Now he remembered what he had been sent to do. He was to follow the St. Thomas road to the top of the hill overlooking the lower river bottoms, see if there were any cattle in the mesquite flats down there, and investigate them if there were. A preliminary survey would save both man and horse.

Now at the top, Melvin forgot about cattle. Here was a bright red

Maxwell racing car, with a boy about his own age standing beside it. Mel promptly went to investigate.

"Having trouble?" he asked as he rode up. "What seems to be wrong?"

"I've thrown the main rod, looks like. There's just no way to make it move."

"Been here long?"

"Since late yesterday afternoon. No one passed in the whole time, but the mailman this morning, and he didn't hardly slow down."

Mel was instantly on the ground and looking the machine over.

"It's thrown the rod, all right. You'll likely have to tow it to Las Vegas, but that would likely cost more than it's worth — ninety miles is a long ways."

"It would likely cost more than it's worth, but where could I find someone to tow it?"

"Would you take thirty dollars for it as it stands?" Mel ventured.

"It's worth more than that! It's worth ten times more than that!"

"It would be if you had it in Las Vegas, but you can't get it there like it is. I've got three ten-dollar bills here in my pocket, but it's all I got, and no way to get more."

Just then a large car carrying a man, woman, and a little boy came up and stopped. The situation was clear; the man stated it without hesitation.

"Either stay here with the car until you can get it towed in to Las Vegas for repairs, or take what you can get for it, and go on into Las Vegas with us. From there you can telephone your parents, and they'll have to face up to the fact the car is a total loss."

Clearly the boy did not want to spend another night alone here on the desert without food or water, so he took Mel's three ten-dollar bills and started for the back seat of the big car. He was quickly reminded that there were papers to sign and be witnessed before he left.

Melvin came home post haste, a little worried about what Pa would say.

"It would be worth thirty dollars just to have a car set in front of the house," Pa assured him.

Melvin had some little trouble getting the necessary rod that was

[282]

broken; Gus Pendleton didn't have one, but he encouraged Melvin to think he had really made a good deal, even if he had to order the part.

Though he had little faith that he would find the rod at Mesquite, Mel went over. And he did find it! In the junk yard behind the one service station was a driving rod that fit so perfectly that he put it in without any help, and the little car hummed along as good as new. Pa would later tell this as proof that God's hand was in it.

Now Pa wanted to try his own hand at driving. He was too big a man for this little machine, but somehow he jackknifed himself under the wheel. Melvin got the engine running and set it at about fifteen miles per hour. Pa had only to guide it around the block. On the end of the second trip, he was ready to stop, and called "Whoa!" a few times. As he came past, Mel stepped on the running board and turned off the key.

The little red Maxwell became the subject of much discussion in the village, but Gus Pendleton's advice seemed the most sensible.

"You take this car to Las Vegas, but don't run around town in it. Park it close to your sleeping quarters and throw a canvas over it. Then when you have a half-day off, go into town and visit the place where they sell Maxwell cars. Get a newspaper and study the ads, and pretend that you are in the market for a used Maxwell in good shape. That'll give you an idea what you can expect from this one. But don't be in a hurry. The prices might change come fall."

Pa wasn't the only man in Bunkerville who tried to stop his car by saying "Whoa!" to it. Brother Bowman also drove his car about the streets with confidence; he approached his garage at just the right angle, drove slowly and carefully right into the center, and then called out "Whoa," as he pulled back on the wheel, while the car went slowly but surely through the back wall. It was said that after replacing that lumber wall a few times, he decided to leave the end open.

By the time I reached home that spring, the boys had already taken the red Maxwell to Las Vegas, Aura had gone straight there from her school in Jiggs, Nevada, and all were set up at the Stewart Ranch. This was headquarters for the Bunkerville crowd for many years.

[283]

The house wasn't large, but it was built over a full rock-walled basement, which was always cool and dark enough to make an ideal place for day sleepers. Then there was a long, heavy-wooded arbor, which was always shady and cooler than the house, especially after it was sprayed and the ground around it sprinkled.

I left Ernie at home with the folks; Mother was always "Ma" to him, and Francis, Dudley, and Mary like older brothers and sisters.

I decided to make my first call at the bakery where I had worked before, and was surprised at the warmth of the welcome. It was as if a close family friend had arrived. The older son was finishing his work for an Eagle Scout badge, and needed time for the out-of-door activities. The younger one had been selected to take some special training in California. The wife wanted nothing less than to work in the shop. So I not only had a job, but at a twenty-five percent raise.

Melvin and Laurel started work at seven in the evening and worked until three in the morning, with time out at about eleven p.m. for food and rest. They had to wear the heaviest clothing: wool-lined caps, ear-muffs, gloves, and shoes, for they were icing cars and loading fresh fruit on the railroad. They were really too young to take such heavy work, but they could find no other, and this paid well. Usually they would sleep in the dark basement until about three in the afternoon. By the time I came home, they would be preparing to leave, so I had very little time with them. It was almost just a "hail–and–farewell," like ships that pass in the night.

The experience was good in one way: it brought them nearer together as brothers, for during some of their earlier years they had not been friends. Now they shared the search for possible sale or trade of the little red Maxwell. Finally they found a Ford which the owner would trade for an additional fifty dollars. They asked overnight to consider, and when I came home were waiting to talk it over with me.

I was quick to encourage them. Aura and I would have to pay more than twenty-five dollars each to go from Las Vegas to Provo by train. Why not give it to go toward the car? It would be better all around; we could get to our destination easier and better; then the family would have a car to fit their needs, one that Pa could enjoy driving — after he learned how to stop it.

[284]

So it was that we all quit work on September 6, the end of the week, and came home in the "new" Ford. Mother's record says that we pulled out of Bunkerville for Provo on September 12, 1924.

How wonderful it was for us to travel in our own outfit! And how we did load it down! Bedding, clothing, cases of fruit; preserves, jams, and jelly; cured ham and bacon; flour and whole-wheat cereal. On one running board was a five-gallon can of water; on the other a three-gallon can of gas. A short-handled shovel was across the spare tire at the back, and most important of all, a box of big-headed matches within reach.

The roads were not improved; only the big canals were bridged. We felt that if we could average twenty miles an hour, we'd be doing very well indeed. The pull out of the town of Mesquite and onto the Johnson Bench made us conscious of the fact that perhaps we were so overloaded that we might burn out a bearing, or otherwise injure the car. Eager to be of help, Aura and I walked to the top to be ready to block the wheels when we stopped. Across the Johnson Bench we took heart, for we chugged almost twenty-five miles an hour. The steep climb to the foot of the mountain had Aura and me out to walk in several places. The engine boiled until we stopped to let it cool down before we put in water. Otherwise it would boil up like a geyser, and shoot out what water we had.

We stopped for lunch on the Santa Clara Creek, but did not slow up in St. George. We didn't need to buy anything, and we had neither time nor desire to visit. By sundown we had passed through Cedar City and pushed on through the little village of Summit. Here we decided to make camp near a ditch with some clear water and plenty of branches for a fire, lying along the fence.

Motels were not yet known; we had never even heard the word. But we could build a campfire with rocks at the sides and our heavy, flat top to hold frying pan or saucepan. We enjoyed our meal of meat, potatoes and onions, with cookies and milk for dessert.

But we were not good frontiersmen when it came to making a bed on the ground. Little Ernie was put into the back seat of the car, with a good outing-flannel quilt and a pillow, so he was comfortable. Melvin had his bedroll well-placed also. But Aura and I cleared a place where the wind from the canyon came head on at us, so that it was impossible to stay warm. Before daylight we started a fire to provide warmth while we loaded up. Ernest could sleep in the car as we traveled, while either Aura or I would try to doze beside him.

We drove all the way to Beaver before breakfast, for we knew this was a dairy town where we might buy fresh milk and perhaps some eggs and cheese to take along. Again we prepared a good, heavy meal, which we ate in the grass by some young cedar trees; again we took delight in the place we were in, just being glad that we had come so far so well.

By the time we reached Levan, we felt the need of another rest stop and a bit of a snack. This time our shelter consisted of some beautiful young locust trees. We did not slow up in Nephi but were duly impressed by the large sign outside the town promoting *The best road in the state.* Here, now, we could make good time for at least forty miles. We needed to, for the day was far spent.

The forty miles of paved road was a real delight. Another brief stop and finally, at nine o'clock, we pulled into 733 North Fifth West, Provo. Congratulating ourselves that we had come all this distance without one minute of trouble, we felt that God's hand had been over us.

The Larsens were expecting us, but of course didn't wait supper, and except for a drink of milk for Ernie, we didn't need it. Melvin put down his bedroll on the back lawn, for the talk at the supper table made him eager to look over the setup at Johnson's, just two houses up. It seems that Johnson's mean old cow had just had a calf, and would threaten to attack anyone who came around. Not Brother Johnson, of course, but anyone else. She gave a lot of milk, a big bucket overflowing, but she was hard to milk.

The next morning Melvin was up very early. He was interested in the cow, and in the possibility of a good riding horse. He had looked the cow over, and made friends with the pony before Brother Johnson came out.

"Shall I milk her for you?" he asked, and proceeded to handle the situation like an expert, giving the calf its share first and then putting it away into its pen while he filled the bucket with rich, foamy milk.

He told Brother Johnson the whole story of bringing his two sisters up to attend the BYU. He had just graduated from high school, and would like to stay and go, too, if he could manage it. His elder sister had lived with Mrs. Larsen last winter, so the car was parked down there.

"Come in and meet my wife," Brother Johnson said. "She'll have to have her say in whatever is done."

So Melvin carried the bucket of milk into the house, proceeded to put the separator together — it was the same brand as ours at home — and ran the milk through it while the Johnsons talked together in the front room. The fact that Mel ran a two-quart bucket of luke-warm water through the separator before he took it apart won Mrs. Johnson completely. To have it taken apart, washed, scalded and left to dry under a clean dishtowel, the cream put away and the skim milk carried out to the calf and pig, seemed a great burden lifted.

Meanwhile, Melvin and Brother Johnson visited in the yard. Mel had tied up most of his money in the car, and now he would either have to take it back home himself or send it back to the family.

As to the little house, Brother Johnson was generous. His son's wife didn't like it, but he himself thought it was a nice little place: solid as a nut, and easy to heat and keep warm. The large room had been well-insulated; the stove was brand-new. No worry about fuel; there was a pile of cottonwood cut and ricked up big enough to last for years, and there was still coal in the bin, more than would be used in one year.

No, there was no water in the house, but the tap was just outside the door, and they had installed electric lights, with outlets for an electric iron or frying pan, or any other gimmick.

Things quickly fell into place. After Melvin had worked a few days in the harvest and at cleaning out ditches, the Johnsons were determined to keep him. He could share a double bed with a young relative of theirs named Huntington. He played the oboe in the band, and practiced for two hours early every morning. During this time, Melvin did the milking and all the other chores, including running the milk through the separator.

For this he had a bed, closet space for his clothing and shoes, access to the bathtub and the inside toilet. But he ate his meals with us, and spent his free time in the little house.

The one thing that really impressed Mrs. Johnson was the fact that Ernie and her little grandson, Roy, played so well together with never a fight or squabble. Mrs. Johnson said nothing about the marriage and divorce of their son and his wife; in all our conversations that was strictly a closed subject. Nor did I ever try to open any conversation concerning it.

For our part, we arranged our classes so that one of us would always be home, just in case of an accident or fight or mischief between the children.

But our greatest problem was really not the two little boys: it was space for the rest of us, for Charity arrived from her mission just two weeks after we arrived for school. What could she do, except come and join us? How could we manage? Simply by moving over. Aura and I already slept in an extra-size double bed with good springs; we just moved over, which placed me in the middle. We just pushed the clothes hangers closer together on the road, and had Charity put her shoes in another corner. Each of the girls had a locker at the ladies' gym, where she took a shower daily; I arranged with Geneva Larsen for the use of their bath tub at regular hours, when everyone else was away.

Our toilet facility was the two-holer outhouse at the back of the lot. Aura had made herself an elegant bathrobe from a bright-colored Navajo blanket, and finished it with a twisted silk rope with an extra tie around the waist. We named it "Old Donder & Blitzen." It was the only really warm item we had, so we all used it. Interested neighbors might see "Old Donder & Blitzen" hurry down to the outhouse and back three times every morning.

Home for Christmas

SOON AFTER THANKSGIVING, Mother wrote that we should plan to come home for Christmas. She had it all arranged, so we needn't worry. Mrs. M., who was teaching the kindergarten and first grade, was living at our house. She had a six-month-old baby boy; Mother tended the child all day, from the time of his morning bath to four o'clock in the afternoon. His mother came home for lunch at noon, but it was such a long walk that she had only time to take the baby for a few minutes, eat, and hurry back. By the end of the day she was too weary to enjoy him.

They both agreed that Mother's care of the baby was worth a dollar a day, but Mrs. M. was sending the husband $50 a month to help him get through the BYU, so that he would be prepared to teach the next winter. He was a brilliant young man, she assured Mother; he would make a fine teacher. Perhaps she would take a year off and have another baby.

She arranged with her husband that we should all come free, in lieu of the dollar-a-day which Mother had passed on to him by her baby tending over more than three months.

We understood that Mr. M. wanted to be off early, so before daylight we were all ready. He had a Ford sedan; we three girls would sit in the back, and the three boys in front. Since there was no heater in the car, we had two hot rocks wrapped in burlap, and a double blanket to cover us in the back seat, with a quilt for Melvin and Ernie.

The driver was so silent that we hardly knew how we should conduct ourselves. We talked to Ernie, who was full of questions, but before long he had gone to sleep in Melvin's arms. Daylight came, but we couldn't see out; the plastic window covers, fastened with little buttons, let in the cold air without giving any view of the outside through the isinglass windows, so narrow and small. We had no watches among us, so could hardly guess the time, but out on a lonely stretch the car sputtered and stopped. An empty gas tank!

Had we passed any service stations? We in the back had no idea. The driver got out — I didn't say it, but we could have carried some extra gasoline in a five-gallon can. Nobody said anything, but before long another car came up alongside and called out to see what was wrong.

The driver got out and came to offer assistance.

"There's a road camp in the valley. You can get gasoline there," he said. "I've got a stay-chain. I'll fasten it here on your front ex, and pull you over."

The driver climbed back into our car, released his brakes, and held on to the wheel. Then, going downhill, he let our car run up too far on the chain, which got wrapped around the wheel and tipped us over against a snowbank. Aura screamed out and cried, but we all climbed out and trooped through knee-deep snow about a quarter-of-a-mile to the road camp tent, while Ernie stayed in the car. Melvin later carried him over on his shoulders. The three men untangled the chain, set the car onto its wheels, and pulled it down to the gas tanks.

It was now almost mid-forenoon and we were only just past Nephi, which meant that we already had our forty miles of pavement behind us. We arrived at home in Bunkerville about midnight, and found the family all up and waiting. While we got our things out, Mrs. M. greeted her husband, her baby sleeping in her arms, and they quickly slipped away. We were all so busy talking and laughing among ourselves that we were hardly conscious of them at all.

Mrs. M. had arranged to stay this night and the one at the end of the week at the Bunker Hotel, but spent the rest of the holiday somewhere south, either at the Darling Ranch or Glendale, or perhaps on to Las Vegas. They went out nowhere in Bunkerville, so Mrs. M.'s husband did not exist so far as anyone knew or cared.

The week was all too short. We reveled in the clear, warm sunshine — "shirt-sleeve weather," we called it, as it really was.

Our trip back was without incident, slow from the river bridge to the summit, but with nothing more difficult than to stop and pour water into the boiling radiator. We felt freer to talk among ourselves, but our driver hardly opened his mouth, though he did share our food. Mother made sure that no one would be hungry on the way back.

Later, when we were alone, I commented to Melvin about the silence of the driver — no more mention of either his wife or baby than if he had none. Mel knew all the time: this man was courting a young lady from a prominent and wealthy Provo family, while he accepted fifty dollars a month from his wife. Soon after school closed in the spring, he would be married to her. If his wife learned of it while he was down, she said nothing of it to our mother, who continued to love and care for the baby until they left.

Now, back into the routine of school, things went very well for us; we all worked Saturdays as before, and all managed some way. I became involved in the debate program and appeared in several inter-class bouts, including one against the University of California, Southern Branch. My colleague was a handsome, blonde young man, a son of the head of the chemistry department. We were awarded a unanimous decision in our favor. Now I could be initiated into Tau Kappa Alpha, the national debating society, and receive a key to wear as evidence. Needless to say, I treasured that.

As graduation time approached, I became more and more conscious that I must have some money. Then one afternoon as I sat reading on a bench just outside Old Main, George A. Smith of Arizona came up and took possession of the other end.

"Looks like I'm going to have to float a loan to get out of this institution," he said, as he pulled a little notebook from his pocket. Tearing out a sheet, he proceeded to write with his left hand in a bold backhand slant, a request of a loan for one hundred dollars, signed it, folded it, and went over to the little open window where he shoved it under the bars.

When I met him the next day, I asked, "Well, did you get your loan from the school?"

"Sure 'nuf, and got it half spent," and he pulled a little roll out just enough for me to get a glance at it.

"Well, if they'll give you a hundred dollars, maybe they'll trust me with fifty," I said, and at once wrote out an application.

"Sorry, our funds are depleted," they answered.

I was angry: angry at myself for not having been about this business earlier. I wanted a yearbook, I'd have to rent a cap and gown, and my shoes were a disgrace. I swallowed my pride and asked the Larsens to lend me enough for my cap and gown. I could get along without new shoes and yearbook.

I went through the ceremonies without any thrill of pride, but with a growing feeling that I would shake the dust off my feet at the BYU, and never again, as long as I lived, have any doings with them.

I did not know that my folks were in the audience. They had traveled almost all night to attend. Bless them! I knew I must be cheerful and not mention my disappointments.

They came prepared to take me and the other family members home if we wanted to go, but Charity and Aura both had good employment. I wanted to attend the summer school at Aspen Grove in the mountains near Provo, where there was to be a visiting professor to work with people who had any desire to write: how to do it; what to avoid; how to make it pay. It all sounded too exciting to miss.

The greatest surprise of all came just one day after graduation — a letter from President Joseph K. Nicholes of Dixie College informing me that Miss Phillips had accepted a position in Lehi, a larger school and nearer her home. Would I be interested in taking her place? Would I! I could think of nothing — not anything — better than this! On the strength of it, I went to the local bank and borrowed one hundred dollars!

From the first, I liked everything about Aspen Grove: the sharing of a tent with Julia Alleman, one of my debate partners; the camplike cooking and washing procedures; the trees, undergrowth, and grass and flowers. I didn't mind the primitive stove with its two cement sides and flat metal top. It would burn anything from sticks and trash to larger pieces of cut wood, a supply of which was ours for the carrying. It seemed almost a fairyland.

I went chiefly to take the course in creative writing under Dr. Brown. I don't remember the title of my first essay, but I'll never forget his criticism of it.

"You'll have to make up your mind what you're writing — prose or poetry. Your sentences swing along like Henry W. Longfellow's *Hiawatha*: simple sentences linked together with an *and*, *but*, or *for* — each like a butterfly impaled on a pin. Break 'em up! Throw in a verbal phrase at the beginning of the sentence. See how many of these prepositional phrases you can reduce to a single, telling word!"

I knew that I had no skill in fiction, nor did I have any real flare for verse. I decided to begin with biography — true stories of real people. The often-told tale of Grandfather Dudley Leavitt's campfire letter to Shanob, the Great God, which had saved him from hostile Indians, would be a good one to start with. It had been told so often that it had become a family legend, dear even to the youngest, embellished with every telling.

So I wrote the story that Grandpa himself had once told me: of the Indians angry at the death of one of their warriors; of how they had taken Dudley captive and were planning his torture, when he suddenly began writing with his pencil and pad, tearing the paper into strips and sending it up to Shanob in the campfire, all the while chanting for his release; of how, after a sudden explosion of lightning and thunder, the Indians had disappeared.

Dr. Brown told me that he thought this was very interesting, but that he and other readers like him, who knew nothing of the Indian lore of the West, would need more background explanation. This story ought not be the first; others should precede it. Briefly, this might be a very good little incident to include in a book dealing with white men among the Indians; it would not do to publish independently. That the answer from heaven came so promptly should have been preceded with more evidence of a thunderstorm. But it had merit. I should keep it to include with other folklore tales.

Just the fact that I admitted that I wanted to write, and had made even this bit of a start, meant very much. He suggested that we keep a pocket notebook in which we could write ideas as they came to us, or the names of stories we might wish to return to, and sketch plots briefly. A writer was like a bee, he suggested — he gathers his pollen from many sources, but in the end it is his own handling that makes it honey.

I made several other attempts, few of which seemed important enough to justify publication. One short poem, "Sunrise over Mt. Timpanogos," was later used in the *Improvement Era.*

With a little more effort I might have made a good story of the first cotton cloth manufactured west of the Mississippi River. This was at Santa Clara — or rather on the Santa Clara Bench before the Swiss settlers arrived on the townsite.

The cotton seed was brought out from the southern states by missionaries in the area and sent down by the first arrivals, Dudley Leavitt and Jacob Hamblin. Zadok Judd was also along with his young wife and family. They cleared and plowed up a two-acre plot, planted some peach pits that Jacob Hamblin had bought from the Indians, and a few pounds of cotton seed.

I wrote the story as I had heard it from family folklore: the peach trees grown from the pits, and making ten feet in height the first season; the squash vines which grew over a rock fence with the squash hanging like giant fruit, the cotton stalk which boasted twenty-seven large bolls. I had heard the stories as told around the quilting frames in Bunkerville. When I read it to Julia, I learned that Brother Zadok Judd had made the first cotton gin, and that the women in Santa Clara could make only the balls of yarn, or "hanks" of yarn, before it was dyed red or yellow with madder root, or brown with some kind of bark.

Julia and I talked this over; she insisted that some of her people had the only loom, and it was at Parowan. This I could hardly believe, for I had heard my own family story: Aunt Hannah, Grandpa's oldest daughter, had told how they were ordered to move to Bull Valley, and her mother couldn't go, because she had a "web" of cloth in the loom and must finish it.

This experience was a wholesome one for me: I determined to take nothing for granted, but to quote only from reliable printed sources. It was time, too, for me to face up to the fact that I would be teaching at Dixie Junior College, and I would do well to get myself settled early.

I was so uncertain about my work in Dixie that I decided not to keep my house for myself, but to board and room with a family, preferably one with children and near the school. I felt a little uncertainty — almost a fear — of taking over Miss Phillips' English–debate combination. This feeling was intensified when the first person I met on campus was Howard Miller, who told me frankly, "You may be OK, but you can never fill Miss Phillips' place."

"I'll not try to fill her place," I answered. "I'll have to make my own place."

I looked for a place, and was fortunate to find ideal room and board in the home of Coach Leland (Lee) Hafen. His wife, Elsie, was an excellent cook and general manager, and their youngest son, Keith, was within months of Ernie's age. Their home was just across the street and two houses down from the college building, where all my work would be centered.

The two little boys became instant friends; they played as happily together as though they had grown up together. This relieved me greatly.

Without a yearbook, a school paper, or any other reminders, I have only pleasant memories of that year. Life at the Hafen home was interesting; their daughter was just at the age that she liked to drive the car, to be out, to share in social activities. I knew — and she knew that I knew — that quite often she slipped out at night with the car. I heard her when she left and when she returned, but I kept silent, figuring that her parents would learn sooner or later. If they did, they said nothing about it to me.

Ernest came to feel like one of the family. One day he said, "Mother, I think I'd like to have Uncle Lee for my Daddy!"

"For this year you may play that he is," I told him.

My classwork was pleasant: we had some inter-class debate; we had at least two oratorical contests; we participated in school elections. And at the end of the year, I went back again to Aspen Grove, where Charity was now employed in the kitchen.

My first year at Dixie had ended on a high note. My classes had been crowded, my debating classes enthusiastic, so I faced the second year with confidence. Now I was ready to rent a place where the students from the Virgin Valley, or at least my own brothers and sisters, would have headquarters.

I found just what I wanted in the Morrell place, which was across the street and a few houses east of the Hafen residence, a large older house with a spacious front room, a fireplace, and carpeting. A kitchen–dining room was behind it, bedrooms to the west and back. It had no indoor toilet — that facility was at the end of a path back in the lot. Students could take daily showers at the college gym, or they could use a #3 tub in front of the kitchen range. Ernest had his baths there, but the older ones used the school facilities.

This year Laurel and Daisy and cousin Sarah Leavitt were with me. They all enjoyed their stay at Dixie, though none of them had "steady" dates. Mabel Jarvis took great pride in teaching Laurel to tango, which routine, as a member of a committee for MIA social activity, she presented as a special act.

Early in the season the State made an announcement that they would award a large silver bowl to the junior college whose debate teams won the most decisions. Now here was something worth going all out after! We were determined that Dixie win this cup. This would be a major achievement for the college. The high school had another program, a different question and no reward except the decision, and the experience of the contest. It seems incredible, but the records show that Dixie Junior College won every debate without a dissenting vote. There were many pictures of the beautiful cup and the winning teams: Elvis Bird Terry, Madge Morrill, Donald Tobler, and Mervin Reber.

Since I had attended summer school in Aspen Grove for two years, in the summer of 1927 I was willing to consider something else. Mother entered this in her ledger book:

Laurel took Juanita & Ernest, Daisy & Eva, to St. George, where they were met by Mr. Clark of Provo, and took them up to pick berries for him. He had written Juanita to engage 15 girls to work in the berries. She to have them in charge. They left St. George June 6, 1927.

This was indeed a challenge, but work for girls was hard to be found. Mr. Clark would use this as an experimental venture, and if it worked out well, he would greatly enlarge his project. He had a large bunk building with about twenty bunks finished, each with a new single mattress covered, with room under the bed for a suitcase and boxes, hangers on the partitions, and some shelves on the back at the foot of the bed.

The kitchen–dining room area was in a different building. The idea was that we girls should decide on the kind of food we wanted, for the expense would be held out of our earnings. Everything was to be run by the clock — up at 5 a.m., out in the field before six — since they were paid only for the number of baskets or cups they picked, and they would want to be on the job.

Each girl picked up a crate with the little regulation containers, and filled them all before she took them to the checking table. All were instructed exactly how this should be done, because these berries went directly to the market as soon as possible after they were picked. Mr. Clark must establish a reputation as a top producer.

They were expected to pick as fast as possible, for the immediate marketing was very important in getting top prices. That he was satisfied with our efforts was best shown by the fact that he immedi ately enlarged his acreage, and set up his housing for the next season for sixty pickers instead of fifteen.

The girls all said that, while the work was hard, they knew nothing that they could have done better on. At the time, I thought that I should take notes and write up some of the stories that were told as the girls lolled around on the grass in the shade of the tall trees on the banks of the canal.

While I was busy about the strawberry-picking project, Charity had answered an ad in the paper for kitchen help at the visitors' center in Yellowstone Park. She had her interview there in Provo, where a temporary office was set up, was accepted, and was on her way before any of us knew that she was interested. Now, with the strawberry picking all finished, and the girls back in their homes, Aura and I found ourselves with time on our hands.

Leona Durrant had been a companion of Charity's in the mission field; her sister Melva was Laurel's girlfriend, so we were friends, too. Her suggestion was that she furnish the car — she had a new Ford — and that Aura and I put in the gas and oil, and we all "go Dutch" on other expenses, and visit Yellowstone Park.

We made some preparation to have food on hand, and supplied ourselves with road maps and a general guidebook, for the distances were long between stops.

We found facilities at Yellowstone very primitive; most of the visitors were bringing their own small tents and bedrolls. We had blankets and quilts, but on no condition would Leona camp out. We rented a small, one-room lumber cottage with bunk beds and mattresses only, and a small wood heating stove.

Near our place, two girls were having a bit of trouble putting up their tent, so Leona — large and capable — gave them a hand. Their final act was to pull out a pair of very large men's boots and set them just outside the tent flap. They looked formidable enough; we all slept better because they were there.

We engaged this cottage for three nights, since there was a small discount on price. We were glad to make a wood fire in the little heating stove and fry our eggs and heat the teakettle on top. After our long trips during the day, it was a luxury to come home to this cabin with its rough beds and table and heater.

We were eager to see all there was to see, so we studied the guidebooks and followed the rangers on all the hiking trails that we could. In the afternoon we would take longer trips in the car, and we always collected the picture post cards and other trinkets to keep as mementoes.

We had been warned not to feed the bears in the park, nor to otherwise disturb them, especially if we were walking. But one day we saw a large one near the road, who came when we stopped as though she knew that we might have goodies for her. She was on my side of the car; Ernie was sitting in the middle. I rolled down the window and we let Ernest give her a cookie. But soon they were all gone.

"No more, no more! All gone," we said, but she was not about to go away, so Leona quickly stepped on the gas and I rolled the window up. After that we were frightened enough to stay as far away from the bears as we could.

Our three days in the park were not nearly long enough, but they were so exciting that we brought back as much as we could in cards and mementoes, promising ourselves privately that on the next trip we would have more time and money.

As for me, I began to be concerned about my school activities for the year ahead. I felt that with the debating honors we had already won, I must try to keep the standards up, especially with regard to the home I was to live in. My responsibility was larger than just schoolwork. I must maintain a home setting in which I could invite family and friends without embarrassment, but homes for rent were few and far between in St. George.

Perhaps I had been foolish to go meandering off to Yellowstone Park when I should have been in St. George giving my new home a general cleaning and face lifting. And yet I could not feel that I had made a mistake to take this trip; it was truly food for the soul. I'd pitch in with the full force to help prepare my home for better living.

To Columbia

I DON'T REMEMBER THE DATE, BUT IT WAS EARLY IN THE SPRING OF 1928 at a regular Monday morning faculty meeting. We met in a classroom adjoining the president's office, and I came in with a chew of squawbush gum in my mouth. For all my scorn of gum and my insistence that students should not chew gum in class, I had not been able to resist this, the result of an afternoon hour along the Santa Clara Creek. I knew that I would discard the gum before class, but had neglected to spit it out as I passed the wastepaper basket.

I had hardly taken my seat before Art Paxman began to sniff the air. "Squawbush gum!" he said. "Who's got squawbush gum?"

I glued my mouth shut, determined not to open it until I got out of there. I knew the odor was pleasant — pungent and different — and evidence that someone had spent some time gathering it. The gum was really not important except that I was embarrassed to have the attention focused on me.

Near the close of the hour President Nicholes announced that the board had consented to give one sabbatical leave each year. This would enable a teacher to take a year off for study on half pay, and come back with a raise in salary the following fall.

Brother Arthur K. Hafen had been longest in service here. Would he care to accept this offer?

"I couldn't possibly leave for a full year," Arthur K. said. "My

[300]

family is large. I cannot take them and I cannot leave them. The older boys are at an age where it is hard for my wife to manage them, and her health is poor."

Next in seniority was H. L. Reid, who declined for the same reason. One or two others were named, but each only shook his head. President Nicholes turned to me.

"Don't look at me," I said. "I'll take it so quick it'll make your head swim."

"I move we give her a hand," Art Paxman said, "and have her explain how come she is here at this hour chewing squawbush gum. You know, of course, that young squaws gather and chew it as a mating bait. Big medicine for them — squawbush gum!"

Everybody laughed, the first bell rang for opening classes, and the meeting was dismissed. I very quickly disposed of the telltale gum and went about my regular classes.

I had given no thought to this possibility, but I knew exactly what I would do: I would go to Columbia University! Later I was often asked why I should choose to go all the way across the continent when I could as easily get a Master's at BYU or the University of Utah, or even at the University of California at Berkeley. I answered that I had always wanted to see the Statue of Liberty and to visit the New England area, and Boston. I wanted to see the homes and surroundings of the writers: Thoreau's Walden Pond, Emerson's, yes, and Louisa M. Alcott's home. Basically, though, it was because of Miss Mina Connell. If Columbia University had been good enough for my Normal Training Course instructor, it would do for me.

I didn't worry about the money, either. I knew that I had enough in savings to take me across the continent and to Columbia, and on $85 a month I could manage.

As I looked through the literature which came in answer to my written request, I was more certain than ever that I was doing the right thing. I would cross the continent on a Pullman Flyer, like the one that had given me such a fright in Moapa years before, and there would surely be adequate housing.

I traveled light: two medium-sized suitcases and a spacious purse held all my necessities. I boarded the train at Modena and arrived in the evening of the second day. We pulled into the underground station and unloaded. I went to the information desk and told a lady that I had come to go to Columbia University, and would like to secure living quarters within walking distance, if possible.

She made a telephone call, and directed me to the Morningside Residence Club, a home for women on the campus. In a very short time I had arrived, signed up and left my check, and was directed to a room on the seventh floor, facing north and east. It was very nice; I could tell even before I turned on the light.

Then I walked across the room, and opened my window to view the scene outside. Instantly a carillon in a nearby church began to play:

> Lead, Kindly Light, amid the encircling Gloom,
> Lead thou me on!
> The night is dark, and I am far from home —
> Lead thou me on!
> Keep Thou my feet, I do not ask to see
> The distant scene — one step enough for me.

This seemed directed at me, especially played for my benefit. At any rate it gave me a new feeling of security, of being right where I should be, and an assurance that things were really working out. From this time on, I tried to be at home every night in time for vespers. They became my private worship.

The next morning I was up and out early, eager to visit the campus. The bookstore was open, so I purchased a notebook, pencils, and a small guidebook covering not only the campus, but the whole area. The young man, seeing that I was from Utah, asked about my home town and background. He was Harold Bentley! Little could he guess how much I knew about him from his little girl friend, my former classmate at BYU.

Yes, Verna was here; she would get her Bachelor's degree in the spring, when he would get his Ph.D., and I hoped to get my Master's.

Verna later seemed happy to meet me, too. They had hoped to find someone to sit with their baby girl two or three hours a week, which I would be glad to do. I was more than happy to have met Hal, for he advised me to take my degree through the University instead of the Teachers' College. I was not interested in training teachers; my business was to teach college students. I learned the time and place for the initiation meeting for potential Master's degree candidates. Here we were told that there would be no record of our activities; we could attend such classes as we cared to; we would work at our own time and pace; we must just pass that final examination. One thing more: we must prepare a written study, a research paper under the direction of a graduate dean, who would work with a group not to exceed twenty students. His grade would be important, but not so important as that of the final test.

Soon after I arrived, the management announced that they were holding open house as a way of helping their people become acquainted, and urged us all to attend. I had not yet spoken to a soul in the building, nor had anyone spoken to me. So I dressed up as well as I could and went to the reception room, where chairs were set up in groups and rows, with a long table filled with plates of cookies and dainties, and at the end coffee, tea, postum, and several cold beverages. Not many had arrived when I served myself and sat in the second row near the center of the room.

Two well-dressed ladies followed soon after and filled in just in front of me. They seemed to be important; at least they were carrying on a lively conversation and greeted most of the others scattered about as if they were well-known.

"I heard the greatest joke the other day," one said to the other. "Doctor Blank told me that there was a Mormon in her department who was going out for his Ph.D. Can you imagine a Mormon getting a Ph.D.?" And they both laughed heartily.

What should I do? Should I sit and hear my people ridiculed and not say a word? And yet, I knew that I would have no influence here; I would be a reason for all the more ridicule. So I sweated it out and waited, as I was prompted to do.

"Oh, Dr. Somebody," one of them called out to another mature lady as she finished filling her plate. "Come over here and sit with us. Dr. Blank here has just told me the greatest joke. There is a Mormon in her department who is going out for his Ph.D.!"

"Where have you girls been? I know many Mormons who have Ph.D's. On our faculty some of our best teachers are Mormons. Dr. Lew Winsor and Dr. Keith Seegmiller are well-known in Cornell. And this man with the Bell Telephone laboratories, Harvey Fletcher, is a Mormon. They say he fills his ranks with University of Utah graduates, and they are getting too great a stronghold."

I returned my empty dishes to their place and left without having met a single person, but my heart was warm with the knowledge that someone else had spoken better for me than I could have spoken for myself.

This business of working alone, without regular classes and occasional tests or reports, was different. I quickly found my reading room area, and on a desk a large book — hardbacked, loose-leaved, bigger than an unabridged dictionary, which contained all the questions that had been asked in the final tests for the previous ten years or so. The pages were pretty well worn when I started my investigation, and I was only over a few pages when a couple of other girls came up, and soon a third. So we decided to read the questions aloud and pool our knowledge.

I found that I knew next to nothing. Such questions as: Who wrote about a tub? A bandersnatch? The Jaberwocky? The Big Indians? Dover Beach? An Idiot Boy? A Walrus and a Carpenter? An Eel?

Never before or since have I felt so ignorant, so totally lost. Who was I to come to an institution like this for a Master's degree, with a background like mine? A high school of forty students! Credits in a Normal school geared to teaching in the sage flats of Nevada! College classes taken because the time scheduled fitted the exchange in hours for caring for the baby and preparing meals! Surely I had made a major mistake to come here!

They told us that we might have two trials to pass the tests; that is, if I failed the first time, I might stay another year and try again. After a second failure, I would not be considered of mental caliber to receive a Master's from Columbia University. So I simply must not fail!

I thought things over, and decided that maybe that test would not be so impossible, after all. The questions, many of them, came from the classics which I had read in my senior year at Bunkerville. Never a main character would be listed, but an important one; in *Silas Marner* it was Dunstan Cass, for example. By reviewing my course in English literature under Mr. Kelly, I revived many characters. I was

[304]

short on the works of Jonathan Swift and Matthew Arnold, and some others. All in all, I did read pretty consistently every day, five days a week. On Saturday I did my general clean-up and shopping. Sunday, of course, was Sunday, with at least one meeting at church.

We would also be expected to produce an essay or dissertation on an assigned subject. Those interested in American literature should meet in one room; those whose major was English should meet in another. It was understood that the questions for finals would be from both fields. Here there might be another division if the group were too large.

Some thirty people assembled in the room for American literature. The leader was a plump young man, not exactly fat, but well-rounded and blonde, with smooth, hairless cheeks.

We would each draw a subject from boxes labeled AMERICAN or ENGLISH. I pulled out a slip which read "American poetry before Ann Bradstreet." *Before* Ann Bradstreet! How in the world could I start? I felt as if the breath had been knocked out of me.

I held my peace; I would wait for others to react, as some of them emphatically did. This, I could see, got them nowhere. As for me, I was too heartsick to speak. I worked diligently, I had several interviews with the instructor, and finally handed in a paper just before the final closing date, which he graded A–.

One of the girls who lived in the apartment house had come to be a speaking acquaintance, though we never said more than a good morning. Then she came to look me up. Would I like to go to the Alumni Banquet of the Naval Military Academy? No, I don't really know where it was held, and I had no reason to want to go. But it seemed very important to her. Her escort was bringing a friend along, and she must supply a date for him. I protested that I had no appropriate clothes. She would rent an outfit for me, and I could help select it. So she brought several dresses, and rigged me out with a wrap and shoes as well, so that I looked like any other girl going to a dance — any other plain girl, that is.

We went together in a cab, and found a place at a round table with an extra man and one other couple quite a distance from the speaker's stand. Everyone seemed in high spirits. When the band played

"The Bells of St. Mary's," most of them kept the time with their spoon and glass, while many joined in singing the chorus.

Soon my escort drew a flask from his pocket and started pouring out the drinks. I had no idea what it was, but I knew that I must not drink it. Of course, I should have kept silent and pretended. But I didn't. When the glass was a little over half-full I held up my hand and said, "Whoa!"

A thunderbolt from heaven could not have created more of a sensation. His mouth dropped open; his hand froze in the air. After a pause, he set the bottle down.

"What did you say?" he asked, slowly and distinctly.

"I said '*Whoa*,'" I answered. "That is a perfectly good word. It means *enough, cease, stop, desist, thank you.*"

"Smells like a barn to me," he said shortly. "What do you know about horses?"

"Well, I own a little bay mare of my own."

"Bay is not a color. It is a body of water almost surrounded by land."

"It is a color of a horse. There are sorrels and blacks, and dappled, but bays are most common."

His evening was ruined. He took his drink at a gulp and poured another. I don't remember what we ate. I remember only that the crowd became so noisy that the chairman rapped again and again for order, but no one paid any attention, and the speaker sat down. Some dance music was playing not far away as we got up from the table. The other two couples went over to dance, but my escort sprawled on a couch as though he had literally passed out. I walked to the ladies' room, and wandered about a little before I settled in a chair. My friends didn't dance long; they had also had more liquor than they could handle.

So we left my escort where he was, and got a taxi to take us home. We rode in silence most of the way — there seemed nothing to say to each other. I got out first and walked on toward the door; my friends followed after they had paid the driver. The girl missed her step as she reached the curb, and fell, in all her finery, into the gutter — or onto the pavement. Her escort seemed unable to give much assistance, but the cab driver came and got them onto their feet and headed toward the door. I paused a little before I went in, stopped a minute or two inside, and then opened the door a crack to look out. They were locked in a tight embrace in the corner.

The next morning I put my outfit back into its box, wrapped and tied it, and left it at the desk downstairs to be delivered to the girl who had ordered it. I did not see her again.

I remember the whole incident with a sense of embarrassment and shame. I wonder if, after the fatal "Whoa!" was out, I had smiled and said "Forgive me, please. That's plenty, thank you," perhaps we could have passed it off and found a subject for discussion which was more fitting to the occasion.

At last the day came which we had all dreaded. Six of us girls had worked in the same reading room and discussed characters and trends and general philosophies, trying as best we could to prepare for this ordeal.

On the day appointed for the Master's examination, the large room was filled with men and women — that is, it was filled because there were at least two empty chairs on every side of each candidate. If any were to cheat, it would not be by assistance from his neighbor.

The false–true–completion test in which answers could be made by a check or a single word filled about ten pages. The first several I did not know, so I decided to read through to the end rather quickly and check all that I was absolutely certain of. When you know, and you know that you know, it isn't at all difficult to answer, so this did not take too long.

Beginning again, I tried to associate the items with possible answers, and was surprised that I found others that I really knew when I gave myself a little more time for association. By this time quite a number of students were leaving. Either they had finished well and felt confident, or they had given up trying to do any better.

But I started again for the third time, and strangely, it was as if a light went on and I remembered terms like "Locksley Hall," "Dover Beach," "The Idiot Boy," "In Memoriam," and many that I had passed over at first as totally hopeless. Even at that I had not answered much more than half of the possible questions. I counted again and stayed on, and found a few more that I was really sure of, so that

I had answered well more than half. In spite of this, I felt certain that I had failed this test.

The next day's examination was an essay type: we wrote at some length in discussion of three out of five possible topics. Here I felt that I did better, for on two topics I felt quite conversant, and I knew something of the third.

We were told that if we needed to leave the campus early, and if we would leave a stamped, addressed envelope at the desk, they would mail our grades to us. Or if we cared to call in person after a certain time, they would hand our grades to us, or we could call by telephone. When I learned that both the girls from South Carolina had failed, I was afraid to ask for my results. I called from a telephone booth right there in the building; it would be easier to take alone. When I asked for my results and gave my name, the secretary paused a while as if she were going through the cards, then she sang out, "Congratulations, Miss Pulsipher! You not only passed, but you're listed in the second-to-the-top group. You may be proud of that!"

I could not trust myself with anything more than a mumbled, "Oh, thank you!" and again, "Thank *you* too, Lord!" I had no way to express my joy. I couldn't jump up and down and clap my hands; there was nobody to hug or swing around the floor. So I just hung up the receiver, said "Thank You, Lord," again, and collected myself enough to hurry out onto the street.

The graduation exercises were most impressive to me; I was proud to be a part of this massive program.

I was ready to leave New York City. My friend and classmate Polly decided that she was ready to leave, too. Why not travel together as far as her home in Lynn, Massachusetts? She'd like so much to have me see her family, and she thought they'd be glad to meet me, for Polly had told them that I had been her guardian angel.

We decided to go by boat; it was cheaper, and it would be a different experience for me. So we took off in the late afternoon, stayed out on deck until dark, then went to our cabin until mess call in the morning. Polly had written or telephoned her family, for her father was there with his car to meet us.

They were overjoyed to have their daughter home again. She took me through the shoe factory where her father worked and to meet her pastor, and was glad of his warm welcome home.

By a lucky coincidence, we passed a "Traveling Teachers' Bus," which had a few vacancies. They were visiting all the places I had wanted to see and they had room for a few more teachers. This was one of the most rewarding experiences of my whole year away. We visited the homes of the poets and writers, and took time to walk through and around them while we discussed their various works. "The House of Seven Gables" was one example, and Herman Melville's holdings. I gathered cards and pictures and general enriching background for which I have always been grateful.

Dean of Women

ON MY RETURN FROM COLUMBIA, PRESIDENT NICHOLES GAVE
ME A DIFFERENT ASSIGNMENT. Instead of debate coach, I would be
Dean of Women, to counsel such girls as came to me with their
troubles and to handle special cases. I might continue with my
English "D" — or the survey course in English literature — for that
was the field I had devoted my time to at Columbia. Though I was
a bit disappointed about debate, I very quickly found that I had all
I could handle. Here, within a very short time, one girl came in to
tell me that she thought she was pregnant. What should she do?
Had she told her mother? No, she'd wait awhile. Within the week
she came in very much relieved.

Another girl, a full four months pregnant, had not told her mother.
She wanted me to go with her to break the news, but I convinced her
that her mother would be all the more humiliated if she had a
stranger in on it.

Some girls just needed a sounding board, someone to talk to who
was not family.

My first real case was that of a little girl who had been given the
nick-name of "California Rose." She was small, and so pale as to be
ashen, though her hair, too, was light. She looked so out of place in
that audience of healthy, vigorous young people. Dr. McGregor
telephoned the office and asked for me. Would I get this little girl

and bring her to his office at four o'clock this afternoon? I should talk to her before we came. Six boys or young men had come in for treatment of a disease which everyone said they got from her. "Rotten before she was ripe," explained her.

I had her come into the office, took her name, birthdate, and the name of her guardian in California. She was just here because she wanted to stay and go to school, but she hadn't completed her registration.

I asked her about the charge that she had gone out with boys. Yes, they would whistle for her and she would go out and get into the cars. Did she know their names? No, they just called each other by their nicknames. Where did they go? To a building in the field just a little ways away; it was empty now but it had been shelter for a hired man. There was a quilt folded on the floor, and a cot in the corner. Then what happened? They would each take a turn. Did they pay anything? Once when she held back they gave her a dime; other times they gave her a candy bar.

She didn't want to go to the doctor, but she would rather go there than to the jail. I was disappointed not to get the names of the boys involved, but Doctor McGregor said that was not necessary; he had them all. Everyone had come in for treatment, and of course he had all the information before he would treat them. He seemed concerned, for one or two were from prominent families; no matter who they were, it was a bad situation for everyone.

The "California Rose" did not come back to any Dixie assemblies; she was taken to another guardian in California.

One experience I shall never forget. We had two general assemblies a week, one on Wednesday and one on Friday. Both were held just before noon; both involved community singing, a prayer, and announcements of various kinds. While the Wednesday meeting was faculty oriented, with an educational half-hour lecture, classical music, and demonstration, the Friday program was by and for the students, with various classes or clubs giving the numbers.

One Friday morning three girls gave a little singing, dancing, and advertising skit. They had put on their costumes in the ladies' room downstairs, and when their act was over, one girl found that the $20 bill that she had left in her sweater pocket was stolen. She had brought it expecting to go to the store and pay for a coat she had fitted for earlier. They were holding it for her.

She came at once to me and reported her loss, and we took it to the general office. I called the clothing stores in town and told them to watch for a girl with a twenty-dollar bill, and report to us. I felt that no young man would go into the ladies' rest room, but how could I learn which girl had taken it? School had not been in session long enough for me to know many of the girls who were not in my classes.

I did not have a class the first hour after noon, so I spent the full hour studying how to find the culprit. In the first place, twenty dollars represented a lot of money; and some girl carried the guilt of a major theft.

My class the second period was one in which all thirty seats were full. The students filed into their places and began pulling out papers and opening texts. I looked up just as a young lady took her place third from the back and nearest the door.

Clearly, "the little man on my shoulder," like Socrates' mentor, said, *"There* is your twenty dollars."

I was shaken to the grass roots. This beautiful girl was such a lady — not one to speak out or volunteer anything in class, but usually ready with the right answer if called upon. She always looked so clean, too.

To cover my confusion and regain my poise, I asked them all to write briefly of their reaction to some part of the assignment. They might do this in about ten minutes. I started at the back to pick up the papers, and when I came to her, I said softly, "Come into my office right after class, will you? Please."

Then there followed a general discussion of the lesson, with questions from the floor, comments, tomorrow's assignment, and the dismissal of class.

I went immediately to my office, a small room, indeed, but all we had. I was there only a few minutes before she came in, and I seated her where the light was full on her face.

"Do you have any idea why I asked you here this afternoon?" I asked.

"No."

"Not the slightest?"

"No."

"Then I'll tell you. You took the twenty dollars from Eleanor's pocket in the rest room during assembly."

"Oh, Mrs. Pulsipher, what makes you think that? Have I ever done anything that would make you think I am a thief?"

"Listen, honey," I said, leaning forward and touching her hand, "I don't *think* that; I know. Now you are *not* a thief. You will be worried to death with this money; you cannot spend it; you won't know what to do with it. The bill is marked; it will be instantly recognized. Just hand it to me, and I'll never breathe it to a single soul; your name will never be mentioned. You can slip out that side door, and not a soul will know you've even been in here. You can forget it, and so will I."

She hesitated a second, then pulled the bill out of her pocket and handed it to me.

"Thank you," I said, rising. "Now there will be three of us happy. As for you, this is blotted out. Forget it. I have already."

After she left, I dropped into my chair, almost faint. Suppose I had been wrong! O, dear Lord, what if I had been wrong! How could I ever have apologized enough? And what would it have done to her to be wrongfully accused? But how wonderful, how positively grand it was to have it settled in this way! I could hardly say, "Thank you, Lord!" And I cried a bit to ease my tension.

Laurel had been called to a mission for the Church, but was released a month early for two reasons: he was having stomach trouble, and he would be late getting into school. He arrived in Bunkerville on September 10, 1929, where he remained until Sunday to report on his mission. He then came on to Dixie, where he expected to register at once in the college.

The first Friday after his arrival there was a basketball game between Dixie and Cedar City, and Bessie Atkin invited the team to her home afterward for refreshment and visiting. Laurel was included at the party, though he was not on the team.

I had gone to bed immediately after the game, but I awoke suddenly some time after midnight. Laurel hadn't come home! I put on my shoes and a housecoat and set off, cutting through the public square behind the public library and to the Woodward School on the corner. Here I found Laurel, slumped down against the wall, too sick to travel. He had eaten cake and ice cream, along with other goodies, all of which his stomach had rejected before he could get home. He was so weak that he had stopped here to rest. I was glad the weather was still so moderate.

I got him to his feet, put his arm over my shoulder, and half supporting him, managed to get him home and into bed.

"I knew that I shouldn't have eaten that cake and pie," he confessed, "but I didn't want to appear snobbish."

The next morning I called Dr. McGregor. Though it was his day off, he told me to bring Laurel over for an examination.

"It sounds to me like the common missionary sickness, which I have come to call "The Missionary Frustration Disease" — or just stomach ulcers. It is caused by the stresses and tenseness of earnest young men who just cannot accomplish all that is expected of them, and the more sincere they are, the worse the sickness. It causes ulcers.

"Now if you two will help me carry out a little experiment, I'll make no charge, and I think we can clear this in a matter of a week or so. It will not be pleasant, but it will be better than an operation.

"I've worked out a plan that I'd like to see tried, and if you will be my guinea pig, I'll not charge a cent. It will involve you, too, Mrs. Pulsipher, and may be almost as hard on you as on him. But an operation to remove stomach ulcers is very expensive in more ways than one. You've already learned that you cannot eat pastry, so I don't need to tell you to watch your diet. What I want now is for you to follow a very strict diet for two weeks, at least.

"See this little apparatus," and he held up a long rubber tube with a funnel on one end. "You push this down your throat all the way to your stomach. Now that will not be easy. You'll gag and choke and maybe think a knife operation would be easier, but you can do it if you think you can. And you, Mrs. Pulsipher, must have this pitcher full of tepid water — just body heat. Pour the full quart into his stomach, let him lean down and drain it back into an old pan of some kind. I think you may be surprised at what comes out. But do it two

[314]

or three times each morning early. Let it go the full twenty-four hours before you wash it out again.

"Then for your diet, you go back to first principles for awhile. Milk, warm and fresh from the cow, a raw egg well-beaten and added to a cup of milk later in the day. After a few days a gravy with some spinach leaves, well-washed and diced fine and just brought to a boil. For lunch, one potato baked and seasoned with butter, and milk. You can't take too much milk if you take just a little at a time. But get the spinach leaves. I noticed when I passed your place that they are having a second crop since they have had water, and they look as thrifty as though it were early spring instead of fall.

"I think you'll be surprised and happy at the results. Let me know."

We were, indeed, happy with the results. Before the end of the second week we took back the equipment, and Laurel was given a clean bill of health. No one needed to tell him that he was well; he knew!

He left at once to go on to Provo to school. Here he would marry Melva Durrant, who had corresponded with him faithfully the two years that he was away. They would take over the Con Adams' basement apartment which Melvin and family had occupied. Best of all, his health was perfect; he forgot that he ever had an ulcer.

To move from one ward to another in St. George was like moving from one village to another. Though the organizations were the same, they were manned by different people, and there were subtle changes in some of the activities and minor routines. The Leavitts had been trained to attend their church services, and for the most part they did that, regardless of which ward they lived in.

Our basic pattern was to go to school five days a week, and to study at night, either at home or in the library. Saturday was cleanup day. We would put the washing out early so that the clothes might be good and dry, but gathered the colored clothes back in ahead of time, so that they might be ironed. The sheets and pillow slips, towels and underwear were left out all day, so that the sun should have them all sterilized.

We had no washing machine, so we rubbed the clothes on the board, and depended upon the boiling-and-punching routine to do the real cleaning. Francis and Dudley put the clothes out on the line, and for some reason or other, chose to hang the sheets lengthwise and by their selvage edge, instead of throwing them over the line and making a straight crease down the middle.

The Benson home, a large brick house with an ample front porch facing east, was our near neighbor on the north, but the lot was some six feet higher than ours and we maintained a rock wall between us. The Benson boys had a basketball bank in the back yard, where they would practice in little one-to-one games.

Menzies Benson and my brother Francis were in the same class, and very good friends, but Menzies felt it was rather sissified for Francis to spend his Saturday forenoon doing the family wash. This troubled Francis not at all; he figured that whatever he could do to help would help pay for the opportunity to get an education.

"I'm big and strong, I need to work out a little on something besides a basketball," he would say.

One Sunday afternoon in mid-September, I took a letter to mail at the Post Office. The Postmaster, Walter Cannon, happened to be in, and hearing my voice as I greeted some friends, came out into the foyer.

"I've been hoping that I could see you before anyone else told you about the Athena Club ruckus last night. Your name came up, and someone asked Bess Benson what she thought of you as a neighbor. Well, she said that she'd never really met you, but you hang out the whitest sheets in this town. She wanted to ask what brand of soap or detergent you used. She would, she said, at the first chance she'd get.

"That was just a bombshell. Most of the women there thought that they put out clean sheets. My own wife was almost insulted. Well, Bess didn't back down; she just insisted that either the fabric itself or the washing powder brought out the whitest sheets she'd ever seen in her long life."

I was too surprised to know how to answer, and embarrassed that I had been discussed in public in that manner. I didn't know all the personnel of that group, but I did know Orilla Hafen, Flo Brooks, and Leo Snow's wife. That is, we would greet each other when we met, and I had some of their children in my classes.

In 1975 I went to St. George to attend the funeral of Marilyn

[316]

Bruhn, a young friend of mine. While there, I called on her ninety-six-year-old grandmother.

"I hoped you'd come down," she said. "I thought you would. I was telling someone the other day what a commotion it raised in some party where a lady said you had the whitest sheets in town. Did you ever tell them what kind of soap you used?" she insisted.

"No, I never did. But I'll tell you now. It was my mother's home-made soap, a compound of pork fat and lye, with a drop of essence of peppermint to give a pleasant odor. This was added after it was done.

"I wouldn't have told them for anything in the world. I didn't think it was any of their business. I'm surprised that such a trifle should be remembered so long.

"There's a difference in soap made from beef tallow or mutton tallow and that of pork, too. Mom just happened to get it almost perfect this time."

Ernie came to me one evening and asked very seriously, "Are we a family? Just me and you, are we a family?"

"Yes, dear," I told him. "We are a family."

"Then why haven't we got a home? A family is supposed to have a home!"

"You are right, son," I said promptly. "A family ought to have a home. We must see what we can do about it."

I set out that very afternoon, after having scanned the "Homes For Sale" section in the paper. Within a week, I had a house located that filled my needs, and was within range of my purse. It was on top of the Red Hill, and it would be almost summer before the final papers could be signed.

Ernie took special pride in our little home on the hill; he loved the outside, from the young poplar trees on the sidewalk, the pomegranate bushes along the east fence just loaded, the grapevines in so many varieties — actually a small vineyard, but it looked to him like something very special. The cement walk from the porch to the gate had some bright marigolds on the border, beautiful to him.

And the porch was different. It not only covered the whole front, but went halfway down the west side, so that whoever had that bedroom could come in at night without having to go through the front room and kitchen. There was only one back door, out of the kitchen.

Ernie thought that the little bushy-tailed animal with stripes down its back was an extra bonus, too. It would run around the porch posts and then dodge into a place underneath; when he learned that it was a skunk, he watched from a distance. Somehow the little animal must have decided to leave; at any rate we never did get "scented."

We moved into the place in May 1930, and spent the whole season there very happily. The next winter Dudley lived with us and attended Dixie College. One incident I remember: Dudley, Reed Heywood, Lee Brooks, and perhaps another who was not named, were trying to brew liquor. Evidently they succeeded in getting a product with some kick, for Dudley was sick to his stomach and vomited on his bedroom floor. He not only had to clean up the mess, but I reported him to President Nicholes. Coach Lee Hafen was much surprised that I would turn in my own brother.

"If I am going to report any at all, I must treat all alike. If Dudley got drunk, I'll report it. This time I had the evidence."

I was glad to be able to tell the coach later that Dudley thanked me for reporting him.

"I had a chance to get acquainted with President Nicholes, and it's worth a lot to know a man like that," he told me. "Better still, he knows me."

Just a-Visiting

IN THE SPRING OF 1931, I was appointed to serve as a member of the stake board of MIA, so I felt obligated to attend the Church's General Conference in Salt Lake City. Charity was married and permanently settled in Blanding, and I took this occasion to arrange a visit prior to returning south.

Before I left St. George I had inquired about anyone likely to be going to southeastern Utah from Salt Lake City or Provo. Vilate Prince, a neighbor, said that she was going as far as Price to visit her family. She was riding with Sheriff Will Brooks, who was en route to Cortez, Colorado, where he would pick up a prisoner and return him to Price. Vilate was taking her daughter along, but there would be plenty of room for me.

A little study of the map convinced me that if I could get as far as Monticello, I could risk getting transportation the remainder of the way by mail truck or chance traveller; I might even write or telephone my friends the Rowleys and ask if they could meet me there.

Through Vilate I received the assurance that the Sheriff had room and would be glad to take me as far as he went in my direction. I had told her that they could pick me up at the B. F. Larsen residence in Provo. I was ready and waiting when they arrived; I knew nothing of the roads, but by scanning a map I could see that it was a long, long trail.

Antone Prince, Vilate's husband, was Deputy Sheriff, which meant that they had many common interests. Besides that, they were established in St. George and knew everybody, so they carried on a lively conversation, some of it of keen interest to me. But I only listened.

It was mid-afternoon before we arrived in Price, so Mr. Brooks refused all invitations to get out and come in. We had too long a road ahead. He immediately invited me to the front seat, "Where you should have been all the time."

At Green River we made a short stop to take on gas, visit the rest rooms, and pick up a sandwich and a glass of milk each. He suggested that we take rooms for the night at Moab, since there were accommodations there — "of a kind." He had been driving since early morning; it would be only good sense to go to bed and relax.

Our conversation was chiefly centered in the college activities, without a mention of the Athena Club. I was strongly tempted to suggest that some of the faculty of Dixie College thought that St. George was a very cold and clannish community. Gladys Harrison felt that faculty wives were ignored; the Athena Club represented the elite of the town, and it was restricted in its membership to people who wanted to play rook. Gladys had confided that she had been in St. George two years, and never once been invited to a home. Well, I had had the same experience, but I might have been responsible in part; I had never invited anyone to dinner in my home, either.

After we had talked a bit about school activities, Will changed the subject. It was a shame to be traveling over this road at night, he thought, for here was some of the most spectacular scenery in all the world, only beginning to be discovered. He suggested I make it a point to return back in the daytime and then not just rush by it. Maybe I could write something about this area, especially if I could get pictures in color.

About ten p.m. we took rooms in the hotel at Moab, I on the main floor and he upstairs. Should he ask the management to call us? Or could I trust myself to waken by six a.m.? I told him I thought I could manage.

I was up and showered and ready to go when he called. Our first stop would be at Monticello, where he had spent several happy years, and where he just might spend the night. He must do his visiting here before he had the prisoner on his hands; there'd be no place in Monticello to keep him overnight.

We arrived just at sunrise. I could see the Sheriff tense as he passed familiar places. As we drove slowly down the main street, we saw a lady out sprinkling her lawn.

He slowed up, pulled over toward the gate, and stopped.

"Good morning, M'Rell," he called. "How are you?"

M'Rell dropped the hose into a rose bush and ran up onto the porch, where she called, "Billy Brooks is here, Mother; Billy Brooks is here!"

She returned immediately, pushing her mother in a wheel chair. Sheriff Brooks jumped out of the car, met her on the porch, and gave her a hearty kiss. Then he turned to shake M'Rell's right hand, and hug her to him a bit with his left arm.

"How lucky you've come today!" M'Rell said. "We're having our Relief Society bazaar tonight. Everybody will be out; they will when we scatter the word that you are in town."

"I must visit Grandma Jones; and Dan and Neen, and . . ."

"Everyone in town," M'Rell insisted. "Ain't a person in town won't be glad to see Billy Brooks."

She seemed so sincere that I was impressed in spite of myself.

"I must take this lady on down to Blanding, but I'll be right back; then we can take some time to visit."

"We'll hold breakfast for you. So don't pass us up."

"You needn't do that. I'll be nigh onto two hours — an hour-and-a-half at the best. That's too long for your mother to wait."

"She can have a cup-a-tea to hold her. She'll be right disappointed if you don't stop for a little while."

The Sheriff promised.

On the road again, he really opened up and talked. He had so many good friends there; one way or another, he had dealings with nearly everyone in town, if only to serve them at the store. Grandma Jones had nursed him through the typhoid fever epidemic when so many died, and but for Grandma Jones, he'd have gone, too.

"It's a wonder I didn't go; Grandma Jones' daughter was among them. I was sick in one room and she right through the wall from me

[321]

in another. I knew the instant she went — didn't nobody need to tell me she was dead."

It must have been hard for him to leave, I ventured.

"Nellie just couldn't see it. But now I'm glad that we left. We have a college in St. George. That is important to a family."

When we stopped in front of the Rowley home, I handed him a ten-dollar bill. He instantly handed a five-dollar one back.

"I really shouldn't take anything, it's been such a pleasant trip," he said, "But some folks don't want to accept favors, it seems."

"I know that cars don't run themselves, and I like to share the expense. Thank you for a very pleasant trip."

That was the last time I spoke to Sheriff Will Brooks for almost a year, for though we both lived in St. George, we were in different wards; he was at the dances in the business of a peace officer, not for his own recreation. He did not dance at all, though some of the other floor managers did.

I was so pleased with Charity's setup. Her fifteen-month-old daughter, Janice, was a perfect doll, happy and busy, with a mass of curls and a line of talk which her mother understood better than I did.

Vernon was in the lumber business, operating a sawmill and with a good market. He had taken on a junior league baseball team, and was training and sponsoring them in general, with everyone enjoying it.

Charity was ward Relief Society president in Blanding, and finding the work very rewarding. A close friend, the wife of Brother Albert R. Lyman, was going directly to St. George; her married daughter there was having a baby and needed her mother. With no public transportation, and with the lady eager for company, I was happy to take the chance. We called it "the hand of the Lord."

On February 19, 1932, the whole town was shocked by the sudden death of Sister Nellie Brooks, wife of Sheriff Will Brooks. For years she had been secretary of the Relief Society, which met in their own private hall, the Lyceum. This was just through the block from her home; she could walk west from her back door to the street, cross it and the sidewalk and enter the door.

She had always made a careful record of the meeting, and today was no exception. The minutes were detailed and beautifully written.

The officers were asked to remain for a few minutes after the dismissal; there were two or three items to consider. When it was done, Nellie stretched her arms up over her head and said, "Well, I'm glad that's over," and instantly crumpled to the floor, dead.

In vain they worked with her; a passing brother was called in, and he did what he could — all in vain. They took the body to the hospital for want of a better place, until her husband could be found.

I had all the details from Mabel Jarvis, who had been trying desperately to locate Mr. Brooks. I did not go to the viewing; I just could not make myself go alone. If Mabel or some other friend had asked me to go I'd have been pleased. I knew the whole Athena Club would be there in groups of three or four, or perhaps as a whole group to sit together. I hadn't the heart to face them.

I remained in my upstairs classroom during the whole afternoon, including the funeral in the tabernacle. Not until the group went to the cemetery did I leave to walk home, taking the cutoff up Diagonal Street and the trail up to the top.

President Nicholes at once became interested in our affairs; at least he never lost an opportunity to say a good word about Will to me. In all his life he had never known a man who treated his wife as well as Will Brooks had. He was always so helpful — he prepared breakfast every morning, and when his wife was pregnant, he had carried her orange juice to the bed. He would even change the baby's diapers.

In April the members of the legislature came to visit St. George, and the college in particular. President Nicholes assigned me to ride in Sheriff Brooks' car. I was genuinely grateful, for the Sheriff knew much more about the history of the St. George area than I did. The tabernacle became a very, very special building through his telling of his own father, George Brooks, who had put ten years of his life into the building. From age seventeen to twenty-seven he put in six-and-a-half days a week working here. And for what? Little colored tickets which passed as cash at the tithing office and at some of the stores.

Near the end of the basketball season, President Nicholes arranged with Sheriff Brooks to take the wives of the coaches and other officials to see the game at Cedar City. This game was always very important, they felt; this year it would determine the championship.

I was never much of a basketball fan, often not even attending the home games, to say nothing of going all the way to Cedar City to watch one. I had a pile of test papers on my desk, besides.

Will called from the court house to say that he would be down in about twenty minutes.

"I hadn't planned to go to Cedar tonight," I said.

But he cut me off with a cheerful, "Thank you! That's just fine! Be seeing you in twenty minutes!"

President Nicholes grew sober. "Now, Juanita, be a good sport! You will embarrass us all if you refuse to go. You just enter into the spirit of the thing, and you'll enjoy yourself, too! Just this one time, and I'll never make plans for you again."

After all, he was my boss, I decided, and forced a smile.

"OK. You win! I'll go through with it, and no one will be the wiser!"

"Good girl! You'll not be sorry!"

The Sheriff was on time, all freshly showered and shaved, and I hadn't had time to go home, though I had tried to freshen up in the ladies' room.

Elsie Hafen and Mamie Paxman climbed into the back seat. Their husbands were the coaches. Iris Bentley and I were in the front. A very small lady, Iris, but a good conversationalist.

If I was more silent than usual nobody mentioned it, for there were plenty willing to discuss players, referee, fumbles and fouls. The conversation never lagged.

"Thanks for going with us tonight," Will said as he stopped in front of my house. "I knew that you didn't really want to go, but neither of us could back out. Our friend, Joseph K., wants to help us. You're not sorry that you went, are you?"

"No. I really enjoyed it. Thanks a lot!"

During the early '30's, the Sons of Utah Pioneers, the Westerners, and perhaps other organizations were busy marking the trail from Salt Lake City to California. Among the most important places was the site of the massacre at Mountain Meadows. After much study and work on the ground, it was decided to erect a marker to the people who had lost their lives there. Many were put into a common grave, which it was felt should be marked by a suitable monument.

Word of this project was sent to eastern points with the hope that some of the descendants would be in attendance, and citizens and officials of all the southern Utah counties were expected to come, which in St. George meant everyone in the court house.

In Dixie College, that meant the college band, the faculty, and as many students as could go. The date was Saturday, Sept. 10, 1932.

My friend, Mabel Jarvis, worked at the court house, and early in the day called to say that Sheriff Brooks was taking the girls there, and would like me to go along and bring Ernest. He was taking his son Clair; the boys could be company for each other.

One of the Pendleton sisters, Alice, I believe, was in the front seat with Sheriff Brooks and Clair. The back seat was ample for Ernest and me along with the two other girls.

It was a pleasant day, cool and quiet and clear. For me, the ride was perfect until we came to a winding, twisting road, which I couldn't take. I was embarrassed to have to get out, but I knew that to stay in would be disaster, indeed.

The Sheriff pulled off the road and stopped, telling the boys they might get out and run a little ahead if they kept well off the tracks. I stayed out of sight behind the car, heaved until I felt that I was literally wrong-side-out, and climbed back into the car, evidently looking like a ghost. When we picked up Ernie and Clair, Ernie said with some concern, "Mother, what makes you so pale?"

"That's just my weakness," I told him. "When I was younger than you, I'd have to ride out on one of the horses. I'd get sick in the back under the wagon cover. But it's nothing. I'll be OK in just a minute."

By the time we arrived at the monument, I was ready to enter into the spirit of the occasion. I read the signs on the trails leading to various points; the monument was still swathed in red and white bunting, awaiting the unveiling. With all the expanse of rolling hills with a distant backdrop of jagged peaks, I couldn't help remembering Brother Johnson's shuddering cry of "BLOOD! BLOOD! BLOOD!"

As the program progressed, I walked away far enough to avoid talking about it. The band played funeral music, soft and mournful.

[325]

The speech was short, and the dedicatory prayer a masterpiece. I wanted only to be alone.

The sun was setting when we gathered to the car. I started for the back seat, but Alice graciously offered me her place in front. Now Ernie and Clair both sat with us.

The ride home seemed longer, with all of us impressed and silent. It was hard to make small talk with a massacre so close behind us. Will took Mabel home first, she lived farthest away — then the two Pendleton sisters.

Ernest was telling Clair about our grapes; he thought that whatever was on our lot was something just extra good. Wouldn't they like to take some home? He was so eager to show them off that he ran into the house and brought out knife and pan; they must have some of the big black grapes, "Lady Downings." These were new and special. At this time in September all would be ripe and overripe.

Will picked at them and seemed pleased to take them, and stood awhile until he had sampled them all. Then as he turned to go he said seriously, "I'm not looking anywhere yet, but when I do start, *you'd* better watch out."

"Oh, I don't know," I parried. "I'll have something to say about that, remember."

"I'm just warning you," and he walked away, to stop and call back, "Thanks for the grapes, and for the company."

I got my Christmas cards out early, especially those that needed to be mailed any distance. I selected one especially for the Sheriff, which I held to post just before I left for home. It was a very nice, appropriate card, but impersonal. After I had dropped it into the box, I wished I had waited, though I *had* waited until we left, which was better than mailing it from Bunkerville.

When I received no card from him, I remembered his comment that for one year he was being faithful to the memory of his wife, which would mean until February 9. Oh, well, everybody sent cards at Christmas and I had identified mine only with an inked *JP* joined together to look almost like a ribbon bow.

We had a happy Christmas at home. Not all of the family were there, but enough to make it Christmas, though we didn't go as a

[326]

group caroling. Mother would have gone alone with her guitar, so Daisy, Eva, and I decided to walk with her to the homes of the two grandmothers. Grandma Hafen was first, since she was farthest away. We sang two or three there, with Eva coming in strong with the alto, and Daisy supporting Mother with the melody. I gave moral support.

Grandma Thirza was sleeping nights at the home of Aunt Mary Ellen, so we sang some there, then around the corner and down a half-block to Uncle Albert, Mother's older brother. We moved across the street to Bishop Earl's, and then, because we had to pass them anyway, to Brother James, the Abbotts, and across the street to Sister Adams; she would remember how they used to sing together so long ago.

The next morning the families gathered in, neighbors called. Some came from Mesquite. Before the day was over, all had dropped in to visit and to have dinner together.

I had several things I wanted to do before I returned to Dixie. First, a new dress that needed a slight alteration. Since I had no sewing machine in St. George, I would use Mother's and work in one sister or another to help me.

By New Year's Day my projects were completed, and Mary had invited me to her home in Mesquite. About noon she answered a knock at the door, and I heard Will's voice asking for Mrs. Pulsipher!

I hadn't expected him to come down here at all!

"You're a hard person to find," Will's voice was loud and clear. "Why don't you tell a fellow where he can find you? I've canvassed both towns, door to door!"

"Well, I didn't expect you. I had no idea you'd come down here."

"Sure you did! Else why did you send me that invitation?"

"Everybody sends Christmas cards."

"Yes, but you're not everybody, and a pretty card like this can mean only an invitation. I'm careful to accept one like this."

And he pulled the card from his pocket, showing it to Mary as proof.

"You've timed it just right. We're just ready to sit up. Come and join us." Mary was cordial.

Will seemed to appreciate the invitation, and Mary's food was delicious. I hadn't remembered her as being such a good cook, but then I hadn't been around her much since she had been married.

After the meal, Fenton and Will went into the livingroom to sit before the fireplace. Out of their hearing, Mary took me by my two arms and shook me.

"You crazy kid!" she said. "He's not either *old*, and *fat*, and *funny*! He's *nice*! You'll do well to get a man like that. Don't you make fun of him ever again! You'll do well to get *him*."

It was time for us to go back to St. George. So we loaded in all our boxes and gifts; Dudley and Ernie sat in the back seat. I could hardly believe that Will had come for the express purpose of bringing me back home.

We had plenty of talk on the way about what gifts everybody had received for Christmas, and the sports in the daytime and the theater one night. And horse races! Some of those fellows would bet as much as five dollars on just a horse race!

When we reached home, I handed the key to Dudley, and did not get out at all. He and Ernie could carry the things onto the porch and I could arrange them later. There would be no need to start a fire; they could just roll into bed. I'd come in a little while.

Without a word of explanation or request, Will started the car and drove along the hill road, past Main Street, past the Sugar Loaf, and turned off to the north to some willows and parked.

Here we did our first love-making, but by whatever name it is currently called — "sparking," "spooning," "petting," "necking," "pitching-the-woo," "rotten-logging" — it all adds up to the same thing in the end: an engagement to be married.

We both knew that our case was different; neither was in a position to be married. We had too many other obligations. We agreed never to be seen together in public. Will must not neglect his duties as an officer of the law; I needed full time for my teaching and counseling program. I would continue to go with the same group of girls. He must not dance with me — since he never had, this would only be a continuation of a set pattern. I was on the stake board of MIA, he was superintendent of Sunday School in his ward.

Saturday evening and night would be ours. We usually went to Cedar City, Kanarraville, Leeds, or Beaver Dam Lodge for dinner.

By the middle of spring we had reached the point where we could declare our intentions to the world. This we did on April 19, 1933. As Mother wrote it:

April 19th. Pa's birthday again. Juanita, Dudley, & Ernest from St. George with Sheriff Brooks. Called at Mesquite for Laurel & Melva, Mary & Fenton & family. She brought a freezer of ice cream from St. George, also a cake and oranges, and gave Pa a gift of a $5.00 bill. She also announced her engagement to Sheriff Will Brooks. Said they planned to be married as soon as school is out, which pleased us very much, as she seems to be happy.

Epilogue: *"Heaven Is..."*

I MARRIED THE BROOKS FAMILY in May of 1933. That fall Nels Anderson came to St. George with his wife, his son Martin, and a secretary. His family took lodging on the same block with us, just around the corner and down the sidewalk, and "kittern" through by a shorter trail from his door to mine. Will was still Sheriff Brooks, the man who knew every person in the county.

Many of the citizens of St. George remembered Nels as the little hobo who in 1908 had been kicked off a freight car in the long, empty stretches of Nevada, who had found his way to the ranch of Lyman Wood in Clover Valley, and was taken in as one of the family. In 1909 he had been baptized into the Church. (Some thought that though he had been dipped, it did not sink in.) Later he had attended Dixie College and the BYU, where he had graduated in 1920. Now in 1933 he returned with a grant-in-aid from the Social Science Research Council and one from the Social Science Council of Columbia University. These grants enabled him to complete research for his dissertation, and to collect material for a book to be written on the last Mormon frontier; it appeared as *Desert Saints* in 1942.

None of us really comprehended Nels' influence. Will had known him when he had attended Dixie College, and now Will became a valuable source of information, especially on social matters like the

[330]

regulation of dances, and the part the wine industry had played in Dixie's history. Since most of the material Nels needed would be found in the St. George temple, I, as the newly-appointed president of the Relief Society, obtained permission to go into the vaults and bring out those documents that he requested.

The heavy volumes contained a wealth of information. Here were the most vivid pictures of Mormon life: patterns in worship, in recreation, in the settlement of differences between neighbors, cooperative ventures, and special programs for the different seasons, including Halloween, Valentine's Day, the Fourth of July, and the Twenty-fourth. Nels used all of this. His secretary copied the articles he wished to use or hold for his files for future studies.

As his work progressed, Nels wanted me to use my own family background and write an article on polygamy as I knew it from the experience of my parents. Flattered by this offer, I set about to do it, but when I had finished, Nels was not satisfied.

"Make it less formal," he told me. "Just take an easy, conversational style and don't be too concerned with statistics. Bring in other families, too, if you can."

By this time Will had been made Postmaster in St. George. Nels was leaving for the East, where he would finish writing his dissertation and within the year take a job with the Federal Emergency Relief Administration in Washington, D.C. He stopped at the Post Office to say goodbye, wrote his name and address on a piece of paper, and left word for me to forward the article as soon as it was finished.

Will said he would tell me, slipped the address into his shirt pocket, and promptly forgot about it. By the time it had run through my Maytag washer and wringer, it was illegible. Now, with this second draft of my polygamy story finished, I had no place to send it. While I waited for Nels to tire of waiting and inquire, in a spirit of bravado I mailed it to *Harper's*. They accepted it! And it was published in the February 1934 issue under the title "A Close-up of Polygamy."

Washington County had begun to receive money from the Federal Emergency Relief Act in the late summer of 1933, but in the months that followed none reached the widows with families, or other unemployed women. The public works had found road work, bridge work, water work, public building repair, vacant lot cleaning, fence building, and other projects to give dignity to the checks the people received. But why not have the elderly tell the stories of their lives to skilled people who would take them in shorthand, and come daily to work the story to an interesting account? This would be good for both parties, since they could take all the time they needed. In our area alone fifteen elderly people began the business of recording their histories; this soon became one of the best projects. The elderly looked forward to the daily interviews. They jotted notes ahead of time, verified dates, and filled in details. There was no hurry; the main concern was that the reports were reliable. This in turn necessitated the use of old newspapers, letters, and pictures, all of which added to the general interest of the undertaking.

As nearly as I can tell, a letter from Nels dated November 1, 1934, marks the inception of the idea that collecting diaries and original manuscripts might be done under a government project.

Dear Mrs. Brooks:

It occurs to me that you should initiate a white collar work project for the unemployed in your area. Better still you might have a study project for the students who are now receiving government aid. In my way of thinking there is no better way of using students than in the gathering of historical documents. Let us call it a collection of Dixiana. Here are some of the subjects that should be included:

Documents, pictures and original materials concerning Dixie places, including Silver Reef. All kinds of stories that people can remember about the Reef. Good and bad stories. Even the fictions and myths should be gathered. Each should be written and filed away.

You have already gathered a lot of autobiographies of the pioneers and I have read many of them, but too many of them are worthless. They strive to convey messages. If one could add to these stories about people and places and actual events. The closest approach to a good one was the little book of John S. Stucki.

Pictures should be reproduced in every case where owners want to keep the originals.

Letters should be collected and preserved.

The old Church records and the Town records should be gathered together and preserved.

Epilogue: "Heaven Is . . ."

Old songs (good and bad) should be written down with music.
I am sending a copy of this to Dr. Dorothy Nyswander of the University of Utah, who is also in charge of women's projects in the Relief Administration of Utah. I hope she can help get the thing started.

Sincerely,

Nels Anderson

As a result of his letter to Dr. Nyswander of the University of Utah, I received a letter from her dated November 10, in which she gave the idea her approval, and passed it on.

> . . . I would suggest that you talk over this project immediately with the County Manager of the Relief Administration of Washington County, who has his office in St. George, to see whether or not he would believe it feasible to carry through a project which has so much of social and permanent value. . . .

I took her advice. The man in charge of the FERA funds was Mr. William O. Bentley, who was also stake president. Since I had been made stake president of Relief Society, we were both conscious of the needs of some of our families. Whatever upstate connections he set up, I do not know. I know only that I offered my guest bedroom rent-free as a place to work. We put in a long table, some typewriters, a manuscript file, and a small table at which I could work, and were in business right away.

The first diary came to me through a long-time friend, Fae Ollerton. She was an assistant to Kimball Young, collecting material for his book, *Isn't One Wife Enough?* She was traveling through southern Utah, interviewing every plural wife she could find. From Panguitch she brought a diary of Martha Spence Heywood, second wife of Joseph L. Heywood, which was the most vivid and complete and revealing of all we found. (Happily it was published by the Utah Historical Society in 1978 after many years of being "lost.")

This whole project was so exciting, so full of potential, and so rewarding to the participants. By the end of the year we had our home cleared. Better still, we had on hand several other diaries and many biographical sketches, which became the source of further research.

Not all of these were literary masterpieces, but collectively they did form a good base of local history, and the wages — $30 a month to begin with, later raised to $32, and then to $36 — were a literal godsend to the participants.

I collected the diaries. We announced in a general stake conference that this project was beginning, and that if people who had diaries or other original records in their possession would bring them in, we would copy them free of charge and return the original and a copy to the owner. In every case I received the original, gave the owner a receipt for it, and returned it in person with a typed copy in a manila folder. I followed leads in all parts of the county and into Iron County as well. On one occasion I was traveling with my cousin Vivian Leavitt Palmer. We were going to Virgin, near Zion Park, I in search of a reported manuscript, she to visit several families. Just before we entered the town we had to cross the Virgin River. It wasn't exactly in flood, but the water was far too high to drive a car into. We sat on the bank and considered; finally, not willing to go back, I pulled off my shoes and stockings and waded across, the water above my knees in some places. After a little hesitation, Vivian followed suit.

Fully dressed, we walked into town. I found the home I was looking for, knocked, gave my name and my reason for coming to the woman who answered the door. She seemed not to comprehend quite just what I was after.

"Who did you say you wuz?" she asked.

"I'm Will Brooks' wife — Sheriff Brooks, from St. George," I explained.

"Why didn't you say that in the first place?" she wanted to know, holding out her hand. "Come right in, come right in. Anything I can do for Sheriff Brooks' wife, I'm more than glad to do."

From that day on, I always introduced myself as the wife of Will Brooks, and always had a warm reception. We found a great deal more material than I would have thought existed.

Again Nels proved helpful. He contacted several levels of officials asking to borrow my carbons for study as source material in his research, until finally Dr. Luther H. Evans of the Library of Congress learned of our project and asked me to send copies of all I had done to him. He was so impressed that he arranged a statewide meeting in Salt Lake City July 10–11, 1936. I was asked to attend. He brought with him the results of our work, and had conceived the idea of enlarging upon it. In the meantime, the Federal Writer's Project had been started in Colorado and in Utah, but its purpose was to encourage creative work. Our project was expanded to become the Historic Records Survey. With the organization on a state level, its headquarters at Ogden, I was relieved of my responsibilities.

Although I was "out," I still remained active in locating and sending in diaries; in fact, I considered myself a "quorum of one" to follow up any lead that I found. The staff in our area was now limited to three or four, and Mabel Jarvis continued long after the others had found more lucrative employment. She was the local correspondent for the *Salt Lake Tribune*, and as a part of her other assignments she did short histories of every settlement in the county, and of every ward in the St. George Stake, which extended at the time to include all the southern Nevada settlements. Many stories of historic buildings, celebrations, and obituaries were thus preserved.

I now became interested in doing a biography of Jacob Hamblin, but my father ordered me to do one of Grandpa Dudley Leavitt instead.

"Everybody talks about Jacob Hamblin," he said, "but my father was with him on his hardest expeditions, and when he had one too hard, he sent Dudley Leavitt and Ira Hatch to do it. That was the trip to Las Vegas when they both nearly lost their lives."

He reminded me that, as the Jacob Hamblin group were returning from their first mission to the Indians across the Colorado, it was Dudley Leavitt who had sacrificed his horse that the men might have food. Camped in the snow at Pipe Springs, they faced literal starvation.

Dudley's family had lived on the frontier and had moved so many times that he had had little schooling. Pa felt that this was all the more reason why Grandpa's story should be written, for he had left no written record of his own life.

I had been trained to obey my father; I did so now, working at the manuscript between home duties and carrying it, a chapter at a time, through the block to the local printer. I was not especially proud of it at the time, though I did collect some good folklore from all the living children.

In the meantime, I had become a pen-pal of Dale L. Morgan, who more than any other person influenced my work and my thinking. All of our exchanges were in writing, for Dale was deaf. We corresponded at length on a number of subjects, and from the first he astounded me with the scope of his knowledge, with his exact and precise and unerring memory. It was as if he had a photographic mind which stored neatly every scrap of information and promptly brought it forth upon demand.

As state supervisor of the Utah Writers' Project of the WPA, Dale was collecting material for *Utah: A Guide to the State*, published in 1941. I went by bus to meet him in Cedar City, and we set out in his car to follow the Old Spanish Trail south toward the Mountain Meadows. The road was not marked at the time; we became lost in the maze of corrals, and finally had to return to St. George and get Will to take us back to the monument. We were glad that we had been lost, for Will had no difficulty, and was full of the lore of the region and its landmarks. This trip was so very typical of Dale's insistence on seeing places first hand.

I have wondered if perhaps Dale's deafness was not, in the end, a blessing. Turned in upon itself, his mind became a remarkable storehouse of facts — names, dates, places, happenings, all in such order and relationship that he could produce them almost on call.

Our correspondence during those years was voluminous. At one time he wrote: "Have you noticed that our last three letters have passed each other in the mail? As nearly as I can figure out, we were writing at exactly the same hour and upon exactly the same subject. Explain that if you can."

> *Salt Lake City, Utah*
> *April 12, 1942*

Dear Juanita:

It is refreshing to have your letters. I often gallop at so frantic a pace that the world gets to spinning pretty furiously, and your good common sense and urbane view of the world is a tonic, even when this

*tonic is far from refreshing to you personally. (It is curious, the effect
we can have on people independent of the effect we are having on ourselves.)*

    *It was nice having you {in Salt Lake City}, but there certainly was
little enough leisure to enjoy life with you. I wanted to break a few
trails for you, so to speak, which you could tread with some assurance
when opportunity offered; I probably was not overwhelmingly successful in that, except that you will know where to lay hands on things
when you want them, I think. . . .*

    *. . . You see, Juanita, in a purely practical sense, I get as much out of
everything I do as anybody who partially or wholely [sic] shares in this
action. For the last several years I have been soaking up everything
about the Mormons I could find. Nothing was without significance.
Any problem existing for anybody, in Mormon research, was a problem
for me. These people . . . with whom I come in contact supply me with
provocative viewpoints on this major interest of my life. In answering
their limited needs, I answer larger needs of my own. For example,
your interest is primarily in southwestern Utah, the Indian missions,
Dixie, etc. I can almost exactly parallel your interest and enthusiasm
(except for a geographical and local knowledge I can't possess); what is
important to you is important to me; and the ways these things are
important to you are also the ways they are imporant to me: but also,
all these individual things are parts of an infinitely complex organism
that I am trying to see whole. . . .*

Dale

Not only was Dale stimulating and helpful and critical (as at
times he had to be) but it was he who opened the next door of
opportunity for me. He was living in Arlington, Virginia, doing
research in the Library of Congress. Among his good friends was
Darel McConkie, who was employed in the Department of Agricul-
ture in Washington, D.C. In late January 1944, Dale wrote that
Darel had attended a party the night before, at a home there in
Arlington, where the secret, supposedly carefully guarded, was whispered: "The Henry E. Huntington Library in Los Angeles has purchased from the descendants of Colonel William Nelson the diaries
of John D. Lee. They paid a fabulous sum. Exact amount unknown."

Dale suggested that I write the library telling them I understood
that they had acquired the diaries of John D. Lee, and asking if
I might see them if I were to come down.

[337]

I did, and the answer came with amazing promptness. Dr. Leslie E. Bliss made no reference to my question, but assured me that they did have a copy of the testimony at the John D. Lee trials, which was open to scholars. "There are other reasons why we should like to have you visit our library," he wrote, and added that he had seen my little book on Dudley Leavitt, and that his family was connected by marriage.

In less than a week I was facing the first footman at the Henry E. Huntington Library. The pass Dr. Bliss had sent me gave instant permission to enter. He met me with outstretched hands, and there on the table was a copy of my little Dudley Leavitt book. He took me to meet Dr. Robert G. Cleland, and after a few minutes' visit I was allowed to examine the Lee diaries, upon condition that I should not mention the fact that they had them. Before I left I was appointed to act as a "Field Fellow" for them in the collecting of Mormon materials.

Thus the door of opportunity was opened for me. I've often said that "Heaven is doing what you would be glad to do for nothing and getting paid for it." I still think that is true.

APPENDIX A

Dale L. Morgan to Juanita Brooks, April 12, 1944

Arlington, Va.

Dear Juanita:

I think that whether you like the idea or not, you cannot escape a strong autobiographical structure for [Quicksand and Cactus]. I believe you are disinclined to accept this necessity, in part because your own life does not seem to you particularly worth writing about (a false humility, by the way), and in part because of a natural reluctance to invade your own privacy. In this respect I think you should remember, Juanita, that in what you write you will have a good chance of doing something of a permanent importance — important enough to justify whatever sacrifices writing a personal book may entail for you. I think also, in deciding on what is and is not to go into your book, you should hold to the long view, and consider the significance your book will have, in course of time, to your children, and to their children. You are granted the privilege of creating your own immortality, of a kind. I can understand your feeling about the tragedy attaching to your first marriage, and the pain that writing about it would involve for you. But would not your son, some day, thank you for a picture of his father he could have in no other way? . . .

I believe that the book, when you think things through, will inevitably take its structure from the pattern of your own life, and its cohesion will come from the sense it gives of your own maturing as a person. The book will give not merely a sense of you as a narrator but of you as a participant in the life you describe, conveying an understanding of how this background shaped you for life — the values it gave you, the understanding of people, the insight into living. I think the book will depict the slowly developing pull of "the

[339]

outside" upon you, and I think it will also reveal clearly the values that brought you back to live there — from choice, not from necessity.

. . . When all is said and done, you must write the book so that it satisfies you, yourself. But at the same time, you will find it infinitely more difficult and devious to write in this manner the book you are going to write than if you were to accept yourself frankly as a central condition of your book and pattern your book on that recognition. At the same time, the frankly autobiographical structure opens to you a kind of simplicity and humanity that will come naturally; those qualities will come out of any other pattern only by dint of the greatest technical proficiency and a very great amount of hard work.

From all this, you can see that my recommendations are for you to relax, so to speak, and just sit down and write your own story, letting your fancy wander into past, present, or future, as the developing content may dictate. All these marvelous stories you have will fall naturally into place, and I think you will get a feeling of inner excitement into the story, a sense of human warmth and of the essential dignity and nobility of human living. . . .

Dale L. Morgan

APPENDIX B

Dale L. Morgan to Bernard DeVoto, August 4, 1944

Arlington, Va.

Dear DeVoto,

In this note I am acting upon a suggestion you made to me quite some time back, that I should bring to your attention any book I thought really worthwhile and deserving of someone's interested attention.

I haven't come across any such book from that time to this. But now I want to ask your advice in connection with a book Juanita Brooks of St. George has in progress.

In correspondence with her in January, I commented on her extraordinary practical knowledge of the southern desert frontier, with which I had again been struck by some comments she had made to me, more or less matter-of-factly, about the appearance of human flesh at varying times after death has taken place, and I demanded to know why she shouldn't write a book about the country and the people she knew so well. It seemed obvious to me that her whole experience of life, and all her interests, had been such as to shape her for writing such a book. The articles she published in Harper's in 1934 and 1941 were obviously segments of this larger story, whether she had realized it or not.

Well, she took fire from the idea, and sat down and wrote me twenty or thirty pages of miscellaneous incidents that might be expanded into a book. It was the most marvelous stuff you ever saw, and I forthwith demanded that she go ahead and write the book. . . . Juanita had some trouble arriving at a framework for the book, largely in consequence of her reluctance to use the natural pattern, her own life. But finally she saw the logic of what I said, and she laid out the whole book, writing some eight or nine chapters in rough draft for me to look at. . . . Its materials are wonderful, alive and colorful;

[341]

it gives you a renewed sense of the dignity of the human soul and the worth of human living; and it also gives you a great feeling of admiration for a modest woman who is a valiant woman in all the meaning of that term.

Accordingly, before writing Juanita further, I write to see if you have any advice that might help her in marketing the book. I might say that her tentative title is "Quicksand and Cactus." On the one hand it is a narrative of her own life — born into a Mormon family on the southern frontier, grandchild of the upstanding polygamists she described in Harper's ten years ago; of life in Bunkerville (described to some extent in Harper's three years ago); the values the family and the community lived by; the relations with outsiders — and finally, and most of all, Juanita's own story, growing up in this environment, going out for a schooling, and finally coming back to make her home in the Dixie country. . . .

I feel that it is a rich and heart-warming and lively and colorful book. But I think that it is a book that no one can read without a renewed sense of the worth of human living, and it is at the same time a book to be read with delight. . . .

Regards,

Dale L. Morgan